T

# Capricorn
# 2025

## DAILY HOROSCOPE
## PLANNER

Authors: Tali Edut, Ophira Edut
Managing Editor: Lisa M. Sundry
Copy Editor: Amy Anthony
Contributing Editors: Felicia Bender, Matthew Swann,
James Kerti, Jennifer Karnik, Stevie Goldstein
Research Editor: Stephanie Gailing

Cover Illustration © 2024 by Bodil Jane
Book Design: Yvette L. Robinson
Interior Illustrations: Will Dudley, Yvette L. Robinson
Cover Photo: Brittany Ambridge

# TABLE OF
# CONTENTS

# the Year of The Divine Pendulum

## WHAT'S IN THE STARS FOR ALL OF US?

Back and forth we go! The planetary pendulum swings into wildly unscripted terrain in 2025, producing a brand-new story arc for humans to grapple with. We're not just talking about a garden-variety Mercury retrograde or supermoon here. The slow-moving outer planets, which shape society and larger trends, are the key players in the consciousness-shifting trajectory of 2025.

Evolutionary Pluto has reached cruising altitude in Aquarius, spending its first full year in this high-minded air sign, its zodiac home until 2044. The Age of Aquarius is officially underway, disrupting every industry and bringing rapid advancements in fields like science, technology, finance, fashion, space travel and medicine. Is there an AI chatbot for that? Bet your Bitcoin there is.

In 2025, three momentous planets—Saturn, Uranus and Neptune—will follow in icy Pluto's wake. Each one swings forward into a new zodiac sign for a portion of the year, giving us a glimpse of what's in store for the second half of the decade. And whoa! The next phase of the game is gonna hit different. Both Saturn and Neptune depart the watery well of Pisces and launch into fiery Aries' field—a big deal for Neptune especially, which has been in its home sign of Pisces since 2011. In between these two heavenly bodies, Uranus zips into ingenious Gemini, pulling out of the Taurean trench it's been stuck in since 2018.

When an outer planet changes signs, humanity takes a step in a new direction. It's been nearly 30 years since Saturn's footprint pressed into Aries from 1996 to 1998. In the case of Neptune and Uranus, many of us will experience these cosmic cycles for the first time in our lives. To wit, Neptune's last visit to Aries was from 1862 to 1875, and Uranus was in Gemini from 1941 to 1949.

But wait! Just as we begin to process these metamorphic transitions, all three planets oscillate back to the same zodiac positions that they started the year with. Record scratch! Was it all a dream? Not exactly. But it's definitely a sneak peek of what's to come. In 2026, Saturn and Neptune return for longer tours through Aries (two and 13 years, respectively) while Uranus buzzes back into Gemini for another seven years. Take notes! You'll need them next year.

If the pendulum swing of 2025 discombobulates us, here's where the "divine" part comes in. On January 11, the fateful lunar North Node slips into esoteric Pisces, opening the gateways to subconscious activity until July 26, 2026. Times of uncertainty can be catalysts for developments in the arts, spirituality and healing. This year, we are invited to reach beyond our day-to-day "3D" reality for a sense of meaning, as well as some emotional relief. It's also a 9 Universal Year, a year of sacred revelations and release as we prepare for a new nine-year numerological cycle to begin in 2026.

While we're all processing our feelings and spiritual downloads, the karmic South Node plants in sensual, pragmatic Virgo for this same 18-month period. There's no ignoring our connection to Mother Earth or the impact of the climate crisis on humanity. To borrow a lyric from Pisces Chappell Roan (who was born while the nodes were in Virgo and Pisces), we're "coming face-to-face with 'I told you so.'"

This Pisces/Virgo "earth magick" vibe explains how a mushroom made its way onto the cover of our 2025 Horoscope book, illustrated by artist Bodil Jane. (Although the amanita muscaria is a visual beauty, it's not one to ingest for, er, medicinal purposes.) These incredible organisms may hold the key to our survival. (Seriously!)

Renowned mycologist Paul Stamets lays out the true magic of mushrooms in his TED Talk, "6 Ways Mushrooms Can Save The World," which at this writing has been viewed over 8 million times. Spoiler alert: It's not about a psychedelic voyage. The mycelium network—the threadlike roots of mushrooms that go deep underground and branch out across the entire planet in a fascinating community of connection—is what Stamets calls "Earth's natural Internet."

Fun(gi) fact: Mushrooms hold soil together and break down nutrients that feed plants and trees, giving rise to the entire ecosystem of living things. They clean up industrial waste and eat polluted soil for lunch. They give us antibiotics to cure viral diseases.

That's not to dismiss their impact on another network, the neurological one. Psilocybin, the hallucinogenic chemical in certain mushroom strains, is being hailed as a groundbreaking treatment for depression, anxiety, ADHD, mood disorders and more. Microdoses of psilocybin have been touted as a way to increase sociability and creativity.

Mushrooms are also due to be hot with Big Pharma for 2025. Projections made by the Canadian drug company Optimi Health—which is licensed to produce GMP-grade psilocybin and functional mushrooms for the health and wellness markets—suggest that the legal psychedelics industry could generate over $10 billion annually by 2027. There's gold in this mold!

Will our connection to the divine all come down to 'dosing? Or maybe it's "dowsing," the metaphysical technique of using a pendulum to answer a probing question.

Jokes aside, we should not sleep on the magic of the simpler things, especially not in 2025. At first glance, a pendulum may appear to be little more than a weight on a string. In reality, this device packs a serious punch.

With gravity as their guide, pendulums have been used to measure time and distance since the era of the Mesopotamians five thousand years ago. Ancient Egyptians used a pendulum to measure and build the Great Pyramid of Giza. Galileo's discoveries about the arc of a pendulum's swing were fundamental to our ability to track hours, minutes and seconds on a clock. In 1851, French physicist Léon Foucault demonstrated the Earth's rotation using a pendulum that is now named after him.

Even as we make our way into outer space, humans are still universally bound by gravity. In the Age of Aquarius, discovering what connects us is more important than splintering ourselves with artificial divisions. During the Year of the Divine Pendulum, our survival may depend on (finally) surrendering the myth of "rugged individualism" and embracing a new, networked way of life.

In other words, what if we become more like the living, breathing branches of mycelium sharing resources, energy and instinctive wisdom? After all, these fantastic fungi have survived for 1.3 billion years, while humans have only been around for roughly 300,000.

Could the new arc of humanity be, "as below, so above"? That certainly sounds like a swing in the right direction, even if it comes with a string attached.

GROUNDED IN LOVE,
# TALI & OPHI

# 2025
## Highlights

## THE FATEFUL LUNAR NODES SWITCH INTO PISCES (NORTH) AND VIRGO (SOUTH) ON JANUARY 11

The ethereal meets the material this January 11, as the destiny-directing lunar nodes launch a new 18-month journey through dreamy Pisces and practical Virgo. This spiritual cycle, which last took place from Jun 23, 2006 – Dec 18, 2007, puts a focus on healing in every way, from our energetic and emotional bodies to our physical ones. Artificial boundaries dissolve under the North Node in Pisces' spell, inviting us to discover new dimensions of the human experience. Meanwhile, the South Node in Virgo challenges us to live in greater attunement with Mother Earth. Goodbye micromanagement, hello mindfulness. It's time to embrace a holistic, heart-centered way of living. This pull toward a spiritual, compassionate and intuitive path will feel like a relief after the warmongering, ideologically divided Aries-Libra nodal cycle that began July 17, 2023 and finally wraps on January 11, 2025. Take stock of the relationship shifts and progress on personal initiatives that you've made since then. We're betting you've grown mightily!

## MOTIVATOR MARS KICKS OFF 2025 IN RETROGRADE

Don't rush those resolutions! Go-getter Mars begins 2025 in full retrograde mode, continuing a reverse commute that began December 6, 2024, in passionate, regal Leo. The feisty red planet remains in reverse until February 23, 2025, backing into domestic Cancer on January 6. While Mars in Leo typically fires us up for bold moves and dramatic action, the retrograde cools that energy, asking us to hold back on launching any major initiatives. Instead of pushing for the spotlight, begin the year by reflecting on your personal power and motivations. Have you been seeking attention for the right reasons? Knowing the difference between fame and notoriety is important now. Keep hotheaded instincts in check. Once Mars slips into emo Cancer on January 6, it could be hard to tear yourself out of your hibernation station. Cozy up, but try not to isolate. With this rabble-rousing energy focused on home and family life, you may need to sort out some post-holiday feelings and set firmer boundaries with your inner circle.

## JUPITER BEGINS THE YEAR IN GEMINI

Curiosity is piquing AND peaking this year as boundless Jupiter continues its yearlong trek through inquisitive, variety-loving Gemini. This cycle, which began on May 25, 2024 and lasts until June 9, 2025, powers up platonic partnerships and peer relationships with excitable, expansive energy. Mingle and network but take your time with formalizing agreements until Jupiter turns direct this February 4. New developments in education, transportation and media can surge in the first half of 2025, but since Jupiter is in a tough "detriment" position here—opposite its home sign of Sagittarius—it might take a while to get these innovations in motion. (Cue the electric vehicle market.) Lead with intellectual curiosity while this cycle lasts through June 9. Consider multiple perspectives rather than rushing to conclusions. With Jupiter's big-talking tendencies and Gemini's double-talking ones, fact-checking everything will be essential, especially in the age of AI and deepfakes.

## MERCURY TURNS RETROGRADE THREE TIMES

Mark your calendar for these celestial speed bumps! Messenger Mercury spins retrograde three times this year, a signal-scrambling cycle which can skew information, screw with schedules and bring back people from the past. The first retrograde, from March 15 to April 7, straddles combative Aries and compassionate Pisces, pushing us to slow down and rethink impulsive choices while diving into our emotional depths. Beware a tendency to slip into denial or romanticize. Rose-colored glasses are NOT the accessory to rock this spring. Round two, from July 18 to August 11, crackles in fiery Leo, creating drama in creativity, leadership and dating. Deploy those ego checks! The final retrograde, November 9 to 29, kicks off in Sagittarius before shifting into intense Scorpio on the 18th, revealing hidden truths. Retrogrades call for reflection, course-correction and lots of patience. Use these forced timeouts to focus on "re" activities: revising, reuniting, reviewing, rethinking.

## ONE ECLIPSE SERIES ENDS (ARIES-LIBRA) AND ANOTHER KEEPS ROLLING ALONG (VIRGO-PISCES)

The eclipses, which move in the same cadence as the lunar nodes, will also say goodbye to Aries and Libra this year and shift into Virgo and Pisces. March 29 marks the final Aries solar (new moon) eclipse, bringing profound personal epiphanies. Where have you been trudging forward on an independent path since April 2023 and what changes need to be implemented in certain partnerships? This eclipse invites you to wrap it up with a bow and a bang. Two weeks later, the first Virgo eclipse since 2016 arrives with the March 14 full moon—a total lunar eclipse. Take inventory of your health and habits: How can you hack your routines to make life flow more seamlessly? The fall eclipse season starts with the September 7 total lunar eclipse in Pisces, throwing life into a surreal two-week crucible. Every belief and boundary may be up for examination until the sensible solar eclipse in Virgo brings back certainty with the September 21 new moon—the second  in a rare back-to-back pair in Virgo this year! With this eclipse series waging on until February 2027, balancing fantasy with reality will be a delicate dance.

## VENUS TURNS RETROGRADE THIS SPRING

Starting March 1, you'll need to get real about your love goals or your overall relationship patterns. Ardent Venus flips into a six-week retrograde, which could create a temporary power outage for all things romantic. This cycle happens every 18 months as Venus shifts from being an evening star (visible in the sky at dusk) to a morning star (rising just before dawn). Metaphorically, we have a chance to put old love stories to bed and rewrite a fresh chapter. During this tense period compassion and compromise may go AWOL. To make matters more complicated, 2025's Venus retrograde in self-centered Aries (March 1 to 27) and gullible Pisces (March 27 to April 12) could mean that your prince or princess may revert into a wretched frog right before your eyes. Don't slip into denial. This is a time to take an unblinking look at reality while also reviewing your past patterns. If you're planning a wedding between March 1 and April 12, we recommend doing a City Hall ceremony beforehand or waiting to sign the marriage license until after April 12. Another option? Renew your vows on your one-year anniversary.

## JUPITER IN CANCER TAKES HOME ON THE ROAD

On June 9, Jupiter heads into cozy Cancer for the first time since 2013-14 Talk about a planetary paradox! Worldly, nomadic Jupiter drops anchor in home-loving Cancer for a year this June 9. If that's not weird enough, Jupiter is actually "exalted" in Cancer, meaning the Crab's castle is its most potent place in the zodiac. After spending a year in "detriment" in Gemini, this transit is quite a code switch for the red-spotted titan. Between now and July 30, 2026, the buzzy energy subsides and our capacity for intimacy and emotional intelligence expands. Jupiter-in-Cancer cycles can bring developments in social protection and care for children and families. Housing, food security and domestic stability can also become key issues to resolve, especially as climate change impacts geographically livable zones. Who are the people in your innermost circle? Whether you're blood related or "chosen family," Jupiter in

Cancer can bring a joyful sense of connection. And since this globe-trotting planet rules travel, the second half of 2025 could be an optimal time to visit your ancestral homeland and connect to your roots.

## SATURN SWINGS BETWEEN PISCES AND ARIES

Among the planets having a "divine pendulum" swing in 2025 is stoic, structured Saturn, who divides the year between spiritual Pisces and aggressive Aries. The ringed taskmaster first parked in Pisces on March 7, 2023. Ever since, it's been challenging us to organize the most chaotic, unscripted parts of our lives, like mental health, spiritual beliefs and artistic expression. While Saturn is a boundary hound, Pisces is a boundary dissolver. Talk about a head trip! Literally, this cycle has dovetailed with developments in psychedelic legalization as treatments for everything from depression to creative blocks. This push-pull continues until May 24, when Saturn darts forward into Aries until September 1. The energy shifts dramatically then, as we flip from introspection to daring initiative. Personal responsibility (rather than Piscean victimhood) becomes the new flex, as Saturn in Aries pushes us to take ownership for our actions and evolve accordingly. We haven't experienced this cycle for nearly three decades, as the ringed planet's last visit to the Ram's realm was from April 1996 to October 1998.

While Saturn in Aries encourages bold action and self-reliance, it also warns against impulsive risks. As it serves lessons in conflict management, it reveals the detrimental impact of warmongering, gun violence and use of weapons of mass destruction. Got some original ideas brewing? You're invited to architect a new, self-directed path, as you lay the groundwork for personal (and societal!) reinvention. But advance slowly with new initiatives under cautious Saturn's watch. This surge of novel, enterprising energy kicks up again when Saturn settles into Aries from February 13, 2026 to April 12, 2028.

## URANUS DOES A PENDULUM PIVOT BETWEEN TAURUS AND GEMINI

Also on the celestial swing set in 2025 is innovative, sci-fi Uranus, who does a back and forth between tenacious Taurus and gregarious Gemini. From July 7 to November 7, the planet of progress will briefly dip into Gemini, cracking the seal on a new set of possibilities. In the first half of 2025, however, Uranus is busy finishing its seven-year tour through earthy, sensible Taurus, where it's been revolutionizing finance, agriculture and labor since May 2018. Uranus in Taurus has transformed our material lives, producing a near-cashless society ("Venmo me!") along with fluctuating interest rates and cryptocurrency's slow but real adoption. In Gemini, the techie planet's focus shifts to the intellectual and interpersonal. Historically, Uranus in Gemini has brought metamorphic shifts in communication technologies, such as the rise of the telegraph and commercial television during its last tour through Gemini from 1941-49. And the telescope! Uranus was discovered by William and Caroline Herschel when it was transiting through Gemini in 1781.

Get ready for rapid developments and total disruptions to Gemini-ruled industries: telecommunications, data security, transportation, education and the media. In a flash, Uranus can break us free from outdated systems and incite us to embrace futuristic replacements. Keep up if you can! Everything from the cars we drive (or fly!) to the way we educate our children is up for grabs. Flexible, hybrid and fractional roles may become the new normal for employees. It's worth noting that past Uranus-in-Gemini transits have dovetailed with many wars—the War of Independence, the Civil War, WW2, the Arab-Israeli War and the Indo-Pakistani War to name a few. As we enter 2025, battles are raging across many continents, indicating that these trends may continue well into the second half of the decade.

## NEPTUNE STEPS INTO ARIES FOR THE FIRST TIME SINCE 1862-75

Here's one for the history books! On March 30, numinous Neptune leaves its home sign of dreamy Pisces for the first time since April 2011 and makes a landmark (in our lifetime) trek into action-oriented Aries. For the past fourteen years Neptune has been on a mindfulness pilgrimage and a deep dive through the human psyche. We have the yoga studios, trauma-informed programs, plant medicine ceremonies and worldwide embrace of the "woo" to show for it. As Neptune surfs into Aries from March 30 to October 22, the shift may feel jarring. Neptune is compassionate, dreamy, fluid and soft. Aries is aggressive, daring, entitled and strong. What happens when the twain meet? We need to look all the way back to 1862-75 for clues. Historically, Neptune in Aries has coincided with periods of radical spiritual and ideological change. We saw this in the 1860s when causes like abolitionism drove the American Civil War. Visionary advances have also exploded, like the first printing press and camera obscura in 1544. Or the opening of the New York Stock Exchange in 1865 and the first "tube," London's Tower Subway, in 1872.

Autocrat alert! There may be a rise in cult-like leaders during Neptune in Aries. Martyr movements motivated by lofty ideals could draw zealots who are willing to fight to the death. On a personal level, this cycle provides the courage to build your dream. Watch out for a veiled thirst for power as you ascend along your path. Although Neptune swings back into Pisces on October 22, take notes! This is a preview of a longer, thirteen-year cycle that begins again when Neptune returns to Aries from January 26, 2026 to March 23, 2039.

## PLUTO SPENDS ITS FIRST FULL YEAR IN AQUARIUS

The Age of Aquarius is officially on! Alchemical Pluto, the planet of transformation, power and rebirth, continues the unbroken leg of its journey through Aquarius, which began on November 19, 2024. Pluto first rolled into Aquarius for a brief spell on March 23, 2023. The entire transit lasts until January 19, 2044. This radical transit, which last occurred from 1778-98 during the end of the American Revolution—and for the whole of the French and Haitian Revolutions—signals profound societal shifts. How do we approach power, wealth and community, especially in this time of space travel, AI, quantum technology and deepfakes? In Aquarius, Pluto burns down our limited ways of thinking. With a push toward collective empowerment, old systems that serve only a few (rather than many) could break down. Over the next nineteen years, "power to the people" could look like radical transformations in all the collective structures that democratic Aquarius rules. It's no secret that climate change has become a crisis. With Pluto in sci-fi Aquarius, there may be groundbreaking developments that reverse the damage as well as a move toward new sources of energy (including nuclear). But will it happen fast enough? And will the entrenched monarchies and oligarchies (governed by Aquarius' opposite sign of Leo) release their stranglehold on the world? We have nearly two decades to find out. Get ready for intense clashes along the way—over everything from airspace to human rights to the ethical use of technology.

## BLACK MOON LILITH BRINGS HER INTENSE WAKEUP CALLS TO THREE ZODIAC SIGNS

Shadow-dancer Lilith, a point in the sky associated with the female journey through scorn, rage, empowerment and sexual liberation, is moving through three zodiac signs in 2025. Until March 27, Lilith tours justice-oriented Libra, challenging us to redefine power within partnerships and to fight oppressive laws. Since this cycle began on June 29, 2024, women's rights became a key issue in the U.S. Presidential Election. On March 27, 2025, Lilith plunges into sultry Scorpio, taking us deeper into the heart of emotional truth and taboo topics. Scorpio's intensity stirs raw conversations about sexuality, control, and power, bringing hidden issues to light, especially in areas like reproductive rights and emotional intimacy . The year wraps with Lilith blazing into truth-seeking Sagittarius on December 20, sparking a desire for freedom, exploration, and unfiltered authenticity. Repressive religious regimes—especially those that restrict women's fundamental rights—could be met with a fiery global resistance as we move into 2026.

## THE YEAR OF THE WOOD SNAKE BEGINS JANUARY 29

The Lunar New Year on January 29 ushers in the Year of the Wood Snake, a time for slow, steady growth and transformation. Like the serpent shedding its skin, we're called to release what no longer serves us, making space for evolution. Like the Western sign of Taurus, which the Snake is associated with, this year favors strategy, patience and precision—encouraging us to plan carefully and strike only when the timing is ideal. While the pace may feel subdued, if you play the long game, you can build something solid. With the Wood element promoting growth, thoughtful, subtle movements lead to lasting change. Trust the process and let the Snake's strategic wisdom guide you. This is the first Year of the Wood Snake since 1965. That year was marked by intensified warfare in Vietnam and Civil Rights action, such as MLK's four-day march from Selma to Montgomery.

## 2025 IS A 9 UNIVERSAL YEAR

Get ready for a sacred year of closure and completion. In numerology, 2025 is a 9 Universal Year (2+0+2+5=9) rounding out the full cycle before we reset with a 1 Universal Year in 2026. Globally, we're tasked with letting go of outdated systems and beliefs that no longer serve the collective good. This year will push us to shift from ego-driven actions to a more compassionate, humanitarian approach. The energy of 9 is a lot like Pisces, the final zodiac sign, encouraging surrender, spiritual growth and embracing flow instead of forcing progress. This is a time for healing, forgiveness and creating space for new beginnings as we lead with our hearts and contribute to building a more connected, compassionate world.

## ZODIAC SIGNS

| | |
|---|---|
| ♈ | ARIES |
| ♉ | TAURUS |
| ♊ | GEMINI |
| ♋ | CANCER |
| ♌ | LEO |
| ♍ | VIRGO |
| ♎ | LIBRA |
| ♏ | SCORPIO |
| ♐ | SAGITTARIUS |
| ♑ | CAPRICORN |
| ♒ | AQUARIUS |
| ♓ | PISCES |

## PLANETS

| | |
|---|---|
| ☉ | SUN |
| ☽ | MOON |
| ♂ | MARS |
| ☿ | MERCURY |
| ♀ | VENUS |
| ♄ | SATURN |
| ♃ | JUPITER |
| ♆ | NEPTUNE |
| ♅ | URANUS |
| ♇ | PLUTO |

## MOONS

| | |
|---|---|
| **FM** | FULL MOON |
| **NM** | NEW MOON |
| **LE** | LUNAR ECLIPSE |
| **SE** | SOLAR ECLIPSE |

# TAROT CARD OF THE YEAR

THE HIGH PRIESTESS

## THE HIGH PRIESTESS
### INTUITION, MYSTERY, INNER WISDOM

In 2025, the mysterious High Priestess emerges as the Tarot card of the year, inviting us to peer within and trust our deepest wisdom. Her presence signals a year of heightened intuition, spiritual awakening, and secrets waiting to be revealed. As the veil between the conscious and unconscious thins, the High Priestess urges us to tune in to the quiet, guiding voice of the soul. Mystical insights and deep self-discovery are on the horizon and in the hidden realms of your psyche.

# CRYSTAL OF THE YEAR

## LEPIDOLITE
### CALM, BALANCE, TRANQUILITY

As Saturn, Neptune, and Uranus pivot between zodiac signs in 2025, Lepidolite's balancing properties provide a steadying force. Known for its high lithium content, this stone is a powerful mood stabilizer, often called upon for calming anxiety and emotional turbulence. While the outer world fluctuates wildly in 2025, Lepidolite (which means "scale" in Greek) supports with balanced clarity and resilience. Its gentle vibrations promote deep relaxation and sleep—fabulous for a year when the enchanting Pisces North Node brings messages through our dreams.

# Capricorn

**DATES** December 21 - January 19

**SYMBOL** The Sea Goat

**ELEMENT** Earth

**QUALITY** Cardinal

**RULING PLANET** Saturn

**BODY PART** Knees, skin, bones, teeth

## BEST TRAITS
Loyal, family-oriented, hardworking, devoted, honest, resourceful, wise, protective

## KEYWORDS
Ambition, structure, goals, long-term plans, prestige, status, achievement, abundance

*Read more about Capricorn*

*Born on a cusp? Calculate your Sun sign with a free chart at astrostyle.com/birthchart*

# THE SUN IN
# 2025

*Also known as: "The Zodiac Seasons"*

# The Zodiac Seasons

Break out the cake and candles! On the third week of every month, the Sun changes signs and initiates a brand-new zodiac "season." These four-week cycles show where opportunities are brightest and where your efforts will yield the sparkliest results. Think of each solar season like a costume party. What is it like to live like a Gemini or a Pisces for a month? Try it on for size!

| season | focus |
|---|---|
| **CAPRICORN**<br>**DEC 21, 2024**<br>**4:21AM**<br>Winter Solstice | Earthy Capricorn's ambitious nature makes this the time to aim higher, and then put in a consistent and persistent effort to reach that goal. Network with the VIPs during Capricorn season; mentor someone younger or newer to the game. |
| **AQUARIUS**<br>**JAN 19**<br>**3:00PM** | Weird is wonderful during eccentric Aquarius season. Allow yourself to stand out in the crowd while also embracing the spirit of community. You can be different and belong when this air sign rules the skies. |
| **PISCES**<br>**FEB 18**<br>**5:07AM** | Compassionate, creative Pisces season is a time to feel and heal. Dare to sit with your uncomfortable emotions during this water sign season. Dissect these feelings and turn them into art. Your empathy will expand in the process. |
| **ARIES**<br>**MAR 20**<br>**5:01AM**<br>Spring Equinox | Fiery Aries is the first sign in the zodiac, making this season all about blazing trails and starting fresh. Get to know what makes you tick by daring to do more things independently. |
| **TAURUS**<br>**APR 19**<br>**3:56PM** | Rooted earth sign Taurus reminds us of the importance of comfort and security. Review your finances, update your accounts, create a budget—both for practical necessities and life-enhancing luxuries. Inspect your personal goods—clothing, furniture, dwelling, accessories—and ensure everything is in good working order. |

| season | focus |
|--------|-------|
| **GEMINI**<br>MAY 20<br>2:55PM | How well do you play with others? Gemini is the air sign of cooperation and communication. Stop making assumptions (or assertions) and start asking questions. That's how you'll master the art of creating win-wins. |
| **CANCER**<br>JUN 20<br>10:42PM<br>Summer Solstice | Home sweet sanctuary! Nurturing Cancer is the water sign that rules family and domestic matters. Get back in touch with relatives. Make your space feel cozy, welcoming and supportive of your current lifestyle. |
| **LEO**<br>JUL 22<br>9:29AM | We all have a special light to shine, as fire sign Leo reminds us. Lift the curtain during this zodiac season and show the world what you're made of. Let your wilder romantic nature come out to play and wear your heart on your sleeve! |
| **VIRGO**<br>AUG 22<br>4:34PM | Earthy Virgo is the sign of service. Where would a random act of generosity make a difference for someone else? Be humble and helpful. The simplest approach is the best during this season. |
| **LIBRA**<br>SEP 22<br>2:19PM<br>Fall Equinox | Peace, love and harmony! Great ideals, but ones that are seldom lived by. When air sign Libra blows through town, we get a chance to practice being kind, considerate and collaborative. Opposites attract so stay open to different types. |
| **SCORPIO**<br>OCT 22<br>11:51PM | Sultry, transformational Scorpio isn't afraid of life's mysteries—or our animal instincts. This intuitive water sign season challenges us to bring sexy back by allowing ourselves to dive into our deepest desires and longings. |
| **SAGITTARIUS**<br>NOV 21<br>8:36PM | What's happening on the other side of the globe, fence or aisle? Fire sign Sagittarius is the zodiac's ambassador. Reach across so-called boundaries to learn what makes others tick during this season. Travel or plan your next amazing journey. |
| **CAPRICORN**<br>DEC 21<br>10:03AM<br>Winter Solstice | The Sun swings back around into Capricorn at the end of every year putting the focus on the traditional side of this sign. Get to know a family custom and look for special ways you can provide support and happiness to your inner circle. |

# THE MOON IN
# 2025

MOTIVATE & MANIFEST WITH THE

# New & Full Moons

**NEW MOONS** mark beginnings and are the optimal time to kick off any new projects or plans. Lay the groundwork for what you want to manifest in the coming six months. Set intentions or initiate action while you have this lunar lift creating momentum.

**FULL MOONS** are ideal manifestation moments to show off and celebrate your hard work of the past six months. Full moons dial up feelings and can provoke emotional outpourings. It's time to cash in or cash out if you're ready for something new.

**SUPERMOONS** are new or full moons that arrive at the closest distance possible between the moon and Earth. The full supermoon will appear brighter. Both new and full supermoons deliver strong feels and potent manifestation energy.

### PLAN YOUR SHORT-TERM GOALS BY THE MOON
Each month, there are four moon phases, spaced one week apart. Set intentions at the new moon, then, do a progress check at the waxing quarter moon. Celebrate results at the full moon, then curate at the waning quarter moon—what to keep and what to set aside.

### PLAN YOUR LONG-TERM GOALS BY THE MOON
Each new moon falls in a specific zodiac sign. Six months later, a full moon occurs in the very same sign, completing the cycle.

| phase | date | focus/celebrate |
|---|---|---|
| FULL MOON CANCER (24°00') | JAN 13 5:27PM | **Celebrate:** Bonds with your family and inner circle of friends, the places where you feel at home, nostalgic memories, creative alone time. |
| NEW MOON AQUARIUS (9°51') | JAN 29 7:36AM | **Focus:** Experiment with new technology and techniques, break out of the box with style and social expression, connect to community, activism and humanitarian work. |
| FULL MOON LEO (24°06') | FEB 12 8:53AM | **Celebrate:** The unique way that you shine, the people who make your heart sing, your romantic nature, fashion sense, childlike wonder, the places where you feel like a natural leader, and your fiercely competitive streak that won't let you quit on yourself. |
| NEW MOON PISCES (9°41') | FEB 27 7:45PM | **Focus:** Connect to your dreams, spiritual exploration, find creative outlets, give back, inspire others, form supportive alliances, express empathy so people feel seen and understood. |
| FULL MOON VIRGO (23°57') | MAR 14 2:55AM | **TOTAL LUNAR ECLIPSE** **Celebrate:** The serenity of a freshly cleaned space, streamlined systems, your helpful spirit, being of service to those in need, taking great care of your body by eating clean and exercising, the magic of nature and natural beauty. |
| NEW MOON ARIES (9°00') | MAR 29 6:58AM | **SUPERMOON + PARTIAL SOLAR ECLIPSE** **Focus:** Sharpen your competitive edge, blaze your own trail, take the initiative with people and activities that matter to you, try new things. |
| FULL MOON LIBRA (23°20') | APR 12 8:22PM | **Celebrate:** The power of partnerships and synergistic connections, dressing up and socializing, transcendent music and the arts, peaceful moments of serenity, the parts of your life that are in beautiful balance. |

| phase | date | focus/celebrate |
|---|---|---|
| NEW MOON TAURUS (7°47') | APR 27 3:31PM | **SUPERMOON** **Focus:** Define your values, set up healthy and rewarding routines, enjoy arts and culture, simplify complexities, budget, get out in nature. |
| FULL MOON SCORPIO (22°13') | MAY 12 12:56PM | **Celebrate:** Your loyal and caring spirit, intense exchanges, the sexiest parts of yourself, the ways you've transformed your struggles into gold, true friendship, resourcefulness and raw creative expression. |
| NEW MOON GEMINI (6°06') | MAY 26 11:02PM | **SUPERMOON** **Focus:** Sharpen your communication style, write and make media, pair up on short-term collaborations, socialize with new people, become active in your local community, flirt and joke! |
| FULL MOON SAGITTARIUS (20°39') | JUN 11 3:44AM | **Celebrate:** The spirit of wanderlust, your unvarnished truths, people you love who live far away, the passport stamps you've collected or hope to one day, visionary ideas that you're bringing to life, diversity and cross-cultural connections. |
| NEW MOON CANCER (4°08') | JUN 25 6:32AM | **Focus:** Nourish yourself with good food and close friends, spruce up your spaces so you feel at home everywhere, connect to family, spend time near water, get in touch with your emotions. |
| FULL MOON CAPRICORN (18°50') | JUL 10 4:37PM | **Celebrate:** People you admire—heroes and mentors, family legacies, customs that you want to carry on, enduring friendships and business relationships, your most ambitious ideas, institutions or organizations that you believe in and support. |
| NEW MOON LEO (2°08') | JUL 24 3:11PM | **Focus:** Express yourself through art and style, enjoy romance and playtime, spend time with kids, take a leadership role, host and attend glamorous parties, find your place to shine. |

| phase | date | focus/celebrate |
|---|---|---|
| FULL MOON AQUARIUS (17°00') | AUG 9 3:55AM | **Celebrate:** Your weirdest ideas, teams and communities where you feel seen and embraced, your sharing and accepting spirit, technology that keeps you connected, hopes and dreams for the future, your idealistic nature that refuses to give up on humanity. |
| NEW MOON VIRGO #1 (0°23') | AUG 23 2:07AM | **Focus:** Embrace healthy routines, work out and eat clean, implement efficient systems, hire service providers and assistants, break projects into actionable steps, be of service, adopt a pet. |
| FULL MOON PISCES (15°23') | SEP 7 2:09PM | **TOTAL LUNAR ECLIPSE** **Celebrate:** Your secret fantasies, your creative spirit, messages from your dreams, people who inspire you to think beyond current limitations, compassion and empathy, blurry lines that don't need to be sharpened, the beauty in "ugly" things. |
| NEW MOON VIRGO #2 (29°05') | SEP 21 3:54PM | **PARTIAL SOLAR ECLIPSE** **Focus:** Organize your physical and digital spaces, refine your eating and workout routines, systematize workflow, volunteer, streamline your schedule to reduce stress. |
| FULL MOON ARIES (14°08') | OCT 6 11:48PM | **Celebrate:** Your inner (and outer) bad bitch, new experiences you're brave enough to try, your competitive nature, every unique feature that makes you a rare individual, your fighting spirit that won't give up. |
| NEW MOON LIBRA (28°22') | OCT 21 8:25AM | **Focus:** Find synergies, network to build your contact list, nurture romantic relationships, enjoy art, music and fashion, and beautify everything. |
| FULL MOON TAURUS (13°23') | NOV 5 8:19AM | **SUPERMOON** **Celebrate:** The simple things that bring you joy, the beauty of nature, your favorite music and artists, finding holiday gifts that are sustainable and earth-friendly, creating a comfortable home environment, and food that you love. |

| phase | date | focus/celebrate |
|---|---|---|
| NEW MOON SCORPIO (28°12') | NOV 20 1:47AM | **Focus:** Build trusted bonds, share secrets, join forces (and finances), form strategic partnerships, explore your erotic nature, give everything you do more sizzle and spice. |
| FULL MOON GEMINI (13°04') | DEC 4 6:14PM | **SUPERMOON** **Celebrate:** Build trusted bonds, share secrets, join forces (and finances), form strategic partnerships, explore your erotic nature, give everything you do more sizzle and spice. |
| NEW MOON SAGITTARIUS (28°25') | DEC 19 8:43PM | **Focus:** Turn each day into an adventure, broaden your social horizons, travel, study and self-development goals, make media, speak your truth. |

# ECLIPSES IN
# 2025

# Eclipses

## THESE YEARLY MOON MOMENTS
## SHAKE UP LIFE AS WE KNOW IT

Eclipses arrive four to six times each year, igniting unexpected changes and turning points. If you've been mired in indecision, an eclipse may force you to act, whether you're ready or not. Unanticipated events arise and demand a radical change of direction. Since eclipses reveal shadows, get ready for buried truths and secrets to explode into the open. Situations that are no longer "meant to be" are swept away without notice. Shocking though their delivery may be, eclipses help open up space for progress.

## SOLAR VERSUS LUNAR ECLIPSES

A solar eclipse takes place when the new moon passes between the Sun and the Earth, temporarily blocking out the light of the Sun. The effect is like a spiritual power outage—you either feel wildly off center or your mind becomes crystal clear in the darkness.

Lunar eclipses arrive at full moons. The Earth passes directly between the Sun and the moon, cutting off their "communication" and casting a blood red shadow on the full moon. Situations could pivot abruptly or come to a sudden, unceremonious halt. There's no way around it. During a lunar eclipse, you have to deal with the stormy feelings that arise.

| MAR 14 | MAR 29 | SEP 7 | SEP 21 |
|---|---|---|---|
| Eclipse #1 | Eclipse #2 | Eclipse #3 | Eclipse #4 |
| 2:55 AM | 6:58 AM | 2:09 PM | 3:54 PM |
| Total Lunar Eclipse in Virgo (23°57') | Partial Solar Eclipse in Aries (9°00') | Total Lunar Eclipse in Pisces (15°23') | Partial Solar Eclipse in Virgo (29°05') |

*All dates and times in Eastern Time Zone*

# Eclipse # 1

### MAR 14 (2:55 AM) TOTAL LUNAR ECLIPSE IN VIRGO (23°57)
The first Virgo eclipse since 2016, this total lunar eclipse shines a spotlight on health, routines and service. It's a powerful moment to reassess how well your daily habits support your overall well-being. With Virgo's analytical energy, you can clean up the details of your life, from workflow to eating habits to your self-care practices. Emotional clarity around relationships and work-life balance may also surface, encouraging you to release perfectionism and embrace more sustainable ways of managing your responsibilities.

# Eclipse #2

### MAR 29 (6:58 AM) PARTIAL SOLAR ECLIPSE IN ARIES (9°00')
This partial solar eclipse in Aries marks the conclusion of a series on the Aries-Libra axis that began in April 2023, bringing closure to themes around self vs. relationships. Take bold, courageous action toward personal goals, especially those that align with your authentic desires. Aries energy is impulsive and pioneering, so this eclipse could propel you into a new chapter of independence, leadership, or self-discovery. Whether you're launching a new project or setting personal boundaries, the key is to prioritize yourself without sacrificing collaboration.

# Eclipse # 3

## SEP 7 (2:09 PM) TOTAL LUNAR ECLIPSE IN PISCES (15°23')

A dreamy and emotional total lunar eclipse in Pisces brings matters of intuition, spirituality, and creativity to the forefront. Let go of rigid structures and embrace flow and surrender. Here's your cue to release old emotional baggage or patterns that have been holding you back from experiencing peace or connection. Since Pisces rules imagination and compassion, this eclipse is perfect for healing wounds, exploring artistic projects and tapping into your intuitive side. Expect heightened sensitivity, but also a sense of relief as you let go of what's no longer serving your emotional and spiritual growth.

# Eclipse # 4

## SEP 21 (3:54 PM) PARTIAL SOLAR ECLIPSE IN VIRGO (29°05')

The second Virgo eclipse of the year, this partial solar eclipse at 29º Virgo brings a fresh start to how you manage your time, resources, and daily responsibilities. Since it's also the second in a rare pair of Virgo new moons (the first was on August 23), you could already be well on your way to handling these matters. Virgo's meticulous energy urges you to refine your plans and focus on practicality, efficiency, and self-care. This eclipse provides a push to set new intentions around your work habits, health routines, or even a project that requires detailed attention. It's a great time to create systems that support long-term growth and well-being, while also letting go of perfectionism.

*All dates and times in Eastern Time Zone*

# INNER PLANETS IN
# 2025

# Mercury

Messenger Mercury is the ruler of information, communication and our intellectual processes. The closest planet to the Sun, Mercury orbits through each zodiac sign for three weeks. These cycles shape our cultural interests. From the topics we're buzzing about to the ways we communicate, whatever sign Mercury is occupying plays a role.

| date | sign | what's going on |
|------|------|-----------------|
| JAN 1 | SAGITTARIUS | Blue-sky conversations are lit with excitement. Discuss expansion plans with a diverse pool of people, but make sure you research the details before you green-light them. |
| JAN 8 | CAPRICORN | Conversations are serious, goal-oriented, and focused on results. Practicality prevails, but communication can feel rigid or overly formal. |
| JAN 27 | AQUARIUS | Communication takes a visionary, innovative turn. Conversations are future-focused and idealistic, but emotions may be overlooked in favor of logic. |
| FEB 14 | PISCES | Words become dreamy, poetic, and intuitive. Interactions are compassionate and imaginative, but clarity can drift and misunderstandings may occur. |
| MAR 3 | ARIES | Communication is fast and direct. Attention spans are short, so speak in bullet points. Watch for impulsive words and fiery reactivity. |
| MAR 15 | RETROGRADE IN ARIES | Tempers flare and harsh tones cause misunderstandings. Slow down before reacting, and double-check plans to avoid miscommunication or rushed decisions. |
| MAR 29 | RETROGRADE IN PISCES | Communication gets foggy, and compulsions override logic. Daydreaming takes over, leading to confusion or missed details. Revisit plans with extra care. |

| date | sign | what's going on |
|---|---|---|
| APR 7 | DIRECT IN PISCES | Clarity returns after a muddled period. Intuition and creativity flow smoothly again, making it easier to express emotions and connect with others on a deeper level. |
| APR 16 | ARIES | Conversations are bold, direct, and action-driven. Expect fast-paced exchanges, but be mindful of bluntness or speaking without thinking. |
| MAY 10 | TAURUS | Conversations slow down and become more thoughtful. People are practical and grounded. Stubbornness may creep in, but decisions are steady and deliberate. |
| MAY 25 | GEMINI | The mind races with curiosity and multitasking rules. Ideas flow quickly, and conversations are lively, but focus can be scattered. |
| JUN 8 | CANCER | Words are infused with emotion. Communication becomes nurturing and intuitive, but mood swings can cloud clarity. Speak from the heart. |
| JUN 26 | LEO | Speak with flair and confidence! Conversations take on a dramatic tone, but watch out for self-centeredness. Creative expression thrives. |
| JUL 18 | RETROGRADE IN LEO | Drama and ego clashes can derail conversations. Watch for overconfidence or misinterpretation. Revisit creative projects and be mindful of how you express yourself. |
| AUG 11 | DIRECT IN LEO | Communication regains its bold, confident flair. Creative projects can move forward, and self-expression becomes clearer—just be mindful of ego trips. |
| SEP 2 | VIRGO | Communication is detailed, analytical, and efficient. It's time to plan, organize, and solve problems, but don't get lost in perfectionism. |
| SEP 18 | LIBRA | Diplomacy and balance rule conversations. It's all about finding harmony and weighing both sides, but decision-making won't be easy. |

| date | sign | what's going on |
|------|------|-----------------|
| OCT 6 | SCORPIO | Conversations go deep and reveal hidden truths. Words can be intense, investigative, and transformative—just avoid obsessiveness or secrecy. |
| OCT 29 | SAGITTARIUS | Communication becomes bold, optimistic, and blunt. It's time to talk big ideas and philosophy, but be mindful of exaggeration or tactlessness. |
| NOV 9 | RETROGRADE IN SAGITTARIUS | Plans go awry, and travel or grandiose ideas need revision. Enthusiasm is high, but avoid jumping to conclusions or making promises you can't keep. |
| NOV 18 | RETROGRADE IN SCORPIO | Secrets come to light, and intense conversations resurface. Emotions run deep, so be cautious with power struggles and avoid obsessive thinking. Reflect before you react. |
| NOV 29 | DIRECT IN SCORPIO | Conversations regain intensity but with more focus and control. Secrets and hidden truths that surfaced during the retrograde can now be addressed with clarity and depth. |
| DEC 11 | SAGITTARIUS (until JAN 1, 2026) | Ideas flow freely, with a focus on big-picture thinking and optimism. You'll crave deep, philosophical conversations, but watch out for exaggeration or glossing over details. |

# Venus

Venus, the planet of romance, beauty and luxury, lends its decadent energy to every zodiac sign for three to five weeks. Who will we swoon for? Venus sets the love language of the moment, determining best moves for pleasure and passion.

| date | sign | what's going on |
|------|------|-----------------|
| JAN 2 | PISCES | Love becomes dreamy, compassionate, and romantic. Emotions are deep and poetic, but boundaries may blur. Idealism rules relationships and creativity. |

| date | sign | what's going on |
| --- | --- | --- |
| FEB 4 | ARIES | Passion ignites as love becomes bold, adventurous, and spontaneous. You're ready to take charge in romance, but impatience and impulsiveness can stir drama. |
| MAR 1 | RETROGRADE IN ARIES | Old flames and unresolved issues resurface, urging you to reflect on your approach to love. Avoid impulsive decisions. Take time to reassess desires. |
| MAR 27 | RETROGRADE IN PISCES | Emotions and past relationships come into focus, sparking nostalgia or confusion. Dreamy connections may cloud judgment, so reflect before committing. |
| APR 12 | DIRECT IN PISCES | Clarity returns in love, and romantic dreams can now unfold with a sense of purpose. Compassion flows, but with stronger boundaries in place. |
| APR 30 | ARIES | Love is fiery, spontaneous, and full of excitement. You're drawn to passionate connections, but impatience or a desire for instant gratification could spark drama in relationships. |
| JUN 6 | TAURUS | Love is sensual, stable, and grounded. Relationships focus on pleasure, loyalty, and comfort, but possessiveness or stubbornness may also creep in. |
| JUL 4 | GEMINI | Flirtation and curiosity dominate as love turns lighthearted, intellectual, and social. Keep conversations lively and fun, but beware of scattered or superficial interactions. |
| JUL 30 | CANCER | Love becomes nurturing, emotional, and protective. You crave deeper connections and security, but watch out for moodiness or clinginess in relationships. |
| AUG 25 | LEO | Romance is grand and dramatic. Self-expression and affection flow boldly, but be mindful of attention-seeking behavior or letting ego drive your love life. |
| SEP 19 | VIRGO | Love takes a practical, devoted turn. You show affection through helpful acts and attention to detail, but watch for perfectionism or over-criticism. |

| date | sign | what's going on |
|---|---|---|
| OCT 13 | LIBRA | Romance thrives on balance, harmony, and beauty. Relationships are diplomatic and fair, but indecision and people-pleasing could hinder deeper connections. |
| NOV 6 | SCORPIO | Love is intense, passionate, and transformative. Deep bonds are formed, but emotional power struggles or jealousy can lead to turbulence. |
| NOV 30 | SAGITTARIUS | Adventure beckons as love becomes free-spirited, bold, and open-minded. You seek excitement and growth in relationships, but commitment might feel restrictive. |
| DEC 24 | CAPRICORN Until JAN 17, 2026 | Love turns serious, responsible, and goal-oriented. You're focused on building lasting commitments, but romance can feel practical and businesslike at times. |

# Mars

Mars is the planet of action, drive, and ambition, pushing you to take bold steps toward your goals. Mars brings a burst of energy when it transits through a sign for six to eight weeks on average and supports with tackling big projects or asserting yourself in key areas of life. Knowing when to harness Mars' dynamic influence helps you plan for periods of high motivation, but be mindful—Mars can also stir up conflict if not channeled wisely.

| date | sign | what's going on |
|---|---|---|
| JAN 1 | RETROGRADE IN LEO | Creative passions slow down, and you may second-guess bold actions. Old conflicts resurface, particularly around ego or pride. Reevaluate your desires before moving forward. |
| JAN 6 | RETROGRADE IN CANCER | Energy turns inward, making emotional confrontations likely. You may feel less motivated or struggle with moodiness, as old family or home-related issues come to the surface for healing. |

| date | sign | what's going on |
|------|------|-----------------|
| FEB 23 | DIRECT IN CANCER | Emotional drive returns, and you feel protective and motivated to take care of home and family. Be mindful of passive-aggressive tendencies or emotional outbursts. |
| APR 18 | LEO | Bold, confident, and dramatic, you're ready to take center stage and fight for what you want. Your energy is high, but watch out for pride or over-the-top reactions. |
| JUN 17 | VIRGO | Energy becomes focused and efficient. You'll want to tackle tasks with precision and productivity, but perfectionism or nitpicking could cause frustration. |
| AUG 6 | LIBRA | Action takes a diplomatic turn as you seek balance in conflict. You'll focus on cooperation and harmony, but indecision or avoiding confrontation can lead to tension. |
| SEP 22 | SCORPIO | Passionate, intense, and fiercely driven, you're ready to pursue your goals with unshakable determination. Watch out for obsession or control issues in relationships or ambitions. |
| NOV 4 | SAGITTARIUS | Energy is adventurous, bold, and optimistic. You'll feel motivated to take risks and explore new horizons, but be careful of impulsiveness or reckless behavior. |
| DEC 15 | CAPRICORN Until JAN 23, 2026 | Disciplined and determined, you're ready to tackle long-term goals with steady ambition. Productivity is high, but avoid becoming too rigid or overworking yourself. |

*All dates and times in Eastern Time Zone*

# OUTER PLANETS IN
# 2025

# Jupiter

Jupiter, the planet of expansion and abundance, blesses you with growth opportunities during its year-long tour through each zodiac sign. Whether it's luck in finances, learning, or personal growth, Jupiter helps you plan for periods of optimism and possibility. This is your time to dream big and pursue goals that push your boundaries!

| date | sign | what's going on |
|------|------|-----------------|
| JAN 1 | RETROGRADE IN GEMINI Since OCT 9, 2024 | Growth slows, and you may revisit old ideas or projects. It's a time to rethink big plans and fine-tune your communication skills. Be cautious of spreading yourself too thin. |
| FEB 4 | DIRECT IN GEMINI | Expansion and learning speed up again. Conversations and opportunities for growth flourish, encouraging curiosity, travel, and exploring new collaborations. |
| JUN 9 | CANCER | Emotional expansion and nurturing energy take the lead. You'll focus on deepening relationships and building a sense of security. This is a time for growth through family, home, and emotional fulfillment. |
| NOV 11 | RETROGRADE IN CANCER Until MAR 10, 2026 | Reflect on how you seek emotional and domestic security. Reassess your connection to family, home, and inner growth, as this retrograde calls for revisiting and realigning emotional priorities. |

# Saturn

Saturn brings structure, discipline and long-term success. The ringed taskmaster lends its sobering energy to a single zodiac sign for two to three years, helping you plan for serious commitments, hard work, and personal growth. Saturn asks you to build a strong foundation before reaching for success. Persistence pays off under its watchful eye.

| date | sign | what's going on |
|------|------|-----------------|
| JAN 1 | PISCES | Discipline meets dreams as Saturn helps you structure your spiritual growth and creative pursuits. It's a time to turn fantasies into reality, but stay mindful of escapism or avoiding responsibilities. |
| MAY 24 | ARIES | Time to take bold, decisive action toward your goals. Saturn's presence in Aries encourages leadership and initiative, but be cautious of impatience or a "my way or the highway" attitude. |
| JUL 13 | RETROGRADE IN ARIES | Reflect on how you've been asserting yourself and pursuing your goals. This retrograde invites you to slow down, reassess your leadership style, and correct impulsive actions. It's a time to refine your strategies for long-term success. |
| SEP 1 | RETROGRADE IN PISCES | Reflect on how you seek emotional and domestic security. Reassess your connection to family, home, and inner growth, as this retrograde calls for revisiting and realigning emotional priorities. |
| NOV 27 | DIRECT IN PISCES | Solidify your dreams with a practical plan. Saturn's direct motion helps you get back on track with your creative and spiritual goals, with a renewed sense of discipline and clarity. |

# Uranus

Uranus is the planet of innovation, surprise and rebellion, shaking things up during its seven-year cycles through each sign. These transits bring unexpected changes, breakthroughs, and moments of liberation. The opportunity? To break free from old patterns and think outside the box.

| date | sign | what's going on |
|------|------|-----------------|
| JAN 1 | RETROGRADE IN TAURUS Since SEP 1, 2024 | Unfinished business around stability, finances, and security is brought to the surface. Progress slows down, offering time to rethink how you approach material comfort and resources. |
| JAN 30 | DIRECT IN TAURUS | Sudden shifts in finances, security, and personal values resume. You may experience breakthroughs in how you create stability and embrace change, especially around money and possessions. |
| JUL 7 | GEMINI | Innovation takes flight in communication, learning, and adaptability. This is a time for experimental ideas and unconventional thinking—expect major shifts in how you connect with others and process information. |
| SEP 6 | RETROGRADE IN GEMINI | Reassess how you communicate and adapt to changing circumstances. This period is about reflecting on new ideas or exciting collabs that require further refinement before moving forward. |
| NOV 7 | RETROGRADE IN TAURUS Until FEB 3, 2026 | Here's another chance to reexamine your relationship with security, finances, and comfort. You're wrapping up unfinished lessons around stability before Uranus leaves Taurus for good in April 2026. |

# Neptune

Neptune, the planet of dreams and spirituality, brings each sign periods of heightened imagination, creativity, and intuition. Its lengthy 14-year stay in each sign allows you to plan for spiritual growth, artistic endeavors, and to draw from the deep well of your psyche. Be careful. Neptune's foggy influence can blur reality, so check those facts.

| date | sign | what's going on |
| --- | --- | --- |
| JAN 1 | PISCES | Intuition and imagination are heightened. Spiritual growth and compassion flow easily, but be mindful of blurring boundaries or escaping into fantasy. |
| MAR 30 | ARIES | Bold dreams and visionary action take the stage. Neptune in Aries pushes you to pursue your ideals with courage and creativity—just watch out for impulsive decisions or chasing unrealistic goals. |
| JUL 4 | RETROGRADE IN ARIES | Revisit your dreams and ideals with a critical eye. This retrograde invites you to reflect on bold actions and fine-tune your approach to turning visions into reality. |
| OCT 22 | RETROGRADE IN PISCES | Dive deeper into spiritual introspection. You'll reflect on your emotional and spiritual growth, reconsidering how well your ideals align with reality. |
| DEC 10 | DIRECT IN PISCES | Clarity returns to your dreams and spiritual pursuits. You'll feel a renewed sense of inspiration, ready to pursue your creative and emotional goals with grounded vision. |

# Pluto

Pluto is the planet of transformation and power, driving deep inner change over its long transits. Each sign experiences Pluto's influence for over a decade, making it a time to plan for profound personal growth, shedding of old identities, and doing important shadow work that allows for emotional and spiritual evolution.

| date | sign | what's going on |
|---|---|---|
| JAN 1 | AQUARIUS | Deep transformation arrives through technology, innovation, and social structures. You're called to embrace personal and collective change—expect radical shifts in how you relate to community and power. |
| MAY 4 | RETROGRADE IN AQUARIUS | Time to revisit and reassess the transformations happening in your social life. This retrograde slows down the revolutionary changes, giving you space to reflect on personal growth and societal shifts. |
| OCT 13 | DIRECT IN AQUARIUS | The pace of transformation accelerates once again. You'll feel empowered to embrace change, take control of your future, and contribute to the collective evolution with renewed determination. |

# The Lunar Nodes

The lunar nodes, with their 18-month cycles, show where destiny calls and where you must release outmoded ways. The North Node points to your growth path, while the South Node guides you in letting go of outdated habits. Plan for karmic shifts, major life changes, and alignment with your higher purpose.

| date | sign | what's going on |
|------|------|-----------------|
| JAN 1 | **NORTH NODE IN ARIES SOUTH NODE IN LIBRA** Since JUL 17, 2023 | Answer the call to embrace independence, courage, and self-leadership. The North Node in Aries spurs bold action and personal empowerment, while the South Node in Libra asks you to release codependency and people-pleasing tendencies in relationships. |
| JAN 11 | **NORTH NODE IN PISCES SOUTH NODE IN VIRGO** Until JUL 26, 2026 | Put some steam behind your dreams. The North Node in Pisces encourages you to tap into your compassion and divine inspiration, while the South Node in Virgo helps you release the need to micromanage and over-analyze, opening up space for creativity and emotional connection. |

# Chiron

Chiron, the "wounded healer," helps you address deep emotional wounds and past traumas. Chiron is a comet that orbits between Saturn and Uranus; it takes about 50 years to move through all 12 zodiac signs. As it moves through a sign, Chiron offers a time for reflection, healing, and personal growth. Plan for moments of vulnerability and the courage to transform pain into wisdom.

| date | sign | what's going on |
|------|------|-----------------|
| JAN 1 | ARIES | Heal through courage and self-empowerment. You're confronting wounds around identity and independence. Embrace vulnerability to build inner strength. |
| JUL 30 | **RETROGRADE IN ARIES** Until JAN 2, 2026 | Reflect on past wounds related to self-worth and personal power. This retrograde encourages deep introspection, helping you uncover and heal old insecurities about asserting yourself. |

*All dates and times in Eastern Time Zone*

# RETROGRADES IN
# 2025

*When planets go "backward," slowdowns and chaos can ensue.*

When a planet passes the Earth in its orbit around the Sun, it's said to be going retrograde. From our vantage point on Earth, the planet appears to be on a reverse commute, backing up through the zodiac instead of advancing ahead degree by degree. While these aren't optimal times to start anything new, they can be powerful periods to review our progress and enjoy nostalgia.

| mercury | dates | retrograde in |
|---|---|---|
| Communication style, social contacts, systems for workflow, short trips and travel plans, contracts and agreement. | MAR 15–29 | ARIES (9°35'–00°00') |
| | MAR 29 – APR 7 | PISCES (29°59'–26°49') |
| | JUL 18 – AUG 11 | LEO (15°34'–4°14') |
| | NOV 9–18 | SAGITTARIUS (6°51'–00°00') |
| | NOV 18–29 | SCORPIO (29°59'–20°42') |

| venus | dates | retrograde in |
|---|---|---|
| Relationships and love, personal values, self-worth, finances and spending habits, aesthetic and style choices. | MAR 1–27 | ARIES (10°50'–00°00') |
| | MAR 27 – APR 12 | PISCES (29°59'–24°37') |

| mars | dates | retrograde in |
|---|---|---|
| Motivation and goals, energy levels, conflict resolution, anger management, physical fitness and health. | DEC 6, 2024 – JAN 6, 2025 | LEO (06°10'–00°00') |
| | JAN 6–FEB 23 | CANCER (29°59'–17°00') |

| jupiter | dates | retrograde in |
|---|---|---|
| Long-term goals, beliefs and philosophy, expansion plans, travel and education, opportunities for growth. | OCT 9, 2024 – FEB 4, 2025 | GEMINI (21°20'–11°17') |
| | NOV 11, 2025 – MAR 10, 2026 | CANCER (25°09'–15°05') |

| saturn | 2025 dates | retrograde in... |
|---|---|---|
| Responsibilities, long-term commitments, structures and foundations, career and ambitions, personal discipline. | JUL 13–SEP 1 | ARIES (1°56'–00°00') |
| | SEP 1–NOV 27 | PISCES (29°59'–25°09') |

| uranus | 2025 dates | retrograde in... |
|---|---|---|
| Independence, innovation and change, technology use, social causes, freedom vs. stability. | SEP 1, 2024 – JAN 30, 2025 | TAURUS (27°15'–23°15') |
| | SEP 6 – NOV 7, 2025 | GEMINI (1°27'–00°00') |
| | NOV 7, 2025 – FEB 3, 2026 | TAURUS (29°59'–27°27') |

| neptune | 2025 dates | retrograde in... |
|---|---|---|
| Dreams and intuition, boundaries, spiritual practices, creative projects, escapism tendencies. | JUL 4–OCT 22 | ARIES (2°10'–00°00') |
| | OCT 22–DEC 10 | PISCES (29°59'–29°22') |

| pluto | 2025 dates | retrograde in... |
|---|---|---|
| Power dynamics, transformation, control issues, deep-seated fears, emotional intensity. | MAY 4–OCT 13 | AQUARIUS (3°49'–1°22') |

| chiron | 2025 dates | retrograde in... |
|---|---|---|
| Emotional wounds, healing practices, personal vulnerabilities, old traumas, self-empowerment strategies. | JUL 30, 2025 – JAN 2, 2026 | ARIES (27°09'–22°35') |

*All dates and times in Eastern Time Zone*

47

# 2025
# Year of THE Wood Snake

Shed your skin and evolve! The Year of the Wood Snake slinks in on January 29, 2025, at the Aquarius new moon, bringing with it twelve months of renewal and growth. Known for its stealthiness and wisdom, the Snake wants you to move with purpose and precision. Relinquish what no longer serves you so you can evolve.

This serpentine energy guides us all until February 16, 2026 so embrace its slow, steady transformation. Changes might not happen overnight, but that's okay. The Snake is associated with pragmatic Taurus in the Western zodiac, an earth sign known for its grounded, deliberate approach to life. As you weave through the year, you can methodically align with your true path. The key lies in trusting the process.

While the pace of 2025 might feel more subdued compared to 2024's Dragon year, don't mistake this for a lack of action. A Snake year rewards those who think ahead, stay calm under pressure, and strike only when the timing is perfect. Summon your inner strategist. It's time to play the long game and build something solid from the ground up.

The Wood element, which governs all years ending in 4 or 5, brings its own unique flavor to the Snake's influence. Wood encourages growth, expansion, and renewal. Visualize a vine winding its way up a trellis, gaining strength with every twist. This is a year to rise strategically, rather than rushing to the top.

The last Wood Snake year was 1965, a time of profound cultural shifts. The world saw the rise of the counterculture movement, the birth of iconic fashion trends like the miniskirt, and a greater push for civil rights and equality. Sixty years later, we might find similar themes echoing back to us with the Wood Snake year, offering opportunities for transformation and renewal on a global scale.

## HOW TO HAVE A SAVVY SNAKE YEAR

**MOVE STRATEGICALLY:** Patience, precision, and strategy will be your greatest allies. Forget impulsive moves or leaping before you look. Slow down, observe and wait for the perfect moment to strike.

**PLAY UP THE INTRIGUE:** Snakes are masters of stealth, so don't be fooled by a calm surface. Major shifts are happening, both personally and globally, just beneath the radar. Be a bit more mysterious to draw people in.

**REGENERATE AND EVOLVE:** The regenerative Snake understands that you have to shed the old to evolve into the new. Growth may require you to release relationships and obligations that no longer serve you—even if there is grief involved.

**ELEVATE YOUR TASTES:** Quiet luxury and timeless elegance: This is what to invest in during a Snake year. Take time to curate the right option and savor the treasure hunting process.

**DETOXIFY AND HEAL:** In traditional Chinese medicine, the Wood element is linked to the detoxifying liver. Incorporate gentle daily exercise, clean eating and sleep sanctification.

**SUBTLE MOVEMENTS, BIG RESULTS:** Tone down the hype! In 2025, the bold, risky moves that caused a stir in the Dragon Year will fall flat. Focus on careful planning and thorough research. Work behind the scenes, laying the foundation for future success.

# 9
# Universal Year

by Felicia Bender, the Practical Numerologist

**2025 is a 9 Universal Year**

$$2+0+2+5=9$$

### *themes*
### OF A 9 UNIVERSAL YEAR

Releasing

Flow

Completion

Compassion

Collectivism

Humanitarianism

Surrender

### *challenges*
### OF A 9 UNIVERSAL YEAR

Stagnation

Control

Resistance

Preservation

Fear

Ignorance

*2024 gave us a crash course in power dynamics—how we empower and disempower; misuse and properly wield authority. The 8 Universal Year was all about money and value, as we saw global economies restructuring, AI taking off and worldwide wars escalating. Now, in 2025, we transition from the power-hungry 8 into the heart-driven 9. It's time to see where this new energy takes us.*

---

As we enter 2025, we're stepping into a year of global closure and completion—a time to reflect on how we want to move forward as a collective. There's a lot on the line. We can either evolve into a new world rooted in compassion and humanity, or we can remain on our current course, risking self-destruction.

2026 will kick off a 1 Universal Year, marking the start of a fresh nine-year cycle. But first, we need to clear out what's no longer working. The 9 Universal Year is like a deep cosmic cleanse.

In numerology, the 9 is a sacred number. It's the number of the compassionate humanitarian, spiritual ascension, letting go and forgiveness. The 9 invites us to step back from materialism and lead with our hearts.

## HOW TO MAKE THE MOST OUT OF THE
# 9 Universal Year

### LET. IT. GO.

The big question for 2025: What do we need to release in order to make space for positive global change? The goal this year is to let go of what's outdated, so we can step into a new, transformative phase for our world. This is a year of sorting, organizing and reevaluating. It's not about launching something brand new just yet. Instead, we're wrapping up the last nine years, preparing the soil for what's to come. Wherever we feel isolated, angry or defeated is exactly where we need to focus our collective healing energy.

### DO WHAT'S BEST FOR THE COLLECTIVE

The 9 is one of the most evolved numbers in Numerology, carrying the energy of all the other numbers within it. It's often seen as sacred, representing loss, letting go and deep spiritual rewards. In a 9 cycle, the focus shifts from personal gain to the well-being of all. It's about aligning with the present, releasing the past and moving forward with curiosity and an open heart.

### HEAL FROM THE INSIDE OUT

The 9 Universal Year is like winter, a time to prune the dead growth, let the soil rest and prepare for spring. We're standing at a pivotal moment in history, both globally and personally.

2025 is a year for global healing—and individual healing, too. We can't build a new paradigm unless we've done our own inner work. That means dealing with our trauma, clearing out our emotional clutter and upgrading our personal operating systems. We're in a period of accelerated growth, when therapy, energy work and spiritual practices can help us level up.

# CAPRICORN
## IN 2025

| ALL THE PLANETS IN CAPRICORN IN 2025 | YOUR 2025 HOROSCOPE | TOP 5 THEMES FOR CAPRICORN IN 2025 | LOVE HOROSCOPE + LUCKY DATES | MONEY HOROSCOPE + LUCKY DATES |
|---|---|---|---|---|

# Capricorn in 2025

## YOUR YEARLY OVERVIEW

So many people, so little time! If you thought your popularity peaked before, guess again. On January 11, the fateful North Node glides into Pisces, energizing your curious, social third house for eighteen months. Across the board, the karmic South Node treks through Virgo, which can stir up restlessness and turn you into a bit of a nomad. You'll want to do, see and enjoy it all, which means managing your schedule is a must. Lucky for you, expansive Jupiter and innovative Uranus will both spend six months of the year in Gemini and your efficiency-boosting sixth house. Lifehacking is your new superpower (and your lifestyle), whether you're streamlining your work habits, adopting new tech to simplify daily tasks or finally finding the fitness routine that keeps you motivated. This year, think of structure not as a restriction, but as a pathway to more freedom and better health. Partnerships get a burst of momentum on June 9, when growth-agent Jupiter heads into Cancer and your seventh house of relationships for a year. But here's the rub: You won't take kindly to anyone clipping your wings. Can you be more of yourself rather than less? For business, pleasure or mind-blowing romance, create solid alliances that feel expansive. Flowy Neptune and your ruler, structured Saturn, dart into Aries for part of the year, giving your home and family zone a creative but grounded shakeup. Whether it's a move, renovation or establishing firmer roots, blend imagination with practicality and craft a home base that supports your aspirations.

# THE PLANETS IN Capricorn

**THE SUN**
DEC 21, 2024–JAN 19, 2025
DEC 21, 2025–JAN 20, 2026

It's birthday season for you, so step out and shine! Seek novelty and take extra initiative during this radiant monthlong phase.

**NEW MOON**

None in Capricorn this year

**FULL MOON**
JUL 10
4:37PM, 18°50'

Ready, set, manifest! Your work of the past six months bears fruit and it's time to harvest the rewards.

**MERCURY**
JAN 8–27

Crown yourself monarch of the social butterflies when popularity-boosting Mercury visits your sign once a year. Circulate and get social—but don't make promises you can't keep!

**VENUS**
DEC 24, 2025–
JAN 17, 2026

You've got the romantic It Factor when the galactic glamazon charges up your powers of seduction each year. Willpower is weak in the face of beauty and luxury. Watch your spending!

**MARS**
DEC 15, 2025–
JAN 23, 2026

Motivation is high when energetic Mars visits your sign every couple years—but check your combative streak and try not to come on too strong.

# Capricorn in 2025
## HIGHLIGHTS

### REFINE YOUR ROUTINES WITH JUPITER AND URANUS IN GEMINI

Work and wellness are two areas of life that will NOT be "business as usual" in 2025. Liberated Jupiter and rebellious Uranus are both spending half the year in Gemini and your sixth house of daily routines. Jupiter, which is halfway through this transit (May 25, 2024 to June 9, 2025), has you longing for more fluidity in your schedule. Want freedom? Curb your complexifying tendencies and simplify instead. When disruptive Uranus pops into Gemini from July 7 to November 7, you'll get a glimpse of a seven-year cycle that begins in earnest on April 25, 2026. Stay flexible and ready for change because this cycle could bring shifts in colleagues, project timelines, even the entire way that you do your job! Implement healthy habits and prioritize self-care—it may be the best way to stay grounded during all these fluctuations.

### COMMUNICATE AND CIRCULATE: THE NORTH NODE IN PISCES

Is it all about who you know or all about what you say? This year, the answer might be, both. On January 11, the fateful lunar North Node begins an eighteen-month trek through Pisces and your articulate third house, encouraging you to share your story. Whether you're recording a podcast, writing a book or just getting out to socialize on a regular basis, you have a lot to say this year. Collaborate, build networks and pass along your knowledge. Across the zodiac wheel, the karmic South Node takes flight in Virgo and your worldly ninth house, helping you reach a wider audience. Traveling could open up important connections, which might even lead you to relocate or become a regular visitor of a second location. From university campuses to YouTube home studios, teaching could become a new (or renewed) passion.

## VENUS RETROGRADE: REFLECT, RESET AND REALIGN

What's your love language, Capricorn? And how fluent are you when it comes to speaking other people's dialects? Romantic Venus drops into her every-584-day-retrograde from March 1 to April 12, giving you a chance to refresh your skills. What's worked for you in the past may be falling flat or drawing in people who just aren't your type anymore. But what ARE you transmitting? These eye-opening six weeks might just teach you to flirt, seduce and even search for love in a new and improved way. Put pride aside and ask friends and family to weigh in with honest  feedback. Where might your communication style be sending out the wrong signals—not just in love, but with friends and business associates? A little fine-tuning goes a long way.

## HOME BASE MAKEOVER: SATURN AND NEPTUNE IN ARIES

The spotlight swings to your domestic life this spring as two outer planets decamp to Aries, giving you a sneak-peek of longer cycles that pick up again in early 2026. From March 30 to October 22, soulful Neptune sweeps through the Ram's realm making you crave a peaceful oasis. Then, from May 24 to September 1, your ruler, stabilizing Saturn, joins Neptune in this fire sign. If you don't love where you live, start looking around. (And watch the tendency to make sacrifices around this area of your life.) Already in your dream home? The activating Aries energy could inspire some decor updates or give you the motivation to entertain regularly. You may need to set new boundaries with family members this year, especially if they've become a little too reliant on you being their rock and provider at your own expense!

## JUPITER IN CANCER: EXPANSIVE RELATIONSHIPS

On June 9, abundant Jupiter shifts gears, heading into Cancer, where it will activate your seventh house of relationships until June 30, 2026. You need partnerships to feel limitless and freeing now. Anyone who tries to control you or hold you back? Uh, good luck, babe. Emerge from the couple bubble and go mingle—both independently and as a pair. Single Capricorns could meet their match while traveling, studying or doing personal development work. You may feel inspired to co-create with your partner. During this yearlong cycle, you could launch a joint venture from your love nest, buy property together or take a life-changing baecation. If there are unresolved issues brewing, Jupiter's truth-seeking energy can help you clear the air and reach a new level of authenticity with one another.

# TOP 5 THEMES FOR
# Capricorn in 2025

| 1 | 2 | 3 | 4 | 5 |
|---|---|---|---|---|
| RITUALIZE YOUR ROUTINES | EXPAND YOUR ROMANTIC PALETTE | TURN HOME INTO A SANCTUARY | SET BOUNDARIES WITH YOUR INNER CIRCLE | BROADCAST YOUR BELIEFS |

# 1

## RITUALIZE YOUR ROUTINES

### JUPITER AND URANUS IN GEMINI

JUPITER: MAY 25, 2024 – JUNE 9, 2025
URANUS: JULY 7 – NOVEMBER 7, 2025 • JANUARY 26, 2026 – MAY 22, 2033

Quick, Capricorn! Grab your copy of James Clear's Atomic Habits and learn all that you can about "temptation bundling" or "reducing friction" around your daily routines. While you're at it, start turning some of those rote tasks into rituals. Two of the most inventive planets, Jupiter and Uranus, are doing laps through Gemini and your systematic sixth house this year. Structure (your sign's favorite word) creates a clear pathway to freedom. Bonus: You might get into the best shape you've been in for years.

### JUPITER IN GEMINI

MAY 25, 2024 – JUNE 9, 2025

Yoga retreat in Bali? Bikini boot camp in So-Cal? Travel and wellness go hand-in-hand in 2025, thanks to intrepid Jupiter. The vitality-boosting planet is halfway through a yearlong journey through Gemini and your salubrious sixth house. Healthy living has been in the spotlight since May 25, 2024, so you may already have made your mark on the Peloton leaderboard or found the perfect Pilates studio for stretching and strengthening.

Still stuck in couch potato mode? No more! Good-news Jupiter is buzzing through Gemini until June 9, 2025, bringing supersized momentum for your fitness goals. Capitalize on a New Year's membership sale and score yourself a birthday present at a fitness studio that has the elegant vibes a Capricorn needs to stay inspired.

Those workouts will help zap stress, which can ratchet up this year. Projects may have ballooned with expansive Jupiter in your industrious sixth house, which is exciting but also brings another set of challenges. Before you wind up with an administrative nightmare on your hand,s put proper workflows, systems and apps in place to keep you organized. If you want to grow, you have to make sure you are ready to handle the crush of new clients, expenses and other details.

Fortunately, the expansive and hopeful planet can bring a sense of purpose to all your efforts. How can you make them feel less dutiful and more self-empowering? You may need to tap a coach or mastermind group who can help you prioritize and stay accountable. Whenever possible, find ways to turn dull-as-dishwater routines into "sacred rituals"; make momentous tasks "challenges."

Jupiter is the traveler of the zodiac, so your job this year may afford you enough frequent flyer points to earn priority status with your airline of choice. If you're on the hunt for fresh work opportunities, expand your search radius or follow enterprising Jupiter's lead. Starting your own business might be in the cards for many Caps this year. Already the CEO of your own venture? Stake out new markets for your offerings, perhaps in a totally different area code (or country code!).

Liberated Jupiter also reminds you of the importance of personal freedom: both the day-to-day, vacations and flex time. You might be able to renegotiate the terms of your employment and work remotely at least occasionally. This alone will give you the time to prepare healthy meals and get regular movement into your life.

Just one (not too tiny) heads-up: Jovial Jupiter is the god of the feast, and it warns that there really IS such a thing as too much of a good thing. Jupiter in the sixth house can inspire overeating if you aren't mindful since your appetite for everything is growing. This is a great time to work with a nutrition coach and learn how to cook more delicious plant-based and protein-rich dishes. In addition to cardio and weight training, add in exercises that ground you and put you in a meditative mindset. Pull that yoga mat out of the closet and let the Vinyasa flow.

## URANUS IN GEMINI

JULY 7 – NOVEMBER 7, 2025
JANUARY 26, 2026 – MAY 22, 2033

If your motivation—or momentum—starts to flag by the June solstice, just hang on till July 7. That day, high-voltage Uranus lands in Gemini for the first time since 1949, inaugurating what's sure to be a dynamic eight-year journey through your sixth house of work, service, wellness and self-care.

The way you move through your days is about to shift dramatically. The new focus is on simplifying steps and increasing ease. How can you do more with less? That's a puzzle you'll be eager to solve. And once you do, feel free to monetize it as your "proprietary method" or make it accessible through an app.

But let's not get ahead of ourselves. In 2025, Uranus only hangs out in Gemini for a brief, four-month stint, until November 7. Nevertheless, that should be enough of a wave to alert you that a seismic lifestyle shift is heading your way. Next year, on April 25, 2026, Uranus plants itself back in Gemini for seven more years, until May 22, 2033. And yes, this will be a game-changer, particularly when it comes to the way you structure your days.

Since May 2018, Uranus has been in Taurus and your glamorous fifth house, where it's been helping you to add more pleasure to your life. Doing so may have felt like an act of revolution for your hard-driving sign. Incorporating play into work? Prioritizing fun over work some days? That's been a radical concept for you to swallow over the past seven years, Capricorn. Here's hoping that you're among the Sea Goats who allowed yourselves to experience joy, even during the hardest hours (like say, a pandemic), while Uranus toured Taurus.

Starting this July 7, your desires shift in a more streamlined direction. The excessive energy of the past seven years will start to feel burdensome; like something that you're "so over." Overdoing it could take a toll on your health, especially if you're running on a cocktail of stress, adrenaline and caffeine. As futuristic, metaphysical Uranus plugs into curious Gemini and your work and wellness sector, it's time to stop silo-ing those two categories. How can you accomplish more and stress less? Get ready to explore. With edgy Uranus in inquisitive Gemini, you'll be as open to holistic healing and naturopathic medicine as you will be to treatments involving lasers, AI and psychedelics.

Don't worry about being bored! Under this innovative cosmic energy, your workaday routines could become charged with excitement in a different way. While your focus may always be on the final result, you'll become at least as interested in the journey as you are the destination.

Still, we must warn you that there's a paradox to contend with here. Rebellious Uranus goes against the grain, while the sixth house follows processes and procedures. From July 7 to November 7, you may feel constrained by "authority figures" and frustrated by people who insist about playing by the rules. Isn't it ironic, Capricorn, since you're essentially railing against the role that you, as the zodiac's CEO, so often play.

During Uranus in Gemini, embrace the metaphoric role of Chief People Officer instead of Chief Executive Officer. Collaborate with innovators, thought leaders and colleagues you consider to be ahead of the curve. Who you work with determines everything, so set yourself up for success by aligning with a team that values your contributions and demands excellence from every person on board.

While this might sound like a tall order, you don't have to charge in with your usual go-getter zeal. Small tweaks can add up to an entire lifestyle shift with minimal inconvenience or discomfort. Start with: Do your routines support your work life or make things more complicated? Could your systems be more organized or streamlined? In savvy Gemini, technologist Uranus can help you hack your way to a more efficient flow. Ditto for any adjustments you've been wanting to make to your nutritional or exercise regimen.

You may already know what would be ideal, Capricorn. Yet, it's that giant leap from knowing to doing that always trips us up. So rather than put undue pressure on yourself, add one or two tiny new things (weekly yoga, cooking at home) at a time as you phase out unhelpful stuff (boozy brunches, working after hours)...or people. Come up with a game plan and a few specific pivots you can make this year. Stay the course, and you'll realize noticeable progress before Uranus spins back into Gemini at the end of April 2026!

# 2 EXPAND YOUR ROMANTIC PALETTE

## JUPITER IN CANCER

JUNE 9, 2025 – JUNE 30, 2026

Ready to add a plus-one to your roster? When Jupiter swings into Cancer on June 9, it lends its exploratory, broad-minded energy to your seventh house of relationships. Two becomes your magic number in the second half of the year, especially if you're willing to stretch beyond the confines of what (and who) you've traditionally pursued. Opposites attract now— and how! Prepare to have your eyes opened and your mind blown during this cycle, which lasts until June 30, 2026.

Pack your bags, Capricorn. Since Jupiter is the cosmic jetsetter, your preferences may meander into new, unexplored terrain. Stay open to people from diverse cultural backgrounds, as well as the hottie who lives long-distance. Put your suburban, four-bedroom Tudor fantasies on ice for a moment, and open your mind to commuting for monthly visits to a lover in another ZIP code. Absence can make the loins grow hotter.

For coupled Capricorns, this thirteen-month cycle provides bountiful opportunities for co-creation. Jupiter's entrepreneurial influence could see you mixing business and pleasure, teaming up with your sweetie on a professional venture, which is a dream come true for work-hard Capricorn. Start saving up for an epic baecation. Nothing seals a bond quite like a pilgrimage with your partner. How about a cruise on the Caspian Sea or visiting the sacred pyramids in Cairo?

If trouble's been brewing in your closest partnerships, look out! Honest-to-a-fault Jupiter rips off the mask and forces you to stop pretending that everything is (clenched teeth) "fine." But stay aware of your own intensity, Capricorn. Whatever you've held in could rush out like a torrent, completely overwhelming your other half. While you don't want to deny or suppress your feelings, try to keep your focus on the long-term objectives that you want to reach together. If you need help processing anger, perhaps sort through your feelings with a neutral third party before broaching these tender topics.

The last time Jupiter visited Cancer was from June 25, 2013 to July 16, 2014. Flip back in your timeline to see what was happening for you then. Similar themes may arise for you in partnerships or you may be completing a cycle that began nearly twelve years ago. This doesn't necessarily portend a breakup, but it could point to a breakthrough. As the zodiac sign that ages in reverse, you become lighter and freer with every year that passes. You may feel ready to shed some heaviness or undue responsibility that you've carried for others. That's nothing to feel guilty about, Capricorn. Jupiter is here to lift excess burdens so you can be fully present (read: not seething with resentment) in your relationships.

That said, free-spirited Jupiter may indeed be here to liberate you from a connection that you've outgrown. That's a hard concept for you as a devoted Capricorn to swallow. You hate to give up once you've invested.

If you've tried everything from tantric retreats to couples' therapy to tandem skydiving and satisfaction is still eluding you, then you may want to face the music. Grief will be unavoidable, but the sooner you feel, the faster you'll heal.

Professional and creative partnerships are also blessed by Jupiter's beams. Since Cancer is your opposite sign, you may find yourself drawn to people who are basically your opposite. You'll do best with a complementary force now, the yang to your yin, rather than a kindred spirit. Plus, it's good sense to ally with people who know how to pick up where you leave off. Jupiter happens to be "exalted" in Cancer, which is its most potent position in the zodiac. Power couple fantasies—which every Capricorn has—could come to life after June 9. Keep your standards high, but not so impossibly rigid that no one gets past the first checkpoint.

# 3 TURN HOME INTO A SANCTUARY

## SATURN AND NEPTUNE IN ARIES

NEPTUNE: MARCH 30 – OCTOBER 22, 2025 • JANUARY 26, 2026 – MARCH 23, 2039
SATURN: MAY 24 – SEPTEMBER 1, 2025 • FEBRUARY 13, 2026 – APRIL 12, 2028

Whether you're putting down roots or pulling them up, get ready for some shifts in your home life this year. Two significant planets—stable Saturn and fluid Neptune—will spend a portion of 2025 in Aries and your domestic fourth house. It's been a very long time since either one visited the sign of the Ram. Saturn last trekked through Aries from 1996 to 1998. Neptune hasn't been here since 1862 to 1875!

The energy of Aries is fiery, independent and active, which is an interesting vibe to have ruling all things "home and family." While Saturn is only in Aries for three months this year, and Neptune for six, things could get lively under your roof. If you've been pondering a change of address, renovations or a new family plan, 2025 could elicit exciting developments. No need to rush, however. In 2026, both planets spin back into Aries for longer cycles—Saturn for two more years and Neptune for another thirteen.

## NEPTUNE IN ARIES

MARCH 30 – OCTOBER 22, 2025
JANUARY 26, 2026 – MARCH 23, 2039

Home sweet sanctuary? Neptune drifts into Aries from March 30 to October 22, casting a spell in your fourth house of family, domesticity and emotional roots. Your concept of personal space and security begins to go through a transformation, one that will be fourteen years in the making. Although Neptune only visits Aries for six months in 2025, the effects will be eye-opening. And once the numinous planet settles back into the Ram's realm for a longer stay, from January 26, 2026 to March 23, 2039, changes can REALLY get underway. Don't resist the call to explore the more subtle, spiritual aspects of your personal life this year, even if all you hear is a whisper.

As someone who values structure and stability, fluid Neptune in this foundational part of your chart can feel destabilizing. It's a definite departure from your pragmatic approach to life! Over the next decade-plus, you will get a master class in relying on intuition as much as logic when it comes to making personal decisions. We're not saying you should ignore statistics or the numbers on your precious spreadsheets. The thing is, they may not align with your deeper instincts—the ones that are calling you to do something "impractical," like selling off an asset, buying a fixer-upper or making a cross-country (or out-of-country!) move.

Spiritual Neptune in self-sovereign Aries turns up the volume on your core desires and could shift your compass in an unexpected direction after March 30. Heck, you might just be entering your "Eat, Pray, Love" era. Pay attention to what (and who!) makes you feel like your truest, most sacred self. This is where you want to be, Capricorn, and also who you should keep around.

During this cycle, your connection to home and family may take on a more mystical or spiritual dimension. You're typically focused on creating a solid, reliable environment, but Neptune's influence will encourage you to infuse your space with a sense of peace, creativity, and emotional warmth. Personal tastes matter mightily when it comes to your home. This spring, you could begin customizing Casa Capricorn or turning an area of your house into a music studio or meditation room.

Where before you only noticed the dust bunnies, don't be surprised if you start to pick up on energy strands and vibes in every room. Soulful Neptune here could inspire you to try metaphysical modalities. Use feng shui to get the chi flowing in the right direction. Enlist a shamanic practitioner to do a house blessing or space clearing.

Don't be surprised if your taste in neighborhoods changes. While Neptune sailed through Pisces (since 2011), you may have preferred to live near water or away from the center of the action. In Aries, Neptune could find you craving a more active, culturally thriving lifestyle. We're not saying you can't find that on a coastal town or even an island. But if you've sequestered yourself away or created a life that teems with too much "stuff," the urge to purge could already begin after March 30. Neptune in Aries is a time to travel lightly, potentially even exploring a nomadic lifestyle.

Some Capricorns could ponder a move closer to family, especially if a relative is in need of support. Note: Neptune is the planet of compassion and sacrifice. Stay aware of how much you're giving on a day-to-day basis. Caretaker burnout is a real concern. You would do anything to provide for your loved ones, but gentle reminder: Draining your reserves (no matter how mighty), will render you incapable of giving anyone a hand.

Have you been estranged from a relative? Forgiveness is Neptune's domain. You may finally have a chance to bury the hatchet with someone in your family. Be cautious of unspoken expectations that could lead to disappointment. This is a time to communicate openly and honestly, ensuring that everyone is on the same page and that you're not carrying the weight of unresolved issues. Conversely, you may realize that it's time to put a hardcore boundary in place with someone whose very presence continually triggers a trauma response in you.

In that vein, Neptune in Aries is a powerful time to process old pain around your childhood. Generational patterns have a way of repeating themselves and now's the time to break free of anything from your lineage that feels unhealthy. Therapeutic Neptune can help you access buried memories and shed light on family dynamics that are ready for a 2025 upgrade. Be mindful of Neptune's tendency to blur reality. Try to stay grounded and avoid idealizing the past or getting lost in nostalgia.

As you ease into this longer Neptune cycle, you may notice yourself softening some of your hardcore judgments. That's especially true when it comes to the judgments that you cast on your own emotions. Some feelings won't fit easily into a behavioral model or be explained in a scientific study. And that's okay, Capricorn! Allow yourself to get a little messy. It might just be the healthiest thing you do this year. The trick is to focus on naming and claiming your feelings instead of falling into Neptune's other trap of denial, avoidance and escapism.

Equally important? Keeping healthy boundaries around food, drink and any addictive substances. Avoid anything resembling a slippery slope when you're going through an issue. In daredevil Aries, Neptune could lead you toward destructive behaviors that may temporarily distract you from your pain. Fortunately, your sensible sign understands the concept of taking on a challenge!

## SATURN IN ARIES

MAY 24 – SEPTEMBER 1, 2025
FEBRUARY 13, 2026 – APRIL 12, 2028

It's not all incense and crystals in Chez Chèvre in 2025. On May 24, your ruler, structure-hound Saturn, joins Neptune in Aries for three months. Until September 1, it's shining its trusty inspector's headlamp into that very same fourth house of home, family and emotional foundations. Similarly to Neptune, Saturn's tour through Aries is a preview of a longer cycle that begins again on February 13, 2026 and lasts for two more years, until April 12, 2028.

When your galactic guardian changes signs, it can profoundly redirect the focus of your life. Since March 7, 2023, Saturn's been stirring up sediment in Pisces and your third house of peers, communication and local activity. The past couple years may have brought significant changes in your social circles. Old friends that you've outgrown may have faded away while other, newer connections have slowly been getting off the ground. Saturn's restraining energy hasn't made it easy for you to express yourself, but when you did, you made every word count.

As Saturn darts forward into Aries for three months, you may feel more playful and free to speak your mind than you have for a while. Home and family matters will now be under traditional Saturn's watch, and there's added gravitas there. So what's a Sea Goat to do? Tuck into your shearling slippers and put a cast-iron pot on the stove. With disciplined Saturn moving through Aries from May 24 to September 1, you may become more of a homebody than you've cared to be for a while.

Top of the agenda? Making your space truly feel like home. If you're already nodding in agreement, wondering why it's taken so long, Saturn is here to get things moving. Remember, Saturn is the zodiac's legendary taskmaster, demanding commitment and diligence. So if you're truly ready to create your dream dwelling, it's time to roll up your sleeves and get strategic.

Being the process-driven soul that you are, it's best to start with a plan. What are the most pressing changes that you'd like to make to your space? If you're contemplating a move, make a list of preferences in order of importance: natural light to keep your moods up, ample square footage so you have privacy but not SO much that cleaning becomes a never-ending chore. What amenities do you want (need!) in your neighborhood: indie businesses, healthy grocery stores, good public schools? Saturn abhors ambiguity (and so do you, as a Saturn-ruled sign). Write lists, make mood boards, get a picture in your mind before you even start the search. The same holds true for any redecoration or renovation you're contemplating. Between now and April 12, 2028, you can methodically work toward these domestic dreams.

Saturn's trek through Aries can also stir up some reflection (and even regrets) around your relationship with a few key relatives. Do you wish you had a better connection to a parent? You might find yourself navigating difficult, but long-overdue, conversations. Whether it's about setting healthy boundaries or strengthening your connection, this period is ripe for working through these issues. And if you have children, Saturn challenges you to establish clear boundaries in your parenting style. Enforcing rules consistently will be vital. (Sorry kids, no more phones at the dinner table!)

With Saturn in self-sovereign Aries, it's equally important to maintain your own identity and not lose yourself in helicopter parenting. This isn't selfish, Capricorn, it's about modeling an important virtue: Living life with a growth mindset rather than stubbornly refusing to evolve after a certain age. Carve out necessary "me time" and make sure everyone else under your roof is pulling their weight. With Saturn in Aries forming a challenging square to your Capricorn Sun, be prepared for some tough compromises. Family life can be both a source of joy and stress, and without firm boundaries, you may feel taken advantage of due to your protective nature and instincts to provide.

Your social circle may shrink during this time, but that's not necessarily a bad thing. You need supportive, reciprocal relationships now more than ever, Capricorn—friends who truly support and uplift you. Saturn values longevity and people who you meet between May 24 and September 1 could be keepers who become part of your inner circle. No need to rush to become besties—that's not Saturn's style. Be aware of a tendency to judge people on status. Elitism is a pitfall that your sign occasionally struggles with. While Saturn's in Aries, some of the cool kids you hang out with could fade away for the more heartfelt, enduring types you normally might look right past.

# 4 SET BOUNDARIES WITH YOUR INNER CIRCLE

## VENUS RETROGRADE IN ARIES AND PISCES

ARIES: MARCH 1 – 27
PISCES: MARCH 27 – APRIL 12

Spring break reunion, anyone? Starting this March 1, you may feel the urge to reconnect with your innermost circle. The reason for this? Convivial Venus slips into her biennial retrograde, backing up through Aries and your family-oriented fourth house until March 27, then rounding out the retreat in Pisces and your social third house until April 12.

Relatives that you haven't talked to in ages could start pinging you on WhatsApp. And while you're scrolling through Insta between appointments, you could go down a rabbit hole of posts that inspire you to reach out to your college besties. Follow those urges, Capricorn, because these reconnections can be extra sweet during Venus retrograde.

Need to get away for an end-of-winter reprieve? If you're in the mood for a change of scenery, you MIGHT opt for a chic resort with spa amenities. But also think about renting an Airbnb with an open-plan kitchen and heated pool. Domestic vibes follow you wherever you go during the first half of the retrograde, which could be unfortunate if you find yourself surrounded by piña-colada-swilling tourists sharing drunken exchanges at a swim-up pool. (Can't they see that you're trying to read?) Enjoying healthy meals and easy downtime in a private space could be more in alignment with the low-key vibes of this cycle.

Home sweet home could be your favorite location during this cycle. Set up the spare bedroom or couch and invite guests to Casa Capricorn, where you can give them the grand tour of your favorite cultural hotspots. If you want to bury the hatchet with a frenemy or difficult relative, skip the trip and take the process in much smaller bites. With peacekeeping Venus off her game, you might rush to "make nice" only to find the unresolved issue rearing up ten times stronger. Start with a phone call and maybe a lunch date on neutral territory after that.

Warning: Family and friends may be less than supportive of your grandiose ideas this March. If so, take a time out from sharing your visions with your inner circle. Their care and concern, while valid, could dampen your motivation. Going forward, be mindful of how you present your "Woe is me!" moments. YOU might bounce back like an elastic band, but you can't expect others to spring back and forth with your moods. If you don't want them worrying about your emotional wellbeing, save these conversations for a therapist or coach, who doesn't have so much skin in the game.

Venus is the planet of love and romance, and this retrograde reminds you that like attracts like. To draw in an emotionally aware partner, you have to be tuned in to your own inner workings. Take time to honor your sentient self, even if that means more alone time or a few extra therapy sessions. You'll find that, as you do, your existing relationships will also improve. Bottom line: It's not frivolous to feel!

With this romantic retrograde going down in your domestic zone until March 27, you may have to negotiate new rules if you share a home with your partner. Do you have adequate space for relaxing in privacy and doing your creative work? If not, you could be quite the cranky member of the lair. Of course, elbowing out your S.O. or family won't work. Look into renting an outside space for your memoir writing or drum practice. If your home and workspaces just don't feel cozy enough, make a few cosmetic upgrades now. But hold off on any massive renovation until Venus is back on track mid-April. Otherwise, you could spend a fortune making your bedroom look like an upscale boutique hotel only to wake up in six weeks to realize it's totally the wrong look.

# 5
## BROADCAST YOUR BELIEFS

### LUNAR NODES IN VIRGO AND PISCES

NORTH NODE IN PISCES, SOUTH NODE IN VIRGO
JANUARY 11, 2025 – JULY 26, 2026

Whatever you're selling, Capricorn, we'll take it in bulk! Your strategic genius is about to hit new levels starting January 11, as the fate-fueled North Node returns to Pisces for the first time in nearly 20 years. Until July 26, 2026, it sprinkles some serious cosmic fairy dust into your communicative third house, setting the stage for a major popularity spike. Get ready to start a buzz!

While you're usually heads and tails above most people, this cycle could connect you to peers who can match your standards and work ethic. Surprise twist? Someone you thought was a competitor could actually be the missing link in your success strategy. Fortunately, your practical Capricorn nature isn't one to hold grudges—you're too focused on results to let pettiness get in the way. The third house rules your siblings, friends, coworkers, and neighbors, so don't be surprised if these folks start playing essential roles in your projects. Just make sure you've got everything in writing. Ambiguity? No thanks. In your world, every contract is ironclad, because unclear expectations breed discontent.

Got a message to broadcast? This is your moment to elevate your voice. Start a blog, podcast, or a series of viral social campaigns. As a Capricorn, you are full of actionable insights that improve systems and get things done. With the North Node in Pisces, you'll find the perfect platforms to share your expertise, perhaps within an industry group or a community organization. Publish those white papers, or become the go-to expert in your field. Either way, 2025 is the year to make your mark as a thought leader.

During this 18-month nodal cycle, you could step into roles ranging from spokesperson to brand ambassador. Of course, being the conscientious Capricorn you are, you'll make sure every endorsement reflects your values—sustainably sourced, ethically produced, and, yes, profitable. Your personal brand will be on point, and everything you touch could turn to gold.

While the fate-fueling North Node is giving you the local spotlight, the karmic South Node will simultaneously travel through Virgo and your nomadic ninth house, reminding you that the world is your oyster. Are you casting a wide enough net? While the North Node showers you with nearby opportunities, the South Node encourages you to think big. Did a 23andMe test reveal some far-flung relatives? Maybe it's time to explore your roots with a meaningful trip. After January 11, these kinds of journeys could be life-altering. Make sure your passport is up-to-date.

For many Capricorns, multi-city living could become the new norm. Maybe you're negotiating to go "permanently remote" or setting yourself up as a digital nomad, hopping between locations without skipping a beat at work. Even if globetrotting isn't in the cards for you long-term, spending a few weeks as a "touring resident" in different cities could add some adventure to your year.

Not ready to pack your bags? No worries—the South Node in Virgo could spark your inner scholar. If higher education has been on your radar, now might be the time to apply for that MBA program or take up a new certification. The ninth house also rules spirituality, so you might find yourself revisiting a practice or philosophy that once brought you peace. Whether you're diving into ancient teachings, developing a new workshop, or writing your memoir (Eat, Pray, Capricorn?), this is the year to go deep and share your wisdom with the world.

2025 is setting you up for a whole new level of success, Capricorn—both locally and globally. Whether you're building powerful partnerships, expanding your knowledge, or becoming the voice of authority in your field, the world is ready to hear from you!

# Love

YOUR 2025 FORECAST

The love rollercoaster is still serving some ups and downs in the first part of the year, so buckle up, Capricorn. Renegade Uranus has trekked through Taurus since May 2018, shaking things up in your fifth house of love. Whether single or attached, this cycle has kept you on your toes, encouraging you to experiment and break free from convention. Relationships may be one area of life that has felt very un-Capricorn since 2018—and frankly, you're probably ready for a bit more of a steady pace.

Fortunately for you, that's coming soon. From July 7 to November 7, Uranus will dart into Gemini and your sensible sixth house, clearing your love life from its chaotic influence. As the year wraps up, Uranus will do one final lap through your Taurus-ruled romance realm (from November 7, 2025 to April 25, 2026) then won't be back for another eighty years. Whew!

This destabilizing energy hasn't been ALL bad; in fact, it may have felt liberating for many Sea Goats out there. No more trying to keep up with the "Love Joneses." Your romantic trajectory has been yours to author and that may have led to some exciting discoveries that you'll carry into this next season of your life. Perhaps you learned to really, REALLY enjoy your own company. Maybe you discovered your edges in partnership or experimented with a different pace in dating.

If you're still not quite certain what turns you on, carpe diem, Capricorn. And if you are? Carpe diem to you, too. While Uranus twerks through Taurus until July 7, you have a hall pass to explore, experiment and let your body do the talking. This can be a high-minded pursuit, even an intellectual one.

You'll get a tantalizing boost from lusty Mars, who is spending half of 2025 in Cancer and Leo—the rulers of your seventh house of partnerships and erotic eighth house, respectively. Caveat: The feisty red planet will be retrograde until February 23, which could turn up the flame a little too high. Anger and frustration could heat up easily or you may rebel against anyone trying to "pin you down."

Once Mars turns direct on February 23, you're ready to get proactive about love again. While Mars moves through Cancer until April 18, pleasure is your priority. Make a point of getting out more often, dressing up and enjoying cultural activity dates. When Mars heads into Leo from April 18 to June 17, your seductive purr could lure one special soul into your lair, where you're sure to break out some showstopping moves.

This passionate period is anything BUT casual, so say goodbye to the neverending situationships and clear the decks for a relationship that feels like a mutual investment.

The biggest news for your love life this year comes on June 9, when lucky, expansive Jupiter bursts into Cancer, showering your seventh house of relationships with its abundant energy for an entire year. The red-spotted titan hasn't blessed this part of your chart since 2013 to 2014, and its impact could spark a major renaissance in your love life. Turn on that soulmate search light and expand your reach. Worldly Jupiter could serve up a compatible match from an incompatible location. However, this is not the year to rule out a long-distance relationship; well, not if you've FINALLY found someone who ticks all your boxes. (A Herculean effort, if you're being honest.)

Existing relationships may expand in fascinating ways under Jupiter's influence. Perhaps you'll pair up on an entrepreneurial venture, move across the country or get plans in motion for a bucket-list trip to Portugal or Peru. Another possibility? Jupiter's indie-spirited influence can nudge you out of the couple bubble and give you the space to explore separate interests. The right amount of autonomy CAN make the heart grow fonder.

Another wave of magnetism sweeps through your love life at the end of the year, as love planets Mars and Venus copilot through Capricorn in December. Red-hot Mars powers into Capricorn from December 15 until January 23, 2026, giving you the confidence to go after what (or who) you want. And just in time for the holidays, Venus joins the party, sweeping into Capricorn on Christmas Eve and riding alongside Mars until January 17.

This charmed energy could bring more than a mistletoe moment or a NYE kiss, if, that is, you want it that way. Single Sea Goats might be perfectly happy to retain that status through the holidays and enjoy the buffet of romantic options. Even the happily coupled Capricorns could find themselves longing for a little variety, which could lead to some steamy fantasies that you can play out with your partner in real time.

---

CAPRICORN: LUCKIEST love DAY

### JUNE 24
The Day of Miracles could bring sweeping surprises for your love life as the shining Sun and lucky Jupiter roll the dice in Cancer and your seventh house of relationships today. Be open to the attractive force of an "opposite" or a situation that expands your view of what love and relationships can look like.

# Money & Career

## YOUR 2025 FORECAST

Capricorn, 2025 is your year to break free from the grind and discover innovative ways to work smarter, not harder. With both Jupiter and Uranus doing laps through Gemini and your sixth house of work, routines and wellness, you're craving liberation from the daily hustle. And, dare we say, it's about damn time!

Jupiter has been transiting through the sign of the Twins since May 25, 2024, showing you the freedom that can come from streamlining, systematizing and outsourcing certain aspects of your work to experts. If that level of efficiency already comes naturally to you, consider memorializing your methodology. From an orientation manual for employees to a published book or a series of online classes, your lifehacks light the way for others to level up.

If work has grown too complex, you may feel like downsizing certain elements of your job—or even let them go completely. While that might require you to tighten up your belt a bit, think of it as a temporary measure.

The gift of time will allow you to think through a new financial strategy that allows you to actually work smarter, not harder.

From July 7 to November 7, game-changing Uranus swoops into Gemini, giving you a sneak preview of a longer seven-year cycle that kicks off in April 2026. Uranus thrives on disruption, cueing you to embrace unconventional methods. Could AI be used to speed up your outflow? Would working as a fractional executive instead of a full-time one open up room for you to finally produce that documentary? You don't have to shake everything up overnight, but don't be surprised if outdated work habits start fading away in the second half of the year, allowing you to experiment with a more liberated, innovative approach to your career.

PS: Capricorn, these changes CAN feel exciting! Starting January 11, the karmic South Node shifts into Virgo and your worldly, entrepreneurial ninth house. During this cycle, which lasts until July 26, 2026, travel or remote work could play a significant role in your career. If ever there were a time to be a digital nomad, tour with your band or expand your business internationally—this could be it.

Your entire approach to money is also going through a profound metamorphosis. Wealth-agent Pluto—who wrapped up a sixteen-year tour of Capricorn on November 19, 2024—is now in its first full year in Aquarius and your second house of financial security and values. While this cycle lasts for a protracted era, until 2044, your eye may already be on some new balls, ones that will create lasting security. (Music to your ears!)

Here's yet another cue to trim back excess and stabilize a few of the pricier moving parts of your life. Pluto's changes are a slow-burn process, but by the end of 2025, you'll start to feel the benefits of a more focused and sustainable approach to your income and spending. Moves you make now can set the foundation for lasting wealth and financial freedom.

Could that involve purchasing a home sweet home? Quite possibly! On March 29, the final solar eclipse in a two-year series lands in Aries and your rooted, domestic fourth house. With your ruler, serious Saturn, also parking in Aries from May 24 to September 1, you could warm to the idea of putting down roots or creating rental income through an investment property.

Business collaborations heat up after June 9, when lucky Jupiter moves on to Cancer and your partnership zone for an entire year. You won't even have to turn on the searchlight to find allies who want to team up to achieve a common vision. Lawyer up, because you could be formalizing a flurry of deals in the second half of the year.

A final burst of motivation comes on December 15, as go-getter Mars revs into Capricorn—its first visit to your sign in two years. While other people are winding down for the year, you could be rolling up your sleeves. Progress is imminent and you'll have the grit to finish 2025 with some impressive accolades. Take the lead and end the year with a windfall.

---

### CAPRICORN: LUCKIEST career DAY

#### AUGUST 10

Go-getter Mars in partnership-powered Libra is at the apex of your chart, helping you lock in VIP collaborators. As it makes an exact trine to wealth-agent Pluto in Aquarius and your money house, you could tap into revenue streams that were previously hidden from your view. Mercury is on its final day of a retrograde, so you'll need to vet whatever you discover today. Look through your past contacts, as you could discover a promising investment partner or the gatekeeper of an opportunity who's already in your database!

# 2025
# CAPRICORN

## 12 MONTH OVERVIEW

# 1

# January
## MONTHLY HOROSCOPE

Happy birthday, Capricorn! The year kicks off with the radiant Sun in your sign, which is a good reason to keep the celebrations going. This extra solar power lasts until January 19, giving you the energy, discipline and confidence to move the needle on your personal goals. Make room to dabble and try new things before you settle on any major plans. Following the spirit of curiosity can lead you on an exciting new path. On January 11, the lunar nodes shift into Pisces and Virgo, marking the start of an 18-month cycle of personal growth through communication, global travel and education. As one of the zodiac's seekers, you'll revel in this transformative period. After January 19, the Sun drifts on to airy Aquarius, giving you a cosmic tailwind in the area of finances and material security. You could whip up new income streams or breeze right into a brand new job during this four-week cycle. Make a budget for luxury and entertainment, because when the Year of the Wood Snake begins on January 29, your appetite for life's finer things will be huge.

*Read your extended monthly forecast for life, love, money and career! astrostyle.com*

# JANUARY
## Moon Phase Calendar

| SUN | MON | TUE | WED | THU | FRI | SAT |
|---|---|---|---|---|---|---|
| | | | **1** ♐ ♒ 5:50AM | **2** ♒ | **3** ♒ ♓ 10:21AM | **4** ♓ |
| **5** ♓ 2:01PM | **6** ♈ 2nd Quarter | **7** ♈ ♉ 5:11PM | **8** ♉ | **9** ♉ ♊ 8:07PM | **10** ♊ | **11** ♊ ♋ 11:24PM |
| **12** ♋ | **13** ♋ Full Moon 5:27PM | **14** ♋ ♌ 4:12AM | **15** ♌ | **16** ♌ ♍ 11:46AM | **17** ♍ | **18** ♍ ♎ 10:33PM |
| **19** ♎ | **20** ♎ | **21** ♎→♏ 11:20AM ♏ 4th Quarter | **22** ♏ | **23** ♏ ♐ 11:29PM | **24** ♐ | **25** ♐ |
| **26** ♐ ♐ 8:43AM | **27** ♐ | **28** ♐ ♒ 2:31PM | **29** ♒ New Moon 7:36AM | **30** ♒ ♓ 5:52PM | **31** ♓ | |

*Times listed are Eastern US Time Zone*

KEY

| | | | | | |
|---|---|---|---|---|---|
| ♈ ARIES | ♌ LEO | ♐ SAGITTARIUS | **FM** | FULL MOON |
| ♉ TAURUS | ♍ VIRGO | ♑ CAPRICORN | **NM** | NEW MOON |
| ♊ GEMINI | ♎ LIBRA | ♒ AQUARIUS | **LE** | LUNAR ECLIPSE |
| ♋ CANCER | ♏ SCORPIO | ♓ PISCES | **SE** | SOLAR ECLIPSE |

JAN 13 5:27PM
# full moon in
# Cancer (24°00')

## CANCER FULL MOON CRYSTAL

### SELENITE

This calm and soothing gemstone forms in long bands and has a high, clear and pure vibration. Named after Selene, the goddess of the Cancer-ruled moon, this crystal is believed to help the flow of bodily fluids and support fertility. Since selenite does not hold negative charges, it is fantastic to use to neutralize your own energy. Like a "crystal crab shell," selenite is often used to make a protective energetic "grid" around your house or workspace.

---

**What's one thing you're celebrating under this full moon?**

---

## CANCER FULL MOON = CELEBRATE!

*Your divine emotional intelligence*

*The importance of creating safe spaces*

*The power of family—blood-related or chosen*

*Intuitive hits that guide you toward your dreams*

*The healing power of water*

*Mother figures and your own maternal instincts*

JAN 29 7:36AM
## new moon in
# Aquarius (9°51')

## AQUARIUS NEW MOON CRYSTAL

### APOPHYLLITE
High vibes: incoming! This spirit-elevating stone enhances Aquarian-ruled hope for the future. As a clear-hued cluster, the light apophyllite emits encourages self-reflection and gratitude while energizing the soul.

---

*What's one fresh intention you're ready to set under this new moon?*

---

## AQUARIUS NEW MOON = FOCUS

*Experiment with new technology and techniques*
*Break out of the box with style and social expression*
*Connect to community, activism and humanitarian work*

**January 2025** Longitude & Retrograde Ephemeris [00:00 UT]

| Day | Sid.time | ☉ | ☽ | +12h☽ | ☿ | ♀ | ♂ | ♃ | ♄ | ♅ | ♆ | ♇ | ☊ | ☊ | ⚸ | ⚷ | Day |
|---|---|---|---|---|---|---|---|---|---|---|---|---|---|---|---|---|---|
| **1** We | 06:43:36 | ♑10°48'49 | ♑23°54'55 | ♒00°39'41 | DS 19°52 | ♒27°42 | R 01°55 | R 13°12 | ♓14°31 | R 23°38 | ♓27°17 | ♒01°03 | R 01°29 | R 00°52 | ♎20°33 | ♈19°00 | **1** We |
| **2** Th | 06:47:32 | ♑11°50'00 | ♒07°27'28 | ♒14°17'31 | ♐21°10 | ♒28°47 | ♌01°35 | ♊13°06 | ♓14°36 | ♉23°36 | ♓27°18 | ♒01°05 | ♈01°26 | ♈00°41 | ♎20°40 | ♈19°00 | **2** Th |
| **3** Fr | 06:51:29 | ♑12°51'10 | ♒21°09'56 | ♒28°03'59 | ♐22°29 | ♒29°50 | ♌01°14 | ♊13°00 | ♓14°40 | ♉23°35 | ♓27°19 | ♒01°07 | ♈01°23 | ♈00°33 | ♎20°47 | ♈19°00 | **3** Fr |
| **4** Sa | 06:55:26 | ♑13°52'21 | ♓04°59'50 | ♓11°56'49 | D 23°50 | ♓00°54 | ♌00°53 | ♊12°54 | ♓14°45 | ♉23°33 | ♓27°20 | ♒01°09 | ♈01°20 | ♈00°28 | ♎20°53 | ♈19°00 | **4** Sa |
| **5** Su | 06:59:22 | ♑14°53'31 | ♓18°55'12 | ♓25°54'25 | ♐25°11 | ♓01°57 | ♌00°31 | ♊12°48 | ♓14°50 | ♉23°32 | ♓27°21 | ♒01°11 | ♈01°17 | ♈00°26 | ♎21°00 | ♈19°01 | **5** Su |
| **6** Mo | 07:03:19 | ♑15°54'40 | ♈02°54'48 | ♈09°55'52 | ♐26°34 | ♓03°00 | ♌00°09 | ♊12°42 | ♓14°55 | ♉23°31 | ♓27°22 | ♒01°13 | ♈01°13 | D 00°26 | ♎21°07 | ♈19°01 | **6** Mo |
| **7** Tu | 07:07:15 | ♑16°55'50 | ♈16°57'57 | ♈24°00'35 | ♐27°58 | ♓04°03 | ♋29°47 | ♊12°37 | ♓15°00 | ♉23°30 | ♓27°23 | ♒01°15 | ♈01°10 | R 00°26 | ♎21°13 | ♈19°01 | **7** Tu |
| **8** We | 07:11:12 | ♑17°56'58 | ♉01°04'06 | ♉08°07'55 | ♐29°22 | ♓05°05 | ♋29°24 | ♊12°31 | ♓15°05 | ♉23°28 | ♓27°24 | ♒01°16 | ♈01°07 | ♈00°25 | ♎21°20 | ♈19°02 | **8** We |
| **9** Th | 07:15:08 | ♑18°58'07 | ♉15°12'19 | ♉22°16'35 | ♑00°48 | ♓06°07 | ♋29°01 | ♊12°26 | ♓15°10 | ♉23°27 | ♓27°25 | ♒01°18 | ♈01°04 | ♈00°23 | ♎21°26 | ♈19°02 | **9** Th |
| **10** Fr | 07:19:05 | ♑19°59'15 | ♉29°20'53 | ♊06°24'22 | ♑02°14 | ♓07°09 | ♋28°38 | ♊12°21 | ♓15°15 | ♉23°26 | ♓27°26 | ♒01°20 | ♈01°01 | ♈00°17 | ♎21°33 | ♈19°03 | **10** Fr |
| **11** Sa | 07:23:01 | ♑21°00'22 | ♊13°27'02 | ♊20°27'58 | ♑03°41 | ♓08°10 | ♋28°14 | ♊12°16 | ♓15°20 | ♉23°25 | ♓27°27 | ♒01°22 | ♈00°58 | ♈00°09 | ♎21°40 | ♈19°04 | **11** Sa |
| **12** Su | 07:26:58 | ♑22°01'30 | ♊27°27'04 | ♋04°23'22 | ♑05°08 | ♓09°10 | ♋27°51 | ♊12°12 | ♓15°25 | ♉23°24 | ♓27°28 | ♒01°24 | ♈00°54 | ♓29°59 | ♎21°46 | ♈19°04 | **12** Su |
| **13** Mo | 07:30:55 | ♑23°02'36 | ♋11°16'46 | ♋18°06'20 | ♑06°36 | ♓10°11 | ♋27°27 | ♊12°07 | ♓15°31 | ♉23°23 | ♓27°30 | ♒01°26 | ♈00°51 | ♓29°48 | ♎21°53 | ♈19°05 | **13** Mo |
| **14** Tu | 07:34:51 | ♑24°03'42 | ♋24°52'04 | ♌01°33'10 | ♑08°05 | ♓11°10 | ♋27°03 | ♊12°03 | ♓15°36 | ♉23°22 | ♓27°31 | ♒01°28 | ♈00°48 | ♓29°36 | ♎22°00 | ♈19°06 | **14** Tu |
| **15** We | 07:38:48 | ♑25°04'48 | ♌08°09'46 | ♌14°41'18 | ♑09°34 | ♓12°10 | ♋26°39 | ♊11°58 | ♓15°42 | ♉23°22 | ♓27°32 | ♒01°30 | ♈00°45 | ♓29°26 | ♎22°06 | ♈19°07 | **15** We |
| **16** Th | 07:42:44 | ♑26°05'53 | ♌21°08'06 | ♌27°29'48 | ♑11°04 | ♓13°08 | ♋26°15 | ♊11°55 | ♓15°47 | ♉23°21 | ♓27°33 | ♒01°32 | ♈00°42 | ♓29°17 | ♎22°13 | ♈19°08 | **16** Th |
| **17** Fr | 07:46:41 | ♑27°06'58 | ♍03°46'56 | ♍09°59'22 | ♑12°35 | ♓14°07 | ♋25°51 | ♊11°51 | ♓15°53 | ♉23°20 | ♓27°35 | ♒01°34 | ♈00°39 | ♓29°11 | ♎22°20 | ♈19°09 | **17** Fr |
| **18** Sa | 07:50:37 | ♑28°08'02 | ♍16°07'50 | ♍22°12'20 | ♑14°06 | ♓15°04 | ♋25°27 | ♊11°47 | ♓15°59 | ♉23°19 | ♓27°36 | ♒01°36 | ♈00°35 | ♓29°08 | ♎22°26 | ♈19°10 | **18** Sa |
| **19** Su | 07:54:34 | ♑29°09'07 | ♍28°13'46 | ♎04°12'18 | ♑15°37 | ♓16°02 | ♋25°03 | ♊11°44 | ♓16°05 | ♉23°19 | ♓27°37 | ♒01°38 | ♈00°32 | ♓29°07 | ♎22°33 | ♈19°11 | **19** Su |
| **20** Mo | 07:58:31 | ♒00°10'10 | ♎10°08'53 | ♎16°03'47 | ♑17°09 | ♓16°58 | ♋24°40 | ♊11°40 | ♓16°10 | ♉23°18 | ♓27°39 | ♒01°40 | ♈00°29 | D 29°08 | ♎22°40 | ♈19°12 | **20** Mo |
| **21** Tu | 08:02:27 | ♒01°11'14 | ♎21°58'03 | ♎27°51'59 | ♑18°42 | ♓17°54 | ♋24°16 | ♊11°37 | ♓16°16 | ♉23°18 | ♓27°40 | ♒01°41 | ♈00°26 | ♓29°09 | ♎22°46 | ♈19°13 | **21** Tu |
| **22** We | 08:06:24 | ♒02°12'17 | ♏03°46'37 | ♏09°42'18 | ♑20°15 | ♓18°50 | ♋23°53 | ♊11°35 | ♓16°22 | ♉23°17 | ♓27°42 | ♒01°43 | ♈00°23 | R 29°09 | ♎22°53 | ♈19°14 | **22** We |
| **23** Th | 08:10:20 | ♒03°13'19 | ♏15°40'03 | ♏21°40'08 | ♑21°49 | ♓19°45 | ♋23°31 | ♊11°32 | ♓16°28 | ♉23°17 | ♓27°43 | ♒01°45 | ♈00°19 | ♓29°08 | ♎23°00 | ♈19°16 | **23** Th |
| **24** Fr | 08:14:17 | ♒04°14'22 | ♏27°43'33 | ♐03°50'29 | ♑23°24 | ♓20°39 | ♋23°08 | ♊11°30 | ♓16°34 | ♉23°16 | ♓27°45 | ♒01°47 | ♈00°16 | ♓29°05 | ♎23°06 | ♈19°17 | **24** Fr |
| **25** Sa | 08:18:13 | ♒05°15'23 | ♐10°01'49 | ♐16°17'36 | ♑24°59 | ♓21°32 | ♋22°46 | ♊11°27 | ♓16°41 | ♉23°16 | ♓27°46 | ♒01°49 | ♈00°13 | ♓29°00 | ♎23°13 | ♈19°18 | **25** Sa |
| **26** Su | 08:22:10 | ♒06°16'24 | ♐22°38'33 | ♐29°04'32 | ♑26°35 | ♓22°25 | ♋22°25 | ♊11°25 | ♓16°47 | ♉23°16 | ♓27°48 | ♒01°51 | ♈00°10 | ♓28°52 | ♎23°20 | ♈19°20 | **26** Su |
| **27** Mo | 08:26:06 | ♒07°17'25 | ♑05°36'05 | ♑12°12'50 | ♑28°11 | ♓23°17 | ♋22°04 | ♊11°23 | ♓16°53 | ♉23°16 | ♓27°49 | ♒01°53 | ♈00°07 | ♓28°43 | ♎23°26 | ♈19°21 | **27** Mo |
| **28** Tu | 08:30:03 | ♒08°18'25 | ♑18°55'05 | ♑25°42'12 | ♑29°48 | ♓24°09 | ♋21°43 | ♊11°22 | ♓16°59 | ♉23°15 | ♓27°51 | ♒01°55 | ♈00°04 | ♓28°34 | ♎23°33 | ♈19°23 | **28** Tu |
| **29** We | 08:33:60 | ♒09°19'24 | ♒02°34'17 | ♒09°30'30 | ♒01°25 | ♓24°59 | ♋21°23 | ♊11°20 | ♓17°06 | ♉23°15 | ♓27°53 | ♒01°57 | ♈00°00 | ♓28°25 | ♎23°40 | ♈19°25 | **29** We |
| **30** Th | 08:37:56 | ♒10°20'22 | ♒16°30'46 | ♒23°34'03 | ♒03°04 | ♓25°49 | ♋21°04 | ♊11°19 | ♓17°12 | ♉23°15 | ♓27°54 | ♒01°59 | ♓29°57 | ♓28°18 | ♎23°46 | ♈19°26 | **30** Th |
| **31** Fr | 08:41:53 | ♒11°21'19 | ♓00°40'12 | ♓07°48'07 | ♒04°43 | ♓26°38 | ♋20°45 | ♊11°18 | ♓17°18 | D 23°15 | ♓27°56 | ♒02°01 | ♓29°54 | ♓28°13 | ♎23°53 | ♈19°28 | **31** Fr |
| **Δ Delta** | 01:58:16 | 30°32'30" | 396°45'16" | 397°08'26" | 44°50' | 28°55' | -11°09' | -1°54' | 2°47' | -0°22' | 0°38' | 0°57' | 1°35' | 2°39' | 3°19' | 0°28' | **Delta** |

Ephemeris tables and data provided by **Astro-Seek.com.** All times in UTC.

# I

# NOTES & THOUGHTS

| S | M | T | W | T | F | S |
|---|---|---|---|---|---|---|
|   |   |   | 1 | 2 | 3 | 4 |
| 5 | 6 | 7 | 8 | 9 | 10 | 11 |
| 12 | 13 | 14 | 15 | 16 | 17 | 18 |
| 19 | 20 | 21 | 22 | 23 | 24 | 25 |
| 26 | 27 | 28 | 29 | 30 | 31 |   |

## MONTHLY INTENTION

---

**1** WED
● ♑

♒ 5:50AM

---

**2** THU
☽ ♒
Venus in Pisces until Feb 4 (10:24PM)

---

**3** FRI
☽ ♒
♓ 10:21AM
Mars-Pluto opposition

---

**4** SAT
☽ ♓

**JANUARY 2025**

| S | M | T | W | T | F | S |
|---|---|---|---|---|---|---|
|   |   |   | 1 | 2 | 3 | 4 |
| 5 | 6 | 7 | 8 | 9 | 10 | 11 |
| 12 | 13 | 14 | 15 | 16 | 17 | 18 |
| 19 | 20 | 21 | 22 | 23 | 24 | 25 |
| 26 | 27 | 28 | 29 | 30 | 31 |   |

## WEEKLY INTENTION

## TOP 3 TO-DOS

○

○

○

**5** SUN                                            ◐♓︎
                                                ♈︎ 2:01PM

**6** MON                                            ◐♈︎
Mars retrograde enters Cancer (5:44AM)
Mercury-Neptune square
Waxing Quarter Moon in Aries (6:56PM)

**7** TUE

☉♈
♉ 5:11PM

---

**8** WED

☉♉
Mercury enters Capricorn until Jan 27 (5:30AM)

---

**9** THU

☉♓
♊ 8:07PM

---

**10** FRI

☉♊

---

**11** SAT

☉♊
♋ 11:24PM
North Node in Pisces
South Node in Virgo
until Jul 26, 2026

**JANUARY 2025**

| S | M | T | W | T | F | S |
|---|---|---|---|---|---|---|
|   |   |   | 1 | 2 | 3 | 4 |
| 5 | 6 | 7 | 8 | 9 | 10 | 11 |
| 12 | 13 | 14 | 15 | 16 | 17 | 18 |
| 19 | 20 | 21 | 22 | 23 | 24 | 25 |
| 26 | 27 | 28 | 29 | 30 | 31 |   |

## WEEKLY INTENTION

## TOP 3 TO-DOS

○

○

○

**12** SUN

○ ♋
Mars-Neptune trine

**13** MON

○ ♋
Sun-Uranus trine
**FULL MOON IN CANCER**
(5:27 PM, 24°00′)

**14** TUE

○♋
♌ 4:12AM
Venus-Jupiter square

---

**15** WED

○♌
Sun-Mars opposition

---

**16** THU

○♌
♍ 11:46AM

---

**17** FRI

○♍

---

**18** SAT

○♍
♎ 10:33PM
Venus-Saturn meetup #1 of 3

**JANUARY 2025**

| S | M | T | W | T | F | S |
|---|---|---|---|---|---|---|
|   |   |   | 1 | 2 | 3 | 4 |
| 5 | 6 | 7 | 8 | 9 | 10 | 11 |
| 12 | 13 | 14 | 15 | 16 | 17 | 18 |
| **19** | **20** | **21** | **22** | **23** | **24** | **25** |
| 26 | 27 | 28 | 29 | 30 | 31 |   |

## WEEKLY INTENTION

## TOP 3 TO-DOS

◯

◯

◯

**19** SUN

Sun in Aquarius (3:00PM)

**AQUARIUS SEASON UNTIL FEB 18**

**20** MON

**21** TUE       ◑ ♎

♏ **11:20AM**
Waning Quarter Moon in Scorpio (3:31PM)
Sun-Pluto meetup

---

**22** WED       ◑ ♏

---

**23** THU       ◐ ♏

♐ **11:29PM**
Mercury-Mars opposition
Mercury-Uranus trine

---

**24** FRI      

---

**25** SAT      

Venus-Mars trine #1 of 2

**JANUARY 2025**

| S | M | T | W | T | F | S |
|---|---|---|---|---|---|---|
|   |   |   | 1 | 2 | 3 | 4 |
| 5 | 6 | 7 | 8 | 9 | 10 | 11 |
| 12 | 13 | 14 | 15 | 16 | 17 | 18 |
| 19 | 20 | 21 | 22 | 23 | 24 | 25 |
| 26 | 27 | 28 | 29 | 30 | 31 |   |

## WEEKLY INTENTION

## TOP 3 TO-DOS

○

○

○

**26** SUN

● ♐
♑ 8:43AM

**27** MON

● ♑
Mercury in Aquarius until Feb 14 (9:53PM)

**28** TUE

●♑
♒ 2:31PM

---

**29** WED

●♒

## NEW MOON IN AQUARIUS
### (7:36 AM, 9°51')
Mercury-Pluto meetup
Lunar New Year's Eve

---

**30** THU

●♒
♓ 5:52PM
Year of the Wood Snake begins
Uranus retrograde ends (11:22AM)
Sun-Jupiter trine

---

**31** FRI

●♓

---

## MONTHLY REFLECTION

1

# JANUARY
## MONTHLY HOTSPOTS

### JAN 1 (NEW YEAR'S DAY) WAXING CRESCENT MOON IN CAPRICORN UNTIL 5:50AM; THEN, AQUARIUS

If you break dawn on NYE, you might wind up holding an impromptu brainstorming session (or board meeting!) over bubbles. The moon holds court in Capricorn until 5:50AM EST, igniting everyone's ambitions as 2025 dawns. Capture those ideas in a voice memo, then set them aside. In the early hours of the day, la luna shifts into social, idealistic Aquarius, turning the black tie vibes into a casual athleisure affair. Spend the day sending friendly texts to the people who matter most and meeting as many of them as you can for a hair-of-the-dog hangout or an inspired vision-boarding session.

### JAN 2–FEB 4 VENUS IN PISCES

How perfectly poetic! On the second day of 2025, ardent Venus glides into romantic Pisces, bringing artists and romantics a cure for the impending winter blahs. Pisces is the love planet's favorite (exalted) position in the zodiac, which is sure to turn anything "mundane" into pure magic between now and February 4. Rethink any punishing or hardcore resolutions you were about to adopt. Instead, how about transforming them into pleasure-enhancing rituals that feed your mind, body and spirit? Turn your living room into a club for cardio dance routines. Trade massages with your partner and set up a smoothie bar in your kitchen. While this boundary-blurring transit works well for cuddling by the fireplace, it can make business dealings dodgy. Don't drop your guard completely with people you've just met. Before you sign a contract or send out your top-secret pitch deck, run the background checks to make sure they're "as advertised."

## JAN 3 MARS-PLUTO OPPOSITION

Clash of the titans! Ferocious Mars is retrograde in fiery Leo, which has already set everyone's teeth on edge. Today, the feisty red planet locks into the second of two exact oppositions to powermonger Pluto in Aquarius. Whether you're wearing a crown, leading a rebellion or trying to wrangle your family back to a non-holiday schedule, check your authoritative style. Today comes with a strong warning to not abuse your power. Entitlement and egos can masquerade as "doing the right thing," but if you wind up polarizing the people you need in your corner, you'll only shoot yourself in the foot.

## JAN 6

### MARS RETROGRADE ENTERS CANCER (JAN 6–FEB 23)

Don't say the quiet part out loud. Firecracker Mars has been retrograding through ferocious Leo since December 6, 2024, making everyone's roar a little (or a lot) more intense. Today, the red planet goes into "silent simmer" mode, as it retreats into Cancer for the rest of its backspin, until February 23. Sensitivities are heightened and you may feel like you're wading through a minefield of mixed messages. Cut stressful people a wide berth and bring awareness to the emotional energy you bring into a room. Moods are especially contagious now, and it's easy to get passive aggressive instead of being direct. Strong emotions could surge up around family, especially if you're processing generational trauma or navigating complex dynamics that reared up over the holidays. If you're planning to move or renovate, try to wait until Mars is direct in Cancer after February 23. Not an option? Do everything you can to eliminate stress from the process.

### MERCURY-NEPTUNE SQUARE

Mercury in adventurous Sagittarius is eager to gallop out of the starting gate, but not so fast! That could spell wasted energy, thanks to a befuddling beam from hazy Neptune who's fogging up the picture in Pisces. What looks like a "next step" could be a wrong turn into quicksand. And with both planets in mutable signs, every option may seem as enticing as the next. Hold off on decision-making and, instead, do some whiteboarding, mind mapping or "wouldn't it be crazy if...?" visioning. Ponder all the possibilities, from both the left and right hemispheres of your brain.

## WAXING QUARTER MOON IN ARIES (6:56PM)

CEO, MVP, Queen of (fill in the blank). As you set your sights on your 2025 goals, today's quarter moon in competitive Aries brings a burst of excitement to your imagineering process. Visualize yourself at the top of your game and start thinking about what it will take to get there. Is there something you want to be known for this year? Since this is a moderating quarter moon, don't set the bar so high that it becomes impossible to reach. Beware of shiny object syndrome, too. As exciting as the new and trendy option may be, there's a chance it's not worth its weight in glitter.

## JAN 8–27 MERCURY IN CAPRICORN

Strategic socializing is the name of the game as Mercury buzzes through Capricorn, the sign of the mogul, until January 27. Over the next few weeks, go rub shoulders with well-connected people who might help you get ahead. Join mastermind groups and online courses; apply to be part of a club where people with similar aspirations gather. Got a business idea brewing? Stop the guesswork and seek expert guidance. This can save you costly mistakes and help you map out a path to lasting success. Speedy Mercury can feel constrained when buzzing through cautious, conservative Capricorn, but don't put the pedal to the metal. Slowing down will bring results that are worth the wait.

## JAN 11–JUL 26, 2026 NORTH NODE IN PISCES, SOUTH NODE IN VIRGO

Calling all sirens, narwhals and merfolk! Life on Earth may soon feel like a chapter in your favorite fantasy lit novel. (And maybe an underwater dive to the lost city of Atlantis.) For the first time since December 2007, the destiny-driven lunar North Node sets sail on a fantastic voyage through Pisces. The veil will be thin during this 18-month transit, which could bring a global spiritual awakening. Across the zodiac wheel, the lunar South Node hunkers down in analytical Virgo, bringing common sense into the equation. As magical as the tidal wave of Pisces energy can be, we will need periodic reality checks. In comes the Virgo South Node to remind us that the Wizard of Oz was really just a "man behind the curtain." Fittingly, this is a powerful time to tune up both the front end and the back end of your life. Virgo's systems and routines support the free-flowing enchantment of Pisces. What levers must be pulled in order to achieve the Fish's elevated state? Both Virgo and Pisces are associated with healing, which could stretch across all modalities—and both the 3D material plane and 5D ethereal realm—during this 19-month transit. Give your body AND your soul some love.

## JAN 12 MARS-NEPTUNE TRINE

Flashes of feelings will be too strong to ignore today as insistent Mars dances into a powerful water trine with psychic Neptune. Serendipities, coincidences and "signs" are everywhere you turn, practically announcing themselves in bold neon lights. Conversations could feel so connected that you and the other person keep finishing each other's sentences. Don't dismiss these directives from the universe, but don't take them at face value, either. Since Mars is retrograde, emotional biases may cloud your ability to view your findings objectively. Follow up with a fact-check before you continue to pursue any intriguing leads. Couples could find the perfect balance of lust and trust, as compassionate Neptune softens the red planet's raw intensity. Single? A sultry person with a strong spiritual side will be more appealing than the sparkly unicorn with sheer animal magnetism.

## JAN 13

### SUN-URANUS TRINE

Hot damn! Ingenious ideas emerge at every turn as the unstoppable Capricorn Sun syncs up with innovative Uranus in Taurus. Energy is electric and people will be eager to jump into action around world-changing projects and revolutionary ideas. Put your surge protector in place! Uranus is still retrograde until January 30, which could send you on a wild goose chase as you pursue what seems like the next viral hit. Get excited, then, take a deep breath and run the background checks. With a little due diligence dynamic dreams can come to life.

## CANCER FULL MOON (5:27PM; 24°00')

It's peak cozy season today as the first full moon of 2025 glows in warm-fuzzy Cancer. Emotions that have been simmering below the surface may spill out under these stirring moonbeams. And thanks to luna's flowing trine to compassionate Neptune, your sentimental side could be caught in 4K. Naked vulnerability is 100 percent acceptable when you're having lunch with your work wife or gushing to besties in a group thread. Try to keep it professional when the situation requires. Just because you can turn a client into a confidante doesn't necessarily mean that you should. The full moon cuts a close connection to retrograde Mars, dialing up the intensity level of your exchanges. Be gentle when delivering feedback to avoid bruised egos or ruffled feathers. Under Cancer's domestic influence, home life is equally top of mind. First major project of the New Year? Redoing your closets, updating your bedroom furniture—or changing your address entirely!

## JAN 14 VENUS-JUPITER SQUARE

How green is the grass beneath your feet? As Venus in quixotic Pisces butts heads with "more is more" Jupiter in variety-loving Gemini, you'll be hard-pressed to find satisfaction. Comparing is despairing: under this biannual transit, which can make you feel like everyone else has the better deal. Venus and Jupiter are considered the two "benefic" planets because of their primarily positive qualities; yet today's square may prove that it's possible to have too much of a good thing. In romance, people will be fickle, rocking the rose-colored glasses one minute, then suddenly losing interest the next. Hold off on making any irreversible decisions, especially when it comes to your dating life or a pricey purchase that is final sale only.

## JAN 15 SUN-MARS OPPOSITION

You could feel pulled in two directions with equal force under today's headstrong tug of war between the Sun and Mars. Instigator Mars is retrograde in domestic Cancer, driving up family drama. Meanwhile, the

Capricorn Sun is fixated on your career goals. Distractions from home will be impossible to screen out, no matter how desperate you are to give a professional initiative your undivided attention. While it's never wise to leave your loved ones in a lurch, do your best to set boundaries around your time—especially with people who play the helpless role to get attention. Jumping in and making sacrifices won't do either of you any good.

## JAN 18 VENUS-SATURN MEETUP #1 OF 3

Matters of the heart feel heavy and serious as Venus bumps into stern Saturn for the first of three conjunctions in Pisces this year. This odd-couple mashup can put a reality check on fantasies that have spun wildly out of control. No more riding on assumptions. Couples should sit down to talk through agreements, like how you budget and divide up household duties. While you may be wholeheartedly enjoying a situationship, this eye-opening transit could reveal long-term disparities, such as different political views. Saturn rules experts, so if you're at an impasse, a coach or couple's therapist could help you navigate your way through it. Ready to cut someone off who's draining your resources? Make a smooth and steely exit now—no explanations required.

## JAN 19–FEB 18 SUN IN AQUARIUS (3:00PM)

Group hug! The Sun beams into communal Aquarius, the sign of collective and humanitarian efforts. This is peak season for activism, and there's no shortage of important causes to rally behind in 2025. How can you make your corner of the world a safer, more egalitarian place for all? The Sun in "one love" Aquarius shines a light on innovative solutions. Crowdfunding, crowdsourcing or any pooling of resources gets a thumbs up now. Aquarius rules science and technology, making it chic to be a geek now. If you're sitting on an invention or an idea for a must-have app, start talking to people who can help you bring it to life. (Have them sign an NDA to protect your intellectual property, though!) Learn software or figure out how to use AI to scale your business. If you can visualize it, you can do it.

## JAN 21

### SUN-PLUTO MEETUP

Once every year, the dazzling Sun makes an appointment with stormy Pluto, an event that can feel as intense as a Queen's Gambit chess match. The Sun reveals, Pluto conceals, which automatically puts them at cross purposes. As they meet up in communal Aquarius for the first time since the late 1700s, the world stage feels like an improv show. Competitive vibes could amplify to a cutthroat level while alliances emerge in the most unexpected places. If you don't have a team that you trust, start taking steps to amend that at once. And even if you do, keep one eyebrow raised at any suggestions that are brought to the collective. What seems like a generous act could be a power play in disguise.

### WANING QUARTER MOON IN SCORPIO (3:31PM)

How wisely have you invested? From the way you spend your time to the people you share it with, stop and do an audit. Last week's full moon in Cancer revealed relationships that felt nourishing to your soul. Today's quarter moon in devoted, discerning Scorpio puts everyone under the microscope. Heartwarming exchanges don't tell the whole story—not by a long shot! Dig a little deeper into people's personal history and don't be afraid to probe, should the "facts" not seem to line up. This could be a good thing! You could uncover data that helps you make a more informed choice and build a stronger bond of trust.

## JAN 23

### MERCURY-MARS OPPOSITION

You know what you want, but as shrewd Mercury in Capricorn opposes combative Mars retrograde in Cancer, your ideas might be diametrically opposed to what other key players have in mind. There's no easy way around this. Trying to convince people to follow your "proven methodology" will make you look stubborn and rebellious. At the same time, giving in to other people's demands can make you feel weak. Accept that you're going to have to compromise somewhere, and hopefully you can choose your battles.

## MERCURY-URANUS TRINE

Let your imagination wander off leash today, as mindful Mercury in Capricorn trines mad scientist Uranus in Taurus. With both planets in practical earth signs, you probably won't stray too far from reality, but nudge yourself a bit further from your comfort zone than usual. Slide into the DMs of a professional prospect. Put feelers out to see who might want to join you for a crypto conference or self-development seminar. Don't shy away from the oft-taboo topic of money because these conversations could spawn all sorts of income-generating ideas.

## JAN 25 VENUS-MARS TRINE #1 OF 2

If you catch yourself doodling someone's name in a heart, there's no need to blush. Blame it on today's flowing trine between the love planets Venus and Mars. If you want to cop to your crush, you're in luck. This passionate pair is canoodling in water signs—Venus is in Pisces and Mars is in Cancer—setting the stage for a tender exchange of feelings. But with reactive Mars still retrograde, defenses may be higher than usual, too. Try not to read into your person's every twitch and tick. There's a good chance those bodily responses have nothing to do with you. Coupled? Study your partner's nuances now and, instead of criticizing them, celebrate these unique traits.

## JAN 27–FEB 14 MERCURY IN AQUARIUS

Slip off the blazer and slide into your lab coat. As mentalist Mercury shifts out of conventional Capricorn and into mad scientist Aquarius, everything is up for experimentation. New ideas and inventions flood in. Over the next few weeks, you could become obsessed with learning everything there is to know about an offbeat topic. Dive down the rabbit hole! Just make sure the research you find is credible and not funded by someone with a hidden agenda. (Mercury in Aquarius can spin up conspiracy theories.) Under the influence of team-spirited Aquarius, Mercury helps you forge new bonds both IRL and virtually. Community is healing and uplifting, especially during tense times; in fact, "tending and befriending" is a known stress response. Don't isolate!

## JAN 29

### MERCURY-PLUTO MEETUP

Forget about settling for status quo! As inquisitive Mercury unites with investigative Pluto, you want deeper answers. What's really going on here, and what else might be possible? This once-a-year meetup cranks open the discovery vault. Since both planets are touring "anything goes" Aquarius, you might be drawn to subject matter that is dark, mystical and revolutionary. Just be warned that Pluto can pull you into some shadowy places. If you start to feel creeped out or pessimistic, close those browser tabs and go do something to lift your mood!

### AQUARIUS NEW MOON (7:36AM; 9°51') AND LUNAR NEW YEAR'S EVE – WOOD SNAKE

Let's get together and feel alright! The new moon in "one love" Aquarius sends out a strong reminder that we are all connected. And thanks to a globally expansive trine to Jupiter in Gemini, this is a powerful moment for reaching across borders and diversifying your dream team. Each year, the Aquarius new moon dovetails with the Chinese Lunar New Year's Eve. Tonight, the enchanting Wood Dragon disappears in a puff of smoke, handing the magic stick to 2025's reigning creature, the seductive Wood Snake. This is the second of the two-year wood element cycle, which puts the emphasis on growth and cultivating our natural gifts between now and February 17, 2026. Add romantic and artistic gifts to that list! The Snake is ruled by luscious, beauty-loving Venus, a far tamer vibe than the warring Mars energy that the Dragon brought. Send up the prayers for peace!

## URANUS RETROGRADE ENDS

Train your sites on that wild hare and get ready for a hot pursuit! After a five month retrograde that began last September 1, shock-jock Uranus wakes up and jolts us all into action. As the planetary innovator makes a U-Turn in money-minded Taurus, opportunities to improve your economic status could crop up everywhere. Don't get stuck on projects that aren't clicking into place. Business opportunities could arise when you're out doing mundane tasks like picking up your coffee or chatting up another parent at a PTA meeting. No matter what you do for a living, keep your mind open to boundary-pushing and edgy possibilities. Pursuing one of them could lead to quite the bounty in the days ahead. Let's go!

## SUN-JUPITER TRINE

Exactly how wide can you open your mind? Today's free-flowing exchange between the idealistic Aquarius Sun and philosophical Jupiter in Gemini could pull you out of any mental ruts you've been stuck in. Novelty is the antidote to a pedantic mindset so if you need to trigger your own ingenuity, step away from the usual places. If you can't get past a sticking point, could you adopt an attitude of curiosity? Go for a walk (or drive) off your beaten path. Peruse a site that's not in your usual feed. Under the mentally agile influence of this air trine, thinking outside the box can lead to a breakthrough.

# February

## MONTHLY HOROSCOPE

2

Tighten up that belt a bit, Capricorn. With the Aquarius Sun activating your second house of money and values until the 18th, you're ready to be wiser—and more collaborative—about the way you manage your resources. Get your family (chosen or blood-related) involved! With value-driven Venus anchoring down in Aries on the 4th, you could inspire everyone around you to create a more secure life. This Venus cycle also brings out your desire to beautify your space and, if necessary, bring it up to "Capricorn code." Family relationships get a dose of peaceful energy from this harmonizing transit. Smooth over ruffled feathers before Venus turns retrograde from March 1 to April 12. Jupiter turns direct in Gemini on the 4th, bringing a much-needed mindset shift about your work and wellness goals. If you've been feeling sluggish or uninspired, the broad-minded planet pushes you to explore new processes. The Sun sails into Pisces on the 18th, activating your third house of communication. This is a great time for networking, learning and sharing ideas with your community. Finally, Mars turns direct in Cancer on February 23, spicing up your relationships and getting you motivated to take more initiative with the people you love.

*Read your extended monthly forecast for*
*life, love, money and career! astrostyle.com*

# FEBRUARY
## Moon Phase Calendar

| SUN | MON | TUE | WED | THU | FRI | SAT |
|-----|-----|-----|-----|-----|-----|-----|
| | | | | | | **1**<br>♓<br>♈ 8:10PM |
| **2**<br>♈ | **3**<br>♈<br>♉ 10:33PM | **4**<br>♉ | **5**<br>♉<br>2nd Quarter | **6**<br>♉<br>♊ 1:44AM | **7**<br>♊ | **8**<br>♊<br>♋ 6:04AM |
| **9**<br>♋ | **10**<br>♋<br>♌ 12:01PM | **11**<br>♌ | **12**<br>♌ Full Moon<br>8:53AM<br>♍ 8:07PM | **13**<br>♍ | **14**<br>♍ | **15**<br>♍<br>♎ 6:45AM |
| **16**<br>♎ | **17**<br>♎<br>♏ 7:19PM | **18**<br>♏ | **19**<br>♏ | **20**<br>♏→♐ 7:55AM<br>♐ 4th Quarter | **21**<br>♐ | **22**<br>♐<br>♑ 6:09PM |
| **23**<br>♑ | **24**<br>♑ | **25**<br>♑<br>♒ 12:40AM | **26**<br>♒ | **27**<br>♒→♓ 3:46AM<br>♓ New Moon<br>7:45PM | **28**<br>♓ | |

*Times listed are Eastern US Time Zone*

KEY

| | | | | | | |
|---|---|---|---|---|---|---|
| ♈ | ARIES | ♌ | LEO | ♐ | SAGITTARIUS | **FM** FULL MOON |
| ♉ | TAURUS | ♍ | VIRGO | ♑ | CAPRICORN | **NM** NEW MOON |
| ♊ | GEMINI | ♎ | LIBRA | ♒ | AQUARIUS | **LE** LUNAR ECLIPSE |
| ♋ | CANCER | ♏ | SCORPIO | ♓ | PISCES | **SE** SOLAR ECLIPSE |

FEB 12, 8:53AM
# full moon in
# LEO (24°06')

## LEO
## FULL MOON
## CRYSTAL

### TIGER'S EYE
This confidence-boosting stone contains the power of the mid-day Sun, the ruler of Leo. Use Tiger's Eye to enhance creativity and connect to personal agency. With its swirling hues of amber and brown, this talisman directs your attention to what's truly important in your life.

*What's one thing you're celebrating under this full moon?*

## LEO FULL MOON = CELEBRATE

*The unique way that you shine*

*The people who make your heart sing*

*Your romantic nature*

*Your fashion sense*

*Your childlike wonder*

*The places where you feel like a natural leader*

*Your fiercely competitive streak that won't let you quit on yourself*

FEB 27, 7:45PM

# new moon in
# Pisces (9°41')

## PISCES NEW MOON CRYSTAL

### AMETHYST

This relaxing purple crystal increases inner peace and tunes you in to your Pisces-ruled intuition. Keep amethyst by your bedside to sanctify sleep and invite powerful messages from your dreams.

---

*What's one fresh intention you're ready to set under this new moon?*

---

## PISCES NEW MOON = FOCUS

*Connect to your dreams, spiritual exploration*

*Find creative outlets*

*Give back*

*Inspire others*

*Form supportive alliances*

*Express empathy so people feel seen and understood*

**February 2025**

Longitude & Retrograde Ephemeris [00:00 UT]

| Day | Sid.time | ☉ | ☽ | +12h☽ | ☿ | ♀ | ♂ | ♃ | ♄ | ♅ | ♆ | ♇ | ☊ | ☊ | ⚸ | ⚷ | Day |
|---|---|---|---|---|---|---|---|---|---|---|---|---|---|---|---|---|---|
| 1 Sa | 08:45:49 | ♒12°22'15 | ♓14°57'39 | ♓22°07'46 | ♒06°22 | ♓27°26 | ℞ 20°27 | ℞ 11°17 | ♓17°25 | ♉23°15 | ♓27°58 | ♒02°03 | ℞ 29°51 | ℞ 28°10 | ♎24°00 | ♈19°30 | 1 Sa |
| 2 Su | 08:49:46 | ♒13°23'10 | ♓29°18'19 | ♈06°28'25 | ♒08°03 | ♓28°13 | ♋20°10 | ♊11°17 | ♓17°31 | ♉23°15 | ♓27°59 | ♒02°05 | ♓29°48 | D 28°09 | ♎24°06 | ♈19°31 | 2 Su |
| 3 Mo | 08:53:42 | ♒14°24'03 | ♈13°38'04 | ♈20°46'29 | ♒09°44 | ♓29°00 | ♋19°53 | ♊11°16 | ♓17°38 | ♉23°15 | ♓28°01 | ♒02°07 | ♓29°45 | ♓28°10 | ♎24°13 | ♈19°33 | 3 Mo |
| 4 Tu | 08:57:39 | ♒15°24'55 | ♈27°53'48 | ♉04°59'21 | ♒11°25 | ♓29°45 | ♋19°37 | ♊11°16 | ♓17°45 | ♉23°16 | ♓28°03 | ♒02°08 | ♓29°41 | ♓28°11 | ♎24°20 | ♈19°35 | 4 Tu |
| 5 We | 09:01:35 | ♒16°25'46 | ♉12°03'24 | ♉19°05'20 | ♒13°08 | ♈00°29 | ♋19°22 | D 11°16 | ♓17°51 | ♉23°16 | ♓28°05 | ♒02°10 | ♓29°38 | ♓28°12 | ♎24°26 | ♈19°37 | 5 We |
| 6 Th | 09:05:32 | ♒17°26'35 | ♉26°05'30 | ♊03°03'19 | ♒14°51 | ♈01°12 | ♋19°07 | ♊11°16 | ♓17°58 | ♉23°16 | ♓28°06 | ♒02°12 | ♓29°35 | ℞ 28°12 | ♎24°33 | ♈19°39 | 6 Th |
| 7 Fr | 09:09:29 | ♒18°27'23 | ♊09°59'07 | ♊16°52'22 | ♒16°35 | ♈01°54 | ♋18°54 | ♊11°17 | ♓18°05 | ♉23°17 | ♓28°08 | ♒02°14 | ♓29°32 | ♓28°10 | ♎24°40 | ♈19°41 | 7 Fr |
| 8 Sa | 09:13:25 | ♒19°28'09 | ♊23°43'22 | ♋00°31'32 | ♒18°20 | ♈02°35 | ♋18°41 | ♊11°18 | ♓18°12 | ♉23°17 | ♓28°10 | ♒02°16 | ♓29°29 | ♓28°06 | ♎24°46 | ♈19°43 | 8 Sa |
| 9 Su | 09:17:22 | ♒20°28'53 | ♋07°17'10 | ♋13°59'40 | ♒20°05 | ♈03°15 | ♋18°29 | ♊11°18 | ♓18°18 | ♉23°18 | ♓28°12 | ♒02°18 | ♓29°25 | ♓28°00 | ♎24°53 | ♈19°45 | 9 Su |
| 10 Mo | 09:21:18 | ♒21°29'36 | ♋20°39'20 | ♋27°15'33 | ♒21°52 | ♈03°53 | ♋18°17 | ♊11°19 | ♓18°25 | ♉23°18 | ♓28°14 | ♒02°20 | ♓29°22 | ♓27°54 | ♎25°00 | ♈19°48 | 10 Mo |
| 11 Tu | 09:25:15 | ♒22°30'18 | ♌03°48'37 | ♌10°18'00 | ♒23°39 | ♈04°30 | ♋18°07 | ♊11°21 | ♓18°32 | ♉23°19 | ♓28°16 | ♒02°22 | ♓29°19 | ♓27°48 | ♎25°06 | ♈19°50 | 11 Tu |
| 12 We | 09:29:11 | ♒23°30'59 | ♌16°44'00 | ♌23°06'12 | ♒25°27 | ♈05°06 | ♋17°57 | ♊11°22 | ♓18°39 | ♉23°19 | ♓28°18 | ♒02°23 | ♓29°16 | ♓27°42 | ♎25°13 | ♈19°52 | 12 We |
| 13 Th | 09:33:08 | ♒24°31'37 | ♌29°24'58 | ♍05°39'58 | ♒27°15 | ♈05°40 | ♋17°48 | ♊11°24 | ♓18°46 | ♉23°20 | ♓28°20 | ♒02°25 | ♓29°13 | ♓27°38 | ♎25°19 | ♈19°54 | 13 Th |
| 14 Fr | 09:37:04 | ♒25°32'15 | ♍11°51'42 | ♍17°59'55 | ♒29°04 | ♈06°13 | ♋17°39 | ♊11°26 | ♓18°53 | ♉23°21 | ♓28°22 | ♒02°27 | ♓29°10 | ♓27°35 | ♎25°26 | ♈19°57 | 14 Fr |
| 15 Sa | 09:41:01 | ♒26°32'51 | ♍24°05'14 | ♎00°07'33 | ♓00°54 | ♈06°44 | ♋17°32 | ♊11°28 | ♓19°00 | ♉23°21 | ♓28°24 | ♒02°29 | ♓29°06 | ♓27°34 | ♎25°33 | ♈19°59 | 15 Sa |
| 16 Su | 09:44:58 | ♒27°33'25 | ♎06°07'34 | ♎12°05'18 | ♓02°44 | ♈07°14 | ♋17°25 | ♊11°30 | ♓19°07 | ♉23°22 | ♓28°26 | ♒02°31 | ♓29°03 | D 27°34 | ♎25°39 | ♈20°01 | 16 Su |
| 17 Mo | 09:48:54 | ♒28°33'59 | ♎18°01'33 | ♎23°56'26 | ♓04°35 | ♈07°42 | ♋17°20 | ♊11°32 | ♓19°14 | ♉23°23 | ♓28°28 | ♒02°32 | ♓29°00 | ♓27°35 | ♎25°46 | ♈20°04 | 17 Mo |
| 18 Tu | 09:52:51 | ♒29°34'31 | ♎29°50'51 | ♏05°44'57 | ♓06°26 | ♈08°08 | ♋17°14 | ♊11°35 | ♓19°21 | ♉23°24 | ♓28°30 | ♒02°34 | ♓28°57 | ♓27°37 | ♎25°53 | ♈20°06 | 18 Tu |
| 19 We | 09:56:47 | ♓00°35'01 | ♏11°39'43 | ♏17°35'22 | ♓08°18 | ♈08°33 | ♋17°10 | ♊11°38 | ♓19°28 | ♉23°25 | ♓28°32 | ♒02°36 | ♓28°54 | ♓27°39 | ♎25°59 | ♈20°09 | 19 We |
| 20 Th | 10:00:44 | ♓01°35'31 | ♏23°32'55 | ♏29°32'36 | ♓10°09 | ♈08°55 | ♋17°07 | ♊11°41 | ♓19°35 | ♉23°26 | ♓28°34 | ♒02°38 | ♓28°51 | ♓27°40 | ♎26°06 | ♈20°11 | 20 Th |
| 21 Fr | 10:04:40 | ♓02°35'59 | ♐05°35'24 | ♐11°41'35 | ♓12°01 | ♈09°16 | ♋17°04 | ♊11°44 | ♓19°43 | ♉23°27 | ♓28°36 | ♒02°39 | ♓28°47 | ℞ 27°40 | ♎26°13 | ♈20°14 | 21 Fr |
| 22 Sa | 10:08:37 | ♓03°36'26 | ♐17°52'05 | ♐24°07'04 | ♓13°52 | ♈09°35 | ♋17°02 | ♊11°47 | ♓19°50 | ♉23°28 | ♓28°38 | ♒02°41 | ♓28°44 | ♓27°39 | ♎26°19 | ♈20°17 | 22 Sa |
| 23 Su | 10:12:33 | ♓04°36'52 | ♑00°27'26 | ♑06°53'11 | ♓15°43 | ♈09°52 | ♋17°01 | ♊11°51 | ♓19°57 | ♉23°30 | ♓28°40 | ♒02°43 | ♓28°41 | ♓27°37 | ♎26°26 | ♈20°19 | 23 Su |
| 24 Mo | 10:16:30 | ♓05°37'16 | ♑13°25'03 | ♑20°02'52 | ♓17°33 | ♈10°07 | ♋17°00 | ♊11°54 | ♓20°04 | ♉23°31 | ♓28°42 | ♒02°44 | ♓28°38 | ♓27°35 | ♎26°33 | ♈20°22 | 24 Mo |
| 25 Tu | 10:20:27 | ♓06°37'39 | ♑26°47'11 | ♒03°37'32 | ♓19°21 | ♈10°20 | D 17°01 | ♊11°58 | ♓20°12 | ♉23°32 | ♓28°44 | ♒02°46 | ♓28°35 | ♓27°32 | ♎26°39 | ♈20°25 | 25 Tu |
| 26 We | 10:24:23 | ♓07°38'00 | ♒10°34'12 | ♒17°36'27 | ♓21°08 | ♈10°30 | ♋17°02 | ♊12°03 | ♓20°19 | ♉23°33 | ♓28°47 | ♒02°48 | ♓28°31 | ♓27°29 | ♎26°46 | ♈20°28 | 26 We |
| 27 Th | 10:28:20 | ♓08°38'20 | ♒24°44'16 | ♓01°56'39 | ♓22°54 | ♈10°39 | ♋17°04 | ♊12°07 | ♓20°26 | ♉23°35 | ♓28°49 | ♒02°49 | ♓28°28 | ♓27°26 | ♎26°53 | ♈20°30 | 27 Th |
| 28 Fr | 10:32:16 | ♓09°38'38 | ♓09°13'20 | ♓16°33'03 | ♓24°37 | ♈10°45 | ♋17°06 | ♊12°11 | ♓20°34 | ♉23°36 | ♓28°51 | ♒02°51 | ♓28°25 | ♓27°24 | ♎26°59 | ♈20°33 | 28 Fr |
| Δ Delta | 01:46:27 | 27°16'22" | -354°15'40" | -354°25'17" | 48°14' | -13°18' | -3°21' | 0°53' | 3°08' | 0°20' | 0°53' | 0°48' | -1°25' | -0°45' | 2°59' | 1°03' | Delta |

Ephemeris tables and data provided by **Astro-Seek.com.** All times in UTC.

| S | M | T | W | T | F | S |
|---|---|---|---|---|---|---|
|   |   |   |   |   |   | 1 |
| 2 | 3 | 4 | 5 | 6 | 7 | 8 |
| 9 | 10 | 11 | 12 | 13 | 14 | 15 |
| 16 | 17 | 18 | 19 | 20 | 21 | 22 |
| 23 | 24 | 25 | 26 | 27 | 28 |   |

## MONTHLY INTENTION

**1** SAT

●♓
♈ 8:10PM
Venus-Neptune meetup #1 of 3

**FEBRUARY 2025**

| S | M | T | W | T | F | S |
|---|---|---|---|---|---|---|
| | | | | | | 1 |
| 2 | 3 | 4 | 5 | 6 | 7 | 8 |
| 9 | 10 | 11 | 12 | 13 | 14 | 15 |
| 16 | 17 | 18 | 19 | 20 | 21 | 22 |
| 23 | 24 | 25 | 26 | 27 | 28 | |

## WEEKLY INTENTION

## TOP 3 TO-DOS

○

○

○

**2** SUN ☽♈

**3** MON ☽♈
☿ 10:33PM
Mercury-Jupiter trine

**4** TUE ◗♉

Venus in Aries until Mar 27
Jupiter retrograde ends (4:40 AM)

---

**5** WED ◗♉

Waxing quarter moon in Taurus (3:02AM)

---

**6** THU ○♉
♊ 1:44AM

---

**7** FRI ○♊

---

**8** SAT ○♊
♋ 6:04AM

**FEBRUARY 2025**

| S | M | T | W | T | F | S |
|---|---|---|---|---|---|---|
|   |   |   |   |   |   | 1 |
| 2 | 3 | 4 | 5 | 6 | 7 | 8 |
| 9 | 10 | 11 | 12 | 13 | 14 | 15 |
| 16 | 17 | 18 | 19 | 20 | 21 | 22 |
| 23 | 24 | 25 | 26 | 27 | 28 |   |

# WEEKLY INTENTION

## TOP 3 TO-DOS

○

○

○

**9** SUN ○ ♋

Sun-Mercury meetup
Mars-Saturn trine

**10** MON ○ ♋

♌ 12:01PM

Mercury-Uranus square

**11** TUE

☉♌
Sun-Uranus square

---

**12** WED

☉♌
**FULL MOON IN LEO**
(8:53 AM, 24°06′)
♍ 8:07PM

---

**13** THU

☉♍

---

**14** FRI

☉♍
Mercury in Pisces until Mar 3 (7:06AM)

---

**15** SAT

☉♍
♎ 6:45AM

**2**

**FEBRUARY 2025**

| S | M | T | W | T | F | S |
|---|---|---|---|---|---|---|
|   |   |   |   |   |   | 1 |
| 2 | 3 | 4 | 5 | 6 | 7 | 8 |
| 9 | 10 | 11 | 12 | 13 | 14 | 15 |
| **16** | **17** | **18** | **19** | **20** | **21** | **22** |
| 23 | 24 | 25 | 26 | 27 | 28 |   |

## WEEKLY INTENTION

## TOP 3 TO-DOS

○

○

○

**16** SUN ☽♎

**17** MON ☽♎
♏ 7:19PM

**18** TUE

☽ ♏
Sun in Pisces (5:07AM)

**PISCES SEASON UNTIL MAR 20**

---

**19** WED

☽ ♏

---

**20** THU

☽ ♏
♐ **7:55AM**
Waning quarter moon in Sagittarius (12:33PM)
Mercury-Jupiter Square

---

**21** FRI

◑ ♐

---

**22** SAT

◑ ♐
♑ **6:09PM**

**FEBRUARY 2025**

| S | M | T | W | T | F | S |
|---|---|---|---|---|---|---|
|   |   |   |   |   |   | 1 |
| 2 | 3 | 4 | 5 | 6 | 7 | 8 |
| 9 | 10 | 11 | 12 | 13 | 14 | 15 |
| 16 | 17 | 18 | 19 | 20 | 21 | 22 |
| **23** | **24** | **25** | **26** | **27** | **28** | |

# WEEKLY INTENTION

## TOP 3 TO-DOS

○

○

○

**23** SUN ●♐

Mercury-Mars trine
Mars retrograde ends (9:00PM)

**24** MON ●♐

**25** TUE

●♑
♒ 12:40AM
Mercury-Saturn meetup

---

**26** WED

●♒

---

**27** THU

●♒
♓ 3:46AM
**NEW MOON IN PISCES**
**(7:45PM, 9°41')**

---

**28** FRI

●♓

---

## MONTHLY REFLECTION

# FEBRUARY
## MONTHLY HOTSPOTS

### FEB 1 VENUS-NEPTUNE MEETUP #1 OF 3

Shall we dance? Venus in Pisces falls under Neptune's spellbinding sway as the two meet for their first of three conjunctions in 2025. Romance takes on a magical glow as the universe sprinkles stardust on all your encounters. But before you dive headfirst into the fantasy, hit pause. Make sure to look beyond the fairytale sheen to see what's real and what might be an illusion. If you've been caught in a tangled web with a friend or loved one, today's compassionate vibes offer the perfect chance to mend fences and heal those wounds. Let the cosmic currents guide you toward love and forgiveness.

### FEB 3 MERCURY-JUPITER TRINE

It won't be hard to sway the masses today as articulate Mercury in Aquarius and grandiose Jupiter in Gemini sync up in verbose air signs. A dollop of charm and a few pumps of enthusiasm may be enough to turn a "no" to a "yes" for now. But don't rest on any laurels. Big talk needs to be followed up by solid action, the kind that yields results. To avoid getting a reputation as a demagogue, lay out next steps and be sure to make good on them in the coming days. The air-sign trine of Mercury and Jupiter can inflate your reputation. If you're not shining the way you long to be, work on polishing up your personal brand.

### FEB 4

### VENUS IN ARIES (FEB 4-MAR 27)

H-O-T-T-O-G-O! Seductive Venus fire-spins into the bold and brash sign of Aries, heating things up in the Ram's realm for nearly two whole months. Love will be lit during this longer-than-usual cycle, but it also comes with a flame-orange warning flag. On March 1, Venus spins into a six-week retrograde, which could tamp down some of the bold, impulsive energy that her tour through Aries brings. Fortunately, there's a solid month ahead to relish Venus in direct motion. Love may spark quickly and extinguish just as fast in this rapid-fire sign. But don't shy away from the thrill. If your romantic life has slowed to a standstill, Venus in fearless Aries reignites your courage. Note: In the impetuous sign of Aries, Venus finds herself in "detriment," making it tough for the planet of slow seduction to keep a semblance of cool. Unexpected (and intense!) attractions might catch you off-guard. If you're already spoken for, there's no need to act on these impulses. Try to channel that vibrant energy back to your S.O.

## JUPITER RETROGRADE ENDS

Enough with the double talk! After five months of frustrating detours and mental chess games, the road to truth is in sight again. Maximizer Jupiter powers forward in clever, communicative Gemini, where it's been retrograde since last October 9. In the wake of months of introspective rewiring, you may find that you have copious wisdom to share. Plug into articulate Jupiter-in-Gemini to write an article, record a podcast or revive a once-lively group chat. Curiosity may have led you astray since last October, but starting now, it could pave the way to a vibrant social life or a new hobby that you've always wanted to try. Don't be shy about striking up conversations! Tag-team efforts will be blessed with the mighty planet's powers. This is your cosmic cue to think big and assert yourself boldly (well, once you have all the facts). Jupiter in Gemini can amplify your voice and help you reach a global crowd.

## FEB 5 WAXING QUARTER MOON IN TAURUS (3:02AM)

Time for a cosmic check-in! Today's waxing quarter moon in sensible Taurus invites you to fine-tune your goals. Instead of barreling towards the finish line, ease off the accelerator and give all projects a thorough evaluation. Are you clear about the value you're offering? Do you know where you ultimately want to land this plane? Now's the time to fortify your strategies to avoid wasting time and energy. While you may feel like scaling back, don't do minimalism for minimalism's sake. Infuse simplicity with sophistication. Toss out the worn and welcome in the elegant.

## FEB 9

### SUN-MERCURY MEETUP

There is no "I" in "team" as the Sun unites with social Mercury in Aquarius. But that doesn't mean you can't bring your original vibe to a group effort. Under these inclusive skies, band together with a diverse crew and see what you can cook up together. Keep your eyes open for people's hidden potential. The missing link for a project or plan might be someone you've casually interacted with for months. Go ahead and ask the not-so-obvious questions. You could discover mind blowing synergies that you had no clue existed.

### MARS-SATURN TRINE

Gas or brakes? You won't be sure which pedal to ride today as speed-demon Mars in Cancer unites with take-it-slow Saturn in Pisces. Because Mars is retrograde and both planets are in water signs, home and family matters demand attention. Ignore a leaky faucet or a relative's eye rolls at your own peril today. These could quickly snowball into much bigger problems if you don't address them now. It's possible trouble's been brewing unbeknownst to you for a while. Solution-minded Saturn can help you get to the source of the issue and hammer out long-lasting fixes. Keep your temper in check.

### FEB 10 MERCURY-URANUS SQUARE

Pause before you post! Your radical ideas might stir up more chaos than change, as unruly Uranus in bullheaded Taurus clashes with Mercury in rebellious Aquarius. Challenging the norm is one thing, but this feisty energy could drag you into a troll fight that zaps hours of your time. Instead of firing off impulsive rants, take time to refine your message. Being the maverick could backfire spectacularly if you wind up spreading disinformation. If you're pitching a new concept, make sure your arguments are well-structured and backed by solid data. Innovation is valued, but clarity is crucial. Today, aim to be understood, not just heard.

## FEB 11 SUN-URANUS SQUARE

Stay sharp and tread carefully! Today's cosmic climate is extra heated as the Aquarius Sun squares off with abrasive Uranus in Taurus, sparking potential flare-ups and ego battles. This biannual clash tends to magnify power struggles and impulsive reactions. With both celestial bodies in unyielding fixed signs, expect a lot of stubborn "my way or the highway" standoffs. People are likely to react first and think later, making it easy for small disagreements to escalate. Be the calm in the storm. Aim to diffuse tensions and contribute to solutions, not conflicts. Keep your cool and steer clear of unnecessary drama!

## FEB 12 FULL MOON IN LEO (8:53AM; 24°06')

Courage unleashed! Today marks the annual full moon in wholehearted Leo, which emboldens you to live—and love—out loud. Be audacious with your style choices and shameless with the PDA. If you and a certain someone have been coyly circling each other, this could be the day where you bite the bullet and cop to your attraction. The playful, theatrical energy of the day can be fun, but don't be performative at the expense of forging a deeper, emotional connection. With the full moon forming a tense square to unpredictable Uranus and opposing loose-lipped Mercury, be strategic about what you share. If you're divulging personal details to a new friend or unveiling a work project, hold a few details back as you build trust.

## FEB 14—APR 16 MERCURY IN PISCES

Let yourself get swept away this V-Day! Flirty Mercury sets sail in fantasy-fueled Pisces, drifting through this imaginative sign's waters for a solid month. As the messenger planet cranks up the volume on your intuition, you could download all sorts of divine inspiration, from song lyrics to the vision of an installation art piece. Your subconscious will be buzzing, especially after dark. Make time for candlelight meditations, sound baths and any activities that relax your mind so you can receive messages and insights. Don't rush to share them all though! Mercury in Pisces can drive up ambiguity. Since the messenger planet is spinning retrograde (in Pisces and Aries) from March 15 to April 7, you'll need to navigate through some foggy communications. Pay close attention to the unsaid. Body language and subtle signals might reveal more than words ever could!

## FEB 18-MAR 20 SUN IN PISCES (5:07AM)

Pisces season begins today as the Sun casts its line in the watery realm of the Fish, awakening waves of empathy, creativity, and intuition. Compassion reigns supreme for the coming four weeks, a welcome shift after the coolly detached energy of Aquarius season. Forget what the algorithms are serving and tune in to your own soul wisdom. This is a time for dreaming, dancing and flowing with the natural current of the universe—and that requires deep surrender to the unknown. Faith may be tested while the Sun tours this elusive sign since things may not be as they initially appear. During this time, work to cultivate substantial connections rather than fleeting, surface-level interactions. Boundaries can get blurry, so take time to feel your way into situations, making sure that they really do work for you before saying "yes."

## FEB 20

### MERCURY-JUPITER SQUARE

Watch out for a rising tide of know-it-all attitudes today, as fickle Mercury in Pisces clashes with overconfident Jupiter in Gemini. Everywhere you turn, people seem to be making snap judgments and drawing hasty conclusions. The first solution that pops up isn't necessarily the right one, so do your research. Even if you're absolutely sure you're on the money or you're feeling a strong gut instinct, it pays to double-check your facts. Under this mashup, people could be overstating their cases and it's easy to be swayed by an appealing pitch. Challenge for the day: Allow yourself to deeply desire something (or someone) without following the urge to immediately possess it.

### WANING QUARTER MOON IN SAGITTARIUS (12:33PM)

Today's waning quarter moon in straightforward Sagittarius ushers in a wave of clarity and sets the stage for open dialogues. If you've been mulling over an issue since last week's full moon, you may finally see the situation in a new light and discover a silver lining. Ready to wrap up an ideological debate? Focus less on winning or losing and more on understanding different perspectives. Open up the conversation to various viewpoints and strive to see the bigger picture. This broader approach can help resolve conflicts and bring about the peace of mind you've been seeking.

## FEB 23

### MERCURY-MARS TRINE

What have you been stuffing down or keeping inside? Hours before wrapping up its eleven-week retrograde, forthright Mars gets a nudge from communicator Mercury, prompting you to spill. With both planets in emotional water signs, words could rush out like an undammed river. If you feel that swell of energy rising, make sure you're in front of an empathic (and appropriate!) audience. Prickly Mars is retrograde in sensitive Cancer while Mercury in Pisces can make your feelings as clear as a swirling eddy. While it's important to unload, you don't want to pull anyone into an emotional riptide. Best to sort through the emotions that come up before staging any direct confrontations.

### MARS RETROGRADE ENDS

If your 2025 hygge season's been hectic, blame it on aggravating Mars. Since last December 6, the energizer planet has been buried in a frustrating retrograde—in homespun Cancer, no less. Tonight, the red planet resumes forward motion, dialing down that frenetic energy. For the final stretch of winter, set up the craft table and mix up some craft cocktails, as you get into the spirit of cold-weather communing. Vanquish the tension under your roof by decluttering, redecorating and making sure everyone has enough space to do their thing. The red planet's motivational influence may inspire a home-based business or a pre-spring fitness challenge with roommates and relatives. If cabin fever has fanned the flames of conflict, here's your cue to escape to the slopes for a weekend, or maybe the beach!

## FEB 25 MERCURY-SATURN MEETUP

Every word counts today as mouthy Mercury connects the dots with sober Saturn. But with both planets in dreamy, ethereal Pisces, it's almost too easy to make a slip of the tongue. Do your best to pause and think before delivering any sort of judgment—or simply musing aloud. If you're ready to make a serious statement, you can speak with gravitas. To come across as polished and prepared, go easy on the upspeak and vocal fry. This is also a powerful day for consulting experts whose empirical processes can help you turn a lofty vision into a reality.

## FEB 27 NEW MOON IN PISCES (7:45PM; 9°41')

The year's only new moon in Pisces opens up a portal to the divine, marking one of 2025's most potent days for tapping into your own mystical energy. Find at least a few moments during the day to settle into a serene spot, tune out the 3D world and connect to your inner voice. Since new moons make excellent starting blocks, up the ante and begin a 21-day meditation series or sign up for a poetry or Tarot workshop. A sacred healing session or plant medicine ceremony may also be calling your name under these numinous moonbeams. Whatever bubbles up in your imagination is worth taking note of. Guard your nascent dreams from people who are disconnected from their spiritual sides. With Jupiter in Gemini squaring this new moon, one teasing comment could discourage you from pursuing a worthwhile thread.

# NOTES & THOUGHTS

# March

**3**

MONTHLY HOROSCOPE

You're sending out more signals than a satellite tower this March, as the Pisces Sun charges up your third house of communication, learning and community until the 20th. While you're busy networking, info-gathering and swapping ideas, don't neglect your personal life. Both Venus and Mercury will be retrograde in Aries and your home and family zone this month—Venus from March 1 to 27 and Mercury from March 15 to 29. You may need to temporarily distance yourself from a relative or set some boundaries by declaring certain hot-button topics "off-limits." If you've been planning a move or home renovation, expect delays and try to postpone those projects until April. In the meantime, shift your focus to more exciting horizons: The Virgo lunar eclipse on March 14 could bring a serendipitous opportunity for travel or a chance to study with a master teacher. When the Sun enters Aries on March 20, it's time to get serious about making your home life a true reflection of your inner peace. The Aries solar eclipse on March 29 wraps up a two-year cycle in your fourth house, offering a powerful moment to reset your emotional foundations and begin a new chapter in your personal life. Just as you're settling into this shift, Neptune enters Aries on March 30 for the first time since 1875, beginning a 14-year cycle of spiritual growth and transformation in your home and family dynamics. Time to set up your sanctuary!

*Read your extended monthly forecast for life, love, money and career! astrostyle.com*

# MARCH
## Moon Phase Calendar

| SUN | MON | TUE | WED | THU | FRI | SAT |
|---|---|---|---|---|---|---|
| **KEY** | ♈ ARIES<br>♉ TAURUS<br>♊ GEMINI<br>♋ CANCER | ♌ LEO<br>♍ VIRGO<br>♎ LIBRA<br>♏ SCORPIO | ♐ SAGITTARIUS<br>♑ CAPRICORN<br>♒ AQUARIUS<br>♓ PISCES | **FM** FULL MOON<br>**NM** NEW MOON<br>**LE** LUNAR ECLIPSE<br>**SE** SOLAR ECLIPSE | | **1**<br>♓<br>♈ 4:52AM |
| **2**<br>♈ | **3**<br>♈<br>♉ 5:37AM | **4**<br>♉ | **5**<br>♉<br>♊ 7:29AM | **6**<br>♊<br>2nd Quarter | **7**<br>♊<br>♋ 11:29AM | **8**<br>♋ |
| **9**<br>♋<br>♌ 6:59PM | **10**<br>♌ | **11**<br>♌ | **12**<br>♌<br>♍ 3:56AM | **13**<br>♍ | **14**<br>♍ Full Moon<br>& Lunar<br>Eclipse 2:55AM<br>♎ 2:59PM | **15**<br>♎ |
| **16**<br>♎ | **17**<br>♎<br>♏ 3:30AM | **18**<br>♏ | **19**<br>♏<br>♐ 4:17PM | **20**<br>♐ | **21**<br>♐ | **22**<br>♐→♑ 3:29AM<br>♑ 4th Quarter |
| **23**<br>♑ | **24**<br>♑<br>♒ 11:25AM | **25**<br>♒ | **26**<br>♒<br>♓ 3:31PM | **27**<br>♓ | **28**<br>♓<br>♈ 4:36PM | **29**<br>♈ New Moon<br>& Solar Eclipse<br>6:58AM |
| **30**<br>♈<br>♉ 4:16PM | **31**<br>♉ | | | *Times listed are Eastern US Time Zone* | | |

MARCH 14, 2:55AM

## full moon in
# Virgo (23°57')

### VIRGO FULL MOON CRYSTAL

### MOSS AGATE

With its swirls of green, this stone connects you to the healing powers of nature. Moss Agate is known to ease anxiety and reduce people-pleasing and judgment that can creep in under Virgo's watch.

---

*What's one thing you're celebrating under this full moon?*

---

## VIRGO FULL MOON = CELEBRATE!

*The serenity of a freshly cleaned space*

*Streamlined systems*

*Your helpful spirit*

*Being of service to those in need*

*Taking great care of your body by eating clean and exercising*

*The magic of nature and natural beauty*

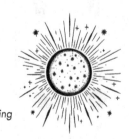

MARCH 29, 6:58AM

new moon in
## Aries (9°00')

ARIES
NEW MOON
CRYSTAL

### CARNELIAN

This vibrant orange stone wakes up the sacral chakra to connect you to your instinctual truth. Use carnelian to enhance confidence and creativity as you step into your Aries-inspired power. This crystal also supports with new beginnings.

**What's one fresh intention you're ready to set under this new moon?**

## ARIES NEW MOON = FOCUS

*Sharpen your competitive edge*

*Blaze your own trail*

*Take the initiative with people and activities that matter to you*

*Try new things*

## March 2025

Longitude & Retrograde Ephemeris [00:00 UT]

| Day | Sid.time | ☉ | ☽ | +12h☽ | ☿ | ♀ | ♂ | ♃ | ♄ | ♅ | ♆ | ♇ | ☊ | ☊ | ⚸ | ⚷ | Day |
|---|---|---|---|---|---|---|---|---|---|---|---|---|---|---|---|---|---|
| **1** Sa | 10:36:13 | ♓10°38'54 | ♓23°55'25 | ♈01°19'02 | ♓26°17 | ♈10°48 | ♋17°09 | ♊12°16 | ♓20°41 | ♉23°38 | ♓28°53 | ♒02°53 | ℞ 28°22 | ℞ 27°24 | ♎27°06 | ♈20°36 | **1** Sa |
| **2** Su | 10:40:09 | ♓11°39'08 | ♈08°43'26 | ♈16°07'17 | ℞S 27°53 | ♈10°50 | ♋17°13 | ♊12°21 | ♓20°48 | ♉23°39 | ♓28°55 | ♒02°54 | ♓28°19 | D 27°24 | ♎27°13 | ♈20°39 | **2** Su |
| **3** Mo | 10:44:06 | ♓12°39'21 | ♈23°30'11 | ♉00°50'53 | ♓29°26 | ℞ 10°48 | ♋17°18 | ♊12°26 | ♓20°56 | ♉23°41 | ♓28°57 | ♒02°56 | ♓28°16 | ♓27°25 | ♎27°19 | ♈20°42 | **3** Mo |
| **4** Tu | 10:48:02 | ♓13°39'31 | ♉08°09'11 | ♉15°24'04 | ♈00°54 | ♈10°45 | ♋17°23 | ♊12°31 | ♓21°03 | ♉23°42 | ♓29°00 | ♒02°57 | ♓28°12 | ♓27°26 | ♎27°26 | ♈20°45 | **4** Tu |
| **5** We | 10:51:59 | ♓14°39'39 | ♉22°35'30 | ♉29°42'42 | ♈02°17 | ♈10°39 | ♋17°29 | ♊12°36 | ♓21°10 | ♉23°44 | ♓29°02 | ♒02°59 | ♓28°09 | ♓27°27 | ♎27°33 | ♈20°48 | **5** We |
| **6** Th | 10:55:56 | ♓15°39'46 | ♊06°45'51 | ♊13°44'22 | ♈03°34 | ♈10°30 | ♋17°36 | ♊12°42 | ♓21°13 | ♉23°46 | ♓29°04 | ♒03°01 | ♓28°06 | ♓27°27 | ♎27°39 | ♈20°51 | **6** Th |
| **7** Fr | 10:59:52 | ♓16°39'50 | ♊20°38'38 | ♊27°28'12 | ♈04°45 | ♈10°19 | ♋17°43 | ♊12°48 | ♓21°25 | ♉23°48 | ♓29°06 | ♒03°02 | ♓28°03 | ℞ 27°28 | ♎27°46 | ♈20°54 | **7** Fr |
| **8** Sa | 11:03:49 | ♓17°39'52 | ♋04°13'33 | ♋10°54'24 | ♈05°49 | ♈10°05 | ♋17°51 | ♊12°53 | ♓21°32 | ♉23°49 | ♓29°09 | ♒03°04 | ♓28°00 | ♓27°27 | ♎27°53 | ♈20°57 | **8** Sa |
| **9** Su | 11:07:45 | ♓18°39'52 | ♋17°31'16 | ♋24°03'55 | ♈06°46 | ♈09°49 | ♋17°59 | ♊12°59 | ♓21°40 | ♉23°51 | ♓29°11 | ♒03°05 | ♓27°56 | ♓27°26 | ♎27°59 | ♈21°00 | **9** Su |
| **10** Mo | 11:11:42 | ♓19°39'50 | ♌00°32'56 | ♌06°58'04 | ♈07°35 | ♈09°30 | ♋18°08 | ♊13°06 | ♓21°47 | ♉23°53 | ♓29°13 | ♒03°06 | ♓27°53 | ♓27°25 | ♎28°06 | ♈21°03 | **10** Mo |
| **11** Tu | 11:15:38 | ♓20°39'45 | ♌13°19'56 | ♌19°38'18 | ♈08°16 | ♈09°09 | ♋18°18 | ♊13°12 | ♓21°55 | ♉23°55 | ♓29°15 | ♒03°08 | ♓27°50 | ♓27°24 | ♎28°13 | ♈21°07 | **11** Tu |
| **12** We | 11:19:35 | ♓21°39'39 | ♌25°53'45 | ♍02°06'04 | ♈08°48 | ♈08°46 | ♋18°28 | ♊13°18 | ♓22°02 | ♉23°57 | ♓29°18 | ♒03°09 | ♓27°47 | ♓27°24 | ♎28°19 | ♈21°10 | **12** We |
| **13** Th | 11:23:31 | ♓22°39'30 | ♍08°15'49 | ♍14°22'48 | ♈09°12 | ♈08°20 | ♋18°39 | ♊13°25 | ♓22°09 | ♉23°59 | ♓29°20 | ♒03°11 | ♓27°44 | ♓27°23 | ♎28°26 | ♈21°13 | **13** Th |
| **14** Fr | 11:27:28 | ♓23°39'19 | ♍20°27'36 | ♍26°30'02 | ♈09°28 | ♈07°53 | ♋18°50 | ♊13°32 | ♓22°17 | ♉24°01 | ♓29°22 | ♒03°12 | ♓27°41 | ♓27°23 | ♎28°33 | ♈21°16 | **14** Fr |
| **15** Sa | 11:31:25 | ♓24°39'06 | ♎02°30'41 | ♎08°29'25 | ♈09°34 | ♈07°23 | ♋19°02 | ♊13°39 | ♓22°24 | ♉24°03 | ♓29°24 | ♒03°13 | ♓27°37 | D 27°23 | ♎28°39 | ♈21°19 | **15** Sa |
| **16** Su | 11:35:21 | ♓25°38'52 | ♎14°26'50 | ♎20°22'52 | ℞ 09°33 | ♈06°52 | ♋19°14 | ♊13°46 | ♓22°32 | ♉24°05 | ♓29°27 | ♒03°15 | ♓27°34 | ♓27°23 | ♎28°46 | ♈21°23 | **16** Su |
| **17** Mo | 11:39:18 | ♓26°38'35 | ♎26°18'11 | ♏02°12'44 | ♈09°22 | ♈06°19 | ♋19°27 | ♊13°53 | ♓22°39 | ♉24°08 | ♓29°29 | ♒03°16 | ♓27°31 | ♓27°23 | ♎28°53 | ♈21°26 | **17** Mo |
| **18** Tu | 11:43:14 | ♓27°38'17 | ♏08°07'15 | ♏14°01'46 | ♈09°04 | ♈05°45 | ♋19°41 | ♊14°00 | ♓22°46 | ♉24°10 | ♓29°31 | ♒03°17 | ♓27°28 | ℞ 27°23 | ♎28°59 | ♈21°29 | **18** Tu |
| **19** We | 11:47:11 | ♓28°37'57 | ♏19°57'04 | ♏25°53'14 | ♈08°39 | ♈05°09 | ♋19°55 | ♊14°08 | ♓22°54 | ♉24°12 | ♓29°33 | ♒03°19 | ♓27°25 | ♓27°23 | ♎29°06 | ♈21°33 | **19** We |
| **20** Th | 11:51:07 | ♓29°37'35 | ♐01°51'07 | ♐07°50'51 | ♈08°07 | ♈04°33 | ♋20°09 | ♊14°16 | ♓23°01 | ♉24°14 | ♓29°36 | ♒03°20 | ♓27°22 | ♓27°23 | ♎29°13 | ♈21°36 | **20** Th |
| **21** Fr | 11:55:04 | ♈00°37'12 | ♐13°53'21 | ♐19°58'45 | ♈07°28 | ♈03°56 | ♋20°24 | ♊14°24 | ♓23°09 | ♉24°17 | ♓29°38 | ♒03°21 | ♓27°18 | ♓27°22 | ♎29°19 | ♈21°39 | **21** Fr |
| **22** Sa | 11:59:00 | ♈01°36'46 | ♐26°07'59 | ♑02°21'14 | ♈06°45 | ♈03°18 | ♋20°39 | ♊14°31 | ♓23°16 | ♉24°19 | ♓29°40 | ♒03°22 | ♓27°15 | ♓27°22 | ♎29°26 | ♈21°43 | **22** Sa |
| **23** Su | 12:02:57 | ♈02°36'19 | ♑08°39'23 | ♑15°02'34 | ♈05°58 | ♈02°40 | ♋20°55 | ♊14°40 | ♓23°23 | ♉24°22 | ♓29°43 | ♒03°23 | ♓27°12 | D 27°22 | ♎29°33 | ♈21°46 | **23** Su |
| **24** Mo | 12:06:53 | ♈03°35'50 | ♑21°31'37 | ♑28°06'33 | ♈05°07 | ♈02°03 | ♋21°11 | ♊14°48 | ♓23°31 | ♉24°24 | ♓29°45 | ♒03°24 | ♓27°09 | ♓27°23 | ♎29°39 | ♈21°50 | **24** Mo |
| **25** Tu | 12:10:50 | ♈04°35'20 | ♒04°48'06 | ♒11°36'04 | ♈04°15 | ♈01°25 | ♋21°28 | ♊14°56 | ♓23°38 | ♉24°26 | ♓29°47 | ♒03°26 | ♓27°06 | ♓27°23 | ♎29°46 | ♈21°53 | **25** Tu |
| **26** We | 12:14:47 | ♈05°34'48 | ♒18°30'57 | ♒25°32'20 | ♈03°22 | ♈00°48 | ♋21°45 | ♊15°05 | ♓23°45 | ♉24°29 | ♓29°49 | ♒03°27 | ♓27°02 | ♓27°24 | ♎29°53 | ♈21°57 | **26** We |
| **27** Th | 12:18:43 | ♈06°34'13 | ♓02°40'25 | ♓09°54'25 | ♈02°30 | ♈00°12 | ♋22°02 | ♊15°13 | ♓23°53 | ♉24°32 | ♓29°52 | ♒03°28 | ♓26°59 | ♓27°25 | ♎29°59 | ♈22°00 | **27** Th |
| **28** Fr | 12:22:40 | ♈07°33'37 | ♓17°14'16 | ♓24°38'47 | ♈01°38 | ♓29°37 | ♋22°20 | ♊15°22 | ♓24°00 | ♉24°34 | ♓29°54 | ♒03°29 | ♓26°56 | ♓27°25 | ♏00°06 | ♈22°03 | **28** Fr |
| **29** Sa | 12:26:36 | ♈08°32'59 | ♈02°07'35 | ♈09°39'12 | ♈00°49 | ♓29°03 | ♋22°38 | ♊15°31 | ♓24°07 | ♉24°37 | ♓29°56 | ♒03°30 | ♓26°53 | ℞ 27°25 | ♏00°13 | ♈22°07 | **29** Sa |
| **30** Su | 12:30:33 | ♈09°32'19 | ♈17°12'59 | ♈24°47'18 | ♈00°04 | ♓28°31 | ♋22°57 | ♊15°40 | ♓24°14 | ♉24°39 | ♓29°58 | ♒03°31 | ♓26°50 | ♓27°25 | ♏00°19 | ♈22°10 | **30** Su |
| **31** Mo | 12:34:29 | ♈10°31'37 | ♉02°21'25 | ♉09°53'43 | ♓29°22 | ♓28°00 | ♋23°16 | ♊15°49 | ♓24°22 | ♉24°42 | ♈00°01 | ♒03°32 | ♓26°47 | ♓27°24 | ♏00°26 | ♈22°14 | **31** Mo |
| **Δ Delta** | 01:58:16 | -29°52'42" | -398°26'00" | 398°34'41" | 3°05' | 12°48' | 6°06' | 3°32' | 3°40' | 1°04' | -1°07' | 0°39' | -1°35' | -0°00' | 3°19' | 1°37' | **Delta** |

Ephemeris tables and data provided by **Astro-Seek.com.** All times in UTC.

3

## MARCH 2025

| S | M | T | W | T | F | S |
|---|---|---|---|---|---|---|
|   |   |   |   |   |   | 1 |
| 2 | 3 | 4 | 5 | 6 | 7 | 8 |
| 9 | 10 | 11 | 12 | 13 | 14 | 15 |
| 16 | 17 | 18 | 19 | 20 | 21 | 22 |
| 23 | 24 | 25 | 26 | 27 | 28 | 29 |
| 30 | 31 |   |   |   |   |   |

## MONTHLY INTENTION

1 SAT

● ♓

♈ 4:52AM

Venus retrograde in Aries (7:36PM)

## MARCH 2025

| S | M | T | W | T | F | S |
|---|---|---|---|---|---|---|
|   |   |   |   |   |   | 1 |
| 2 | 3 | 4 | 5 | 6 | 7 | 8 |
| 9 | 10 | 11 | 12 | 13 | 14 | 15 |
| 16 | 17 | 18 | 19 | 20 | 21 | 22 |
| 23 | 24 | 25 | 26 | 27 | 28 | 29 |
| 30 | 31 |   |   |   |   |   |

**3**

## WEEKLY INTENTION

## TOP 3 TO-DOS

○

○

○

---

**2** SUN ◐♈

Mercury-Neptune meetup
Sun-Jupiter square

---

**3** MON ◐♈

♉ 5:37AM
Mercury in Aries until Mar 29 (4:04AM)

**4** TUE ● ♉

---

**5** WED ● ♉
♊ 7:29AM

---

**6** THU ● ♊
Waxing quarter moon in Gemini (11:32AM)

---

**7** FRI ● ♊
♋ 11:29AM

---

**8** SAT ◐ ♋
Sun-Mars trine

**MARCH 2025**

| S | M | T | W | T | F | S |
|---|---|---|---|---|---|---|
| | | | | | | 1 |
| 2 | 3 | 4 | 5 | 6 | 7 | 8 |
| **9** | **10** | **11** | **12** | **13** | **14** | **15** |
| 16 | 17 | 18 | 19 | 20 | 21 | 22 |
| 23 | 24 | 25 | 26 | 27 | 28 | 29 |
| 30 | 31 | | | | | |

## WEEKLY INTENTION

## TOP 3 TO-DOS

○

○

○

**9** SUN ☽♋
♌ 6:59PM

**10** MON ☽♌

**11** TUE

○♌
Mercury-Venus meetup

---

**12** WED

○♌
♍ **3:56AM**
Sun-Saturn meetup

---

**13** THU

○♍

---

**14** FRI

○♍
**FULL MOON IN VIRGO**
**& LUNAR ECLIPSE**
**(2:55AM, 23°57')**
♎ **2:59PM**

---

**15** SAT

○♎
Mercury retrograde in Aries until Mar 29 (2:46AM)

**MARCH 2025**

| S | M | T | W | T | F | S |
|---|---|---|---|---|---|---|
|   |   |   |   |   |   | 1 |
| 2 | 3 | 4 | 5 | 6 | 7 | 8 |
| 9 | 10 | 11 | 12 | 13 | 14 | 15 |
| **16** | **17** | **18** | **19** | **20** | **21** | **22** |
| 23 | 24 | 25 | 26 | 27 | 28 | 29 |
| 30 | 31 |   |   |   |   |   |

## TOP 3 TO-DOS

◯

◯

◯

## WEEKLY INTENTION

---

**16** SUN ◯ ♎

---

**17** MON ◯ ♎

♏ 3:30AM

**18** TUE ☾ ♏

---

**19** WED ☾ ♏
↗ 4:17PM
Sun-Neptune meetup

---

**20** THU ☾ ↗
Sun in Aries (5:01AM)
Spring Equinox

**ARIES SEASON UNTIL APR 19**

---

**21** FRI ☾ ↗

---

**22** SAT ☽ ↗
♑ 3:29AM
Waning quarter moon in Capricorn (7:29AM)
Sun-Venus retrograde meetup

## MARCH 2025

| S | M | T | W | T | F | S |
|---|---|---|---|---|---|---|
|   |   |   |   |   |   | 1 |
| 2 | 3 | 4 | 5 | 6 | 7 | 8 |
| 9 | 10 | 11 | 12 | 13 | 14 | 15 |
| 16 | 17 | 18 | 19 | 20 | 21 | 22 |
| **23** | **24** | **25** | **26** | **27** | **28** | **29** |
| 30 | 31 |   |   |   |   |   |

**3**

## WEEKLY INTENTION

## TOP 3 TO-DOS

○

○

○

**23** SUN                                                ◐♑

**24** MON                                               ◐♑
                                                   ♒ **11:25AM**
                                    Sun-Mercury retrograde meetup

**25** TUE

**26** WED
♓ 3:31PM

**27** THU
Venus retrograde in Pisces until Apr 12 (4:41AM)
Venus retrograde -Neptune meetup #2 of 3
Black Moon Lilith in Scorpio until Dec 20

**28** FRI
♈ 4:36PM

**29** SAT ●♈
## NEW SUPERMOON IN ARIES & PARTIAL SOLAR ECLIPSE
### (6:58AM, @ 9°00')
Mercury retrograde in Pisces until Apr 7
Mercury retrograde-Neptune meetup

## MARCH 2025

| S | M | T | W | T | F | S |
|---|---|---|---|---|---|---|
| | | | | | | 1 |
| 2 | 3 | 4 | 5 | 6 | 7 | 8 |
| 9 | 10 | 11 | 12 | 13 | 14 | 15 |
| 16 | 17 | 18 | 19 | 20 | 21 | 22 |
| 23 | 24 | 25 | 26 | 27 | 28 | 29 |
| 30 | 31 | | | | | |

**3**

## TOP 3 TO-DOS

○

○

○

## WEEKLY INTENTION

**30** SUN ● ♈

♉ 4:16PM
Neptune in Aries until Oct 22 (8:00AM)

**31** MON ● ♉

# MARCH
## MONTHLY HOTSPOTS

**3**

### MAR 1–APR 12 VENUS TURNS RETROGRADE IN ARIES AND PISCES

Romance hits a six-week speedbump as Venus turns retrograde, first in passionate Aries (until March 27), then, backwards through fantasy-fueled Pisces until April 12. As the planet of love shifts from being an "evening star" (appearing at dusk) to a "morning star" (glimmering in the sky just before dawn) get ready to put old love stories, limiting beliefs and toxic relationships to bed. Arguments can flare between lovers and friends while Venus backs up through combative Aries. As the gloves come off, do your best to not burn an important bridge to the ground. Thankfully, Venus only turns retrograde every 18 months, but this one may be especially feisty. Nostalgia is the magic elixir. Do things that revive a bygone era, like revisiting a place you haven't been to since the honeymoon phase. In autonomous Aries and solitary Pisces, taking time for independent activities that fuel self-love can also restore equilibrium in relationships.

### MAR 2

#### MERCURY-NEPTUNE MEETUP

Fog descending! Esoteric Neptune aligns with Mercury in the dreamy realm of Pisces, making it challenging to distinguish between what's real and what's merely an illusion. Conversations seem enveloped in confusion, and you might find your focus slipping. Don't swim against the current. Instead, lean into your intuition and let your imagination take the lead. Have you been overly critical of others or yourself lately? The empathetic energy of today's skies encourages a more compassionate approach. Buried emotions may surface, so don't be surprised if you find yourself feeling teary. If you've been grappling with a recurring issue, stay open to potentially transformative insights that could lead to healing.

## SUN-JUPITER SQUARE

The magnetic pull of other people's demands can be hard to ignore when the Sun is in Pisces, the sign of sacrifice. But as el Sol squares off with indie-spirited Jupiter for the day, your heart—and the rest of you—could use a break from playing caretaker to everyone around you. That's not to say you should screen out the world. Jupiter is in playful, convivial Gemini, pointing you toward lighthearted engagements with people whose wit you deeply appreciate. While you're out having fun, guard against gullibility. People will be talking a good game—with no real plan for how they'll actually carry it out. Make sure you're not overpromising, either.

## MARCH 3–29 MERCURY IN ARIES

Goodbye, groupthink. Hello, independent thought. Intellectual Mercury charges into bold, fiery Aries today, igniting a spark of daring and outspoken energy. Ready to voice your opinions without hesitation? Aries encourages direct communication. Say exactly what you mean and ensure your words match your intentions. Get those fiery words out fast though! On March 15, Mercury will follow in Venus' footsteps, turning retrograde in both Aries (until March 29), then Pisces (until April 7). Even before the backspin, the line between helpful and harsh can become practically invisible. Have a key point to make? Keep your message crisp and clear. Skip the lengthy explanations and drive home your points with sharp one-liners.

## MAR 6 WAXING QUARTER MOON IN GEMINI (11:32AM)

Embrace the intellectual buzz as today's waxing quarter moon builds momentum in communicative Gemini. Forget about sitting still. It's an optimal day for brainstorming and networking. Gemini's airy influence encourages lively exchanges but beware of scattering your focus. As you get swept up in the flurry of ideas and dialogues, you could lose track of your ultimate goal. To avoid information overload, write up an outline or create a meeting agenda. Inject a bit of Gemini's clever banter to keep your communications fresh.

## MAR 8 SUN-MARS TRINE

Sensitivity is a superpower today as the Pisces Sun trines guardian Mars in Cancer. You may feel an intuitive drive to protect your loved ones or stick up for a random stranger who's in need of an ally. With family front and center, this is the perfect day to heal old wounds. Forthright Mars gives you the courage to approach a long-standing conflict while also leaning into empathy. In some cases, the brave thing may be putting up an iron-clad boundary with someone who consistently takes advantage of your kindness. No guilt! This is best for everyone involved since resentment can poison even the most soulful relationships.

## MAR 11 MERCURY-VENUS MEETUP

Today's spicy sync-up of Mercury and Venus in Aries is like a clarion call for "love warriors." (No surprise Aries Glennon Doyle wrote a book with that title.) Situations could push you to fight for your romantic ideals, or to push past fears of rejection to let your desires be known. Even the usually reserved might find themselves emboldened, ready to engage in some heart-racing flirting. Whether you're typically shy or naturally audacious, today's the day to take the lead in love. For long-term couples, healthy competition can spark up a feisty, sexy dynamic. Meet on the racquetball court, break out a board game, or challenge your partner to a bake-off. Make sure you play with the intention to win!

## MAR 12 SUN-SATURN MEETUP

The effusive Sun holds its once-per-year meetup with sobering Saturn today, teaming up in watery, mystical Pisces. This "Day of Challenges" can feel like an annual inspection as you run your bright ideas through a series of stress tests. While this may turn up some harsh realities, try to adopt a "better safe than sorry" approach. Knowing where your weak points lie can be useful data. Now you can avert a future crisis and know where you should redirect your energy so you aren't wasting valuable time and resources.

## MAR 14 FULL MOON IN VIRGO (2:55AM)
## (TOTAL LUNAR ECLIPSE @ 23°57')

Embrace the clean girl aesthetic today, as the year's only full moon in Virgo—a total lunar eclipse—scrubs away any resistance to taking great care of yourself. This is the first eclipse in discerning Virgo since September 2016, so get ready for an unflinching life edit. If you've been slipping on healthy habits over the winter or slacking at work, you could get a stern wakeup call over the next two weeks. Since eclipses tend to reveal things that are hiding in the shadows, you may be surprised to mildly shocked by what you discover. Before things spiral out any further, lean into these meticulous moonbeams and straighten up your act. Rule of thumb: As you implement new routines, try to keep them simple and manageable. Because this eclipse is opposed by minimalist Saturn and hazy Neptune, the last thing you want to do is set yourself up for failure by over-complexifying your goals. Lean into technology for support with anything that truly is complicated. Is there an app for that? With wizardly Uranus trading friendly fire with the eclipse, an AI companion could lend an incredible assist, especially with Virgoan duties like progress-tracking and scheduling.

## MAR 15–APR 7 MERCURY RETROGRADE IN ARIES AND PISCES

Brace for impact! Mercury darts into its first retrograde of 2025, muddling communication and throwing a wrench into neatly ordered plans. From March 15 to 29, the messenger planet reverses course in the fiery sign of the Ram, sparking a period of heated communications and hasty decisions. Tempers will flare as words fly without thought. Go easy on the smack-talking and careful not to start any needless rivalries. Aries inspires quick action, but retrograde demands caution. It may be necessary to pump the brakes on projects that require a more aggressive approach. Fine-tune personal goals and actions, ensuring they truly align with your ambitions. When Mercury reverses into Pisces on March 29, you can access a deep level of creativity and divine inspiration that supports rapid growth once the retrograde ends on April 7. Patience and precision are your allies now, so adjust your sails accordingly.

## MAR 19 SUN-NEPTUNE MEETUP

The Sun and Neptune come together in ethereal Pisces, turning the world into an enchanted forest for the day. Under this once-per-year spell, you can readily access—and manifest—dreams that have been buried in your psyche. Find time to step back from the noise and do some creative visualization along with some spiritual reflection. Wherever possible, reshuffle your schedule to prioritize projects that can be done while in "flow state." This is a day to lead with vision and let practicalities take a backseat.

## MAR 20-APR 19 SUN IN ARIES (5:01AM; SPRING EQUINOX)

Happy Astrological New Year! The spring equinox marks the start of Aries season each year, refreshing our cosmic calendar in Tropical (Western) astrology. As the Sun catapults into this passionate, adventurous zodiac sign, it's no wonder we all feel too restless to be cooped up indoors. Don't think twice. Grab a jacket, then get outside for springtime bike rides and pickleball dates. Dial up the excitement in your life and love affairs by pushing the envelope a little. 'Tis the season for artfully mismatched patterns and shameless PDA. But keep a steady hand: Aries' fiery spirit can ignite people's competitive and self-centered sides. Set your sights on your ambitions, but make sure to share the glory with the people who help you rise to the top. With both Mercury and Venus retrograde in Aries this cycle, navigating this season comes with its challenges. Keep selfish tendencies in check and curb your impatience, ensuring you don't burn out before you achieve your fullest shine.

## MAR 22

### WANING QUARTER MOON IN CAPRICORN (7:29AM)

Enough deliberating, it's time to take charge. Today's waning quarter moon in commanding Capricorn sharpens your focus on long-term goals and ushers in a refreshing wave of prodcutivity. Last week's total lunar eclipse in Virgo performed a "life audit" on us all and may have illuminated a few tough, but unavoidable, facts. If you haven't quite gotten around to dealing with matters yet, consider this quarter moon your cue to take the reins. In wise, pragmatic Capricorn, this lunar lift advises you to move beyond the binary of right versus wrong. Focus on solutions and figure out what you can improve going forward. A solid plan could emerge today, perhaps one that involves hiring experts or reaching out to a mentor figure.

## SUN-VENUS RETROGRADE MEETUP

It's a pivotal moment for love as the Sun and Venus retrograde converge in Aries, marking an inferior conjunction that occurs once every 584 days during the mid-phase of every Venus retrograde cycle. Much like a new moon, you can think of this as a 'new Venus'—a time to reset your romantic narratives as if the sky has gone dark and the slate is wiped clean. Consider celebrating this moment by setting up a love altar adorned with symbols of your ideal romance or releasing past grievances through a burning ritual. Starting today, Venus disappears from the evening skies, reemerging as a brilliant morning star within a week, heralding a new dawn for love and beauty. Using this metaphorically, what would you like to put to bed when it comes to love? And, uh, who might you finally want to lure INTO your bed? Reflect and write it down, so your vision of love can rise strong and clear after Venus turns direct again on April 7. Until then, keep your mind wide open to possibilities as you parse through what (and possibly who) should stay and what or who should go.

## MAR 24 SUN-MERCURY RETROGRADE MEETUP

Can you verify that data? The Sun syncs up with Mercury retrograde in forthright Aries, shining a light on inconsistencies and flawed thinking. If you plan to challenge anyone's assertions, bring the receipts, proof, timelines and screenshots—whatever it takes to make it an open-and-shut case. Without ample evidence, you could set yourself up for backlash. If you're sharing ideas, open the floor for questions. Allow people to voice any objections and if you can't address them immediately, don't attempt to fudge it. Better to say, "Let me get back to you on that" then to risk getting a reputation as an unreliable source of truth.

## VENUS RETROGRADE IN PISCES (MAR 27–APR 12)

What are your relationship do's and don'ts? As retrograde Venus slides back from assertive Aries into boundary-challenged Pisces, you might need to tape them to your mirror for a firm, daily reminder. Old, counterproductive habits could creep back in between now and April 12, such as making sacrifices to "earn" love or ignoring a date's glaring red flags. Even in healthy relationships, it's important to know where your limits lie so you can avoid poisoning the vibe with resentment. If the walls around your heart resemble the gates of King's Landing, this retrograde could be your cue to soften a little. At the very least, begin to process unresolved emotions so you can find closure. Now for the good news. While Venus slogged through an unhappy detriment (weakened position) in Aries, the love planet absolutely thrives in Pisces, which is its exalted place in the zodiac. Even while retrograde, a Venus-in-Pisces cycle elicits empathy among partners and rekindles soul connections. With the right person, you may practically read each other's minds now.

## BLACK MOON LILITH IN SCORPIO (MAR 27–DEC 20)

Passion, power, erotic liberation! Get ready to plunge into an explicit (and potentially NSFW) exploration of your sexuality as Black Moon Lilith moves out of justice-oriented Libra and into Scorpio's seductive cauldron. Lilith is not a planet but a point in the sky—a void between the Earth and moon that astrologers have come to associate with the scorned, then empowered, feminine aspect of our personalities. This nine-month transit sparks new conversations around sexual liberation and intimacy, encouraging society to break down stigmas and own the full spectrum of our emotions. Since Scorpio rules the reproductive organs, Lilith could evoke a rage-fueled uprising against restrictive laws around abortion, IVF and reproductive freedom for women.

## VENUS RETROGRADE-NEPTUNE MEETUP #2 OF 3

Shall we meet again? Die-hard romantics Venus and Neptune unite for the second of three dances this year—this time in Pisces, where they're turning up the dials on fairy-tale romance. This time around there's a plot twist: Venus is retrograde, cast in the role of Sleeping Beauty instead of the eager seductress. Under this spell, it's easy to miss someone's bids for attention or take a generous partner for granted. With boundaries practically invisible today, you could easily overstep someone's limits without realizing it. Take extra precaution and get consent before making any moves, whether they involve physical touch or doling out well-meaning advice to a struggling friend. Under this tender transit, they may be too triggered to hear it.

## MAR 29

### NEW MOON IN ARIES (6:58AM; SUPERMOON) (PARTIAL SOLAR ECLIPSE @ 9°00')

Wipe the slate clean! Today's new moon in Aries, the only one in 2025, is no ordinary fresh start. It's also a supermoon and a partial solar eclipse, pouring rocket fuel into your tanks and charging up your ventures with unexpected momentum. That's not all! This new moon sits at a friendly angle to expansive Jupiter and powerhouse Pluto. Efforts you initiate today could send you soaring onto the global stage and attract VIP-level support. Even though Mercury and Venus are retrograde, you may have to leap into a groundbreaking project with both feet. (Just make sure you set up a safety net.) Get ready for rapid developments and surprising twists along the way, some that may propel you to leave behind parts of your former self. Over the next six months, leading up to the Aries full moon, ask yourself: How can I transform my passions into tangible outcomes? This is a rare opportunity to harness this fiery energy and shape your future. Make it count!

### MERCURY RETROGRADE IN PISCES (MAR 29–APR 7)

Mercury retrograde slips back from in-your-face Aries to elusive Pisces, throwing interactions into deeper confusion. Take nothing at face value for the next ten days, not even people's expressions of delight or approval. No matter how much you want situations to work out, you can't force them now. One thing spiritual Pisces understands is that "what's meant to be, will be." In the meanwhile, observe what's going on inside of you. How do you deal with waiting for an answer: Are you anxious? Do you start making up disempowering stories about what people are thinking? Do you want to quit and move on rather than face the possibility of "rejection"? Let all feelings arise without interacting with them. They are not wrong or right; they simply "are." There is true power in being able to hold the space of the unknown. In that mystical, in-between state, miraculous solutions can arise. Just plan on taking a lot of long, deep breaths.

## MERCURY RETROGRADE-NEPTUNE MEETUP

Today, Mercury do-si-do's with another planet. This time it's spiritual, numinous Neptune that's connecting to the cosmic messenger for the second of three confabs. With Mercury retrograde for this round, the fog is thick and facts may be imperceptible. Rather than swim upstream, go with the flow! It's an ideal day to color outside the lines or maybe just forget the lines altogether. As you suspend your judgment (and maybe your grip on what is rational), you could dream up the sorts of ideas that, as Pisces Steve Jobs said, "Put a ding in the universe."

## MAR 30–OCT 22 NEPTUNE IN ARIES

Realm shift! Fantasy agent Neptune is switching signs, leaving its home sign of Pisces for the first time since April 4, 2011. From plant medicine ceremonies to astrology and manifestation practices to the lightning-fast transfer of data, the past fourteen years have melted our boundaries between the visible and invisible universe. What on earth could be next? Buckle up as the boundary-dissolving planet takes a wild, hoverboard ride through pioneering Aries for the next seven months—a preview of a longer tour that picks back up again from January 26, 2026-March 23, 2039. This is a huge deal! To put a finer point on it, the last time Neptune trekked through Aries was 1862 to 1875, a time that brought a newly industrialized economy (hello, city life) and the U.S. Civil War. Neptune is the planet of compassion while Aries is on a nonstop combat mission. We may all have to toughen up and develop some grit to make it through this tenuous transition.

# MONTHLY REFLECTIONS

3

# April

## MONTHLY HOROSCOPE

How secure is your foundation? With the Sun hunkered in your fourth house of home and family until April 19, you're focused on your roots, creating a solid base of operations. But before you start laying bricks, slow down. Mercury is retrograde in Pisces and your communication zone until April 7, and Venus is retrograde there until April 12. You may need to refine your communication strategy and clear up any misunderstandings with your partners-in-crime before you can move ahead with ease. Your social charm returns with the Libra full moon on the 12th, which could also bring a peak moment for your career. On April 18, Mars enters bold Leo, firing up your eighth house of seduction, permanent bonds and shared resources. Between now and June 17, you'll feel motivated to fortify relationships and take control of financial matters. Longevity and stability are the goal, so think of each person (or situation) that presents itself as if it were an investment. Taurus season kicks off on April 19, lighting up your fifth house of creativity, romance and self-expression. As the Sun moves into this playful sector, it's time to loosen up, tap into your passions and enjoy life's most decadent pleasures.

*Read your extended monthly forecast for life, love, money and career! astrostyle.com*

# APRIL
## Moon Phase Calendar

| SUN | MON | TUE | WED | THU | FRI | SAT |
|---|---|---|---|---|---|---|
| | | **1** ♉ II 4:26PM | **2** II | **3** II ♋ 6:50PM | **4** ♋ 2nd Quarter | **5** ♋ |
| **6** ♋ ♌ 12:34AM | **7** ♌ | **8** ♌ ♍ 9:40AM | **9** ♍ | **10** ♍ ♎ 9:12PM | **11** ♎ | **12** ♎ Full Moon 8:22PM |
| **13** ♎ ♏ 9:54AM | **14** ♏ | **15** ♏ ♐ 10:37PM | **16** ♐ | **17** ♐ | **18** ♐ ♑ 10:12AM | **19** ♑ |
| **20** ♑→♒ 7:22PM ♒ 4th Quarter | **21** ♒ | **22** ♒ | **23** ♒ ♓ 1:07AM | **24** ♓ | **25** ♓ ♈ 3:24AM | **26** ♈ |
| **27** ♈→♉ 3:17AM ♉ New Moon 3:31PM | **28** ♉ | **29** ♉ II 2:34AM | **30** II | | | |

*Times listed are Eastern US Time Zone*

APRIL 12, 8:22PM

# full moon in
# Libra (23°20′)

## LIBRA FULL MOON CRYSTAL

### ROSE QUARTZ

This pale pink crystal is the stone of pure love, radiating the compassion and romance of Libra. Said to be beneficial for heart healing and fertility, Rose Quartz carries goddess energy and can be used for inspiration and protection.

---

*What's one thing you're celebrating under this full moon?*

---

## LIBRA FULL MOON = CELEBRATE!

*The power of partnerships and synergistic connections*

*Dressing up and socializing*

*Transcendent music and the arts*

*Peaceful moments of serenity*

*The parts of your life that are in beautiful balance*

Supermoon

APRIL 27, 3:31PM

new moon in
Taurus (7°47')

## TAURUS NEW MOON CRYSTAL

### BLUE LACE AGATE

This soothing, soft blue stone helps you relax and tap into a deep inner calm. Blue Lace Agate unblocks the Taurus-ruled throat chakra so you can speak your truth and share what's valuable to you.

*What's one fresh intention you're ready to set under this new moon?*

## TAURUS NEW MOON = FOCUS

*Define your values*

*Set up healthy and rewarding routines*

*Enjoy arts and culture*

*Simplify complexities*

*Budget*

*Get out in nature*

## April 2025

Longitude & Retrograde Ephemeris [00:00 UT]

| Day | Sid.time | ☉ | ☽ | +12h☽ | ☿ | ♀ | ♂ | ♃ | ♄ | ♅ | ♆ | ♇ | ☊ | ☊ | ⚸ | ⚷ | Day |
|---|---|---|---|---|---|---|---|---|---|---|---|---|---|---|---|---|---|
| **1** Tu | 12:38:26 | ♈11°30'52 | ♉17°23'33 | ♉24°49'28 | ℞ 28°44 | ℞ 27°31 | ♋23°36 | ♊15°58 | ♓24°29 | ♉24°45 | ♈00°03 | ♒03°33 | ℞ 26°43 | ℞ 27°22 | ♏00°33 | ♈22°17 | **1** Tu |
| **2** We | 12:42:22 | ♈12°30'06 | ♊02°11'05 | ♊09°27'14 | ♓28°12 | ♓27°04 | ♋23°55 | ♊16°08 | ♓24°36 | ♉24°48 | ♈00°05 | ♒03°34 | ♓26°40 | ♓27°20 | ♏00°39 | ♈22°21 | **2** We |
| **3** Th | 12:46:19 | ♈13°29'18 | ♊16°37'53 | ♊23°42'12 | ♓27°44 | ♓26°39 | ♋24°15 | ♊16°17 | ♓24°43 | ♉24°50 | ♈00°07 | ♒03°35 | ♓26°37 | ♓27°18 | ♏00°46 | ♈22°25 | **3** Th |
| **4** Fr | 12:50:16 | ♈14°28'27 | ♋00°40'29 | ♋07°32'14 | ♓27°22 | ♓26°16 | ♋24°36 | ♊16°27 | ♓24°50 | ♉24°53 | ♈00°10 | ♒03°35 | ♓26°34 | ♓27°17 | ♏00°53 | ♈22°28 | **4** Fr |
| **5** Sa | 12:54:12 | ♈15°27'33 | ♋14°17'59 | ♋20°57'31 | ♓27°06 | ♓25°56 | ♋24°57 | ♊16°36 | ♓24°57 | ♉24°56 | ♈00°12 | ♒03°36 | ♓26°31 | ♓27°17 | ♏00°59 | ♈22°32 | **5** Sa |
| **6** Su | 12:58:09 | ♈16°26'38 | ♋27°31'32 | ♌03°59'59 | ♓26°55 | ♓25°37 | ♋25°18 | ♊16°46 | ♓25°05 | ♉24°59 | ♈00°14 | ♒03°37 | ♓26°28 | D 27°17 | ♏01°06 | ♈22°35 | **6** Su |
| **7** Mo | 13:02:05 | ♈17°25'40 | ♌10°23'39 | ♌16°42'35 | ♓26°50 | ♓25°21 | ♋25°40 | ♊16°56 | ♓25°12 | ♉25°02 | ♈00°16 | ♒03°38 | ♓26°24 | ♓27°18 | ♏01°13 | ♈22°39 | **7** Mo |
| **8** Tu | 13:06:02 | ♈18°24'39 | ♌22°57'36 | ♌29°08'44 | DS 26°50 | ♓25°08 | ♋26°01 | ♊17°06 | ♓25°19 | ♉25°05 | ♈00°18 | ♒03°39 | ♓26°21 | ♓27°20 | ♏01°19 | ♈22°42 | **8** Tu |
| **9** We | 13:09:58 | ♈19°23'37 | ♍05°16'50 | ♍11°21'55 | ♓26°55 | ♓24°57 | ♋26°23 | ♊17°16 | ♓25°26 | ♉25°08 | ♈00°21 | ♒03°39 | ♓26°18 | ♓27°21 | ♏01°26 | ♈22°46 | **9** We |
| **10** Th | 13:13:55 | ♈20°22'32 | ♍17°24'45 | ♍23°25'19 | ♓27°06 | ♓24°48 | ♋26°46 | ♊17°26 | ♓25°33 | ♉25°11 | ♈00°23 | ♒03°40 | ♓26°15 | ♓27°22 | ♏01°33 | ♈22°49 | **10** Th |
| **11** Fr | 13:17:51 | ♈21°21'25 | ♍29°24'22 | ♎05°21'50 | ♓27°22 | ♓24°42 | ♋27°09 | ♊17°37 | ♓25°40 | ♉25°14 | ♈00°25 | ♒03°41 | ♓26°12 | ℞ 27°23 | ♏01°39 | ♈22°53 | **11** Fr |
| **12** Sa | 13:21:48 | ♈22°20'16 | ♎11°18'23 | ♎17°13'56 | ♓27°42 | ♓24°38 | ♋27°32 | ♊17°47 | ♓25°47 | ♉25°17 | ♈00°27 | ♒03°41 | ♓26°08 | ♓27°22 | ♏01°46 | ♈22°57 | **12** Sa |
| **13** Su | 13:25:45 | ♈23°19'05 | ♎23°09'07 | ♎29°03'48 | ♓28°08 | ♓24°37 | ♋27°55 | ♊17°58 | ♓25°53 | ♉25°20 | ♈00°29 | ♒03°42 | ♓26°05 | ♓27°20 | ♏01°53 | ♈23°00 | **13** Su |
| **14** Mo | 13:29:41 | ♈24°17'52 | ♏04°58'38 | ♏10°53'27 | ♓28°37 | D 24°38 | ♋28°18 | ♊18°08 | ♓26°00 | ♉25°23 | ♈00°31 | ♒03°43 | ♓26°02 | ♓27°16 | ♏01°59 | ♈23°04 | **14** Mo |
| **15** Tu | 13:33:38 | ♈25°16'37 | ♏16°48'54 | ♏22°44'52 | ♓29°11 | ♓24°42 | ♋28°42 | ♊18°19 | ♓26°07 | ♉25°26 | ♈00°33 | ♒03°43 | ♓25°59 | ♓27°12 | ♏02°06 | ♈23°07 | **15** Tu |
| **16** We | 13:37:34 | ♈26°15'20 | ♏28°41'58 | ♐04°40'09 | ♓29°49 | ♓24°47 | ♋29°06 | ♊18°30 | ♓26°14 | ♉25°29 | ♈00°36 | ♒03°44 | ♓25°56 | ♓27°07 | ♏02°13 | ♈23°11 | **16** We |
| **17** Th | 13:41:31 | ♈27°14'02 | ♐10°40'05 | ♐16°41'44 | ♈00°30 | ♓24°55 | ♋29°30 | ♊18°41 | ♓26°21 | ♉25°32 | ♈00°38 | ♒03°44 | ♓25°53 | ♓27°02 | ♏02°19 | ♈23°14 | **17** Th |
| **18** Fr | 13:45:27 | ♈28°12'41 | ♐22°45'51 | ♐28°52'26 | ♈01°16 | ♓25°05 | ♋29°55 | ♊18°52 | ♓26°27 | ♉25°36 | ♈00°40 | ♒03°45 | ♓25°49 | ♓26°57 | ♏02°26 | ♈23°18 | **18** Fr |
| **19** Sa | 13:49:24 | ♈29°11'20 | ♑05°02'16 | ♑11°15'25 | ♈02°04 | ♓25°18 | ♌00°20 | ♊19°03 | ♓26°34 | ♉25°39 | ♈00°42 | ♒03°45 | ♓25°46 | ♓26°53 | ♏02°33 | ♈23°22 | **19** Sa |
| **20** Su | 13:53:20 | ♉00°09'56 | ♑17°32'43 | ♑23°54'14 | ♈02°56 | ♓25°32 | ♌00°45 | ♊19°14 | ♓26°41 | ♉25°42 | ♈00°44 | ♒03°46 | ♓25°43 | ♓26°51 | ♏02°39 | ♈23°25 | **20** Su |
| **21** Mo | 13:57:17 | ♉01°08'30 | ♒00°20'49 | ♒06°52'29 | ♈03°51 | ♓25°49 | ♌01°10 | ♊19°25 | ♓26°47 | ♉25°45 | ♈00°46 | ♒03°46 | ♓25°40 | ♓26°50 | ♏02°46 | ♈23°29 | **21** Mo |
| **22** Tu | 14:01:14 | ♉02°07'03 | ♒13°30'05 | ♒20°13'32 | ♈04°50 | ♓26°07 | ♌01°36 | ♊19°36 | ♓26°54 | ♉25°49 | ♈00°48 | ♒03°46 | ♓25°37 | D 26°51 | ♏02°53 | ♈23°32 | **22** Tu |
| **23** We | 14:05:10 | ♉03°05'35 | ♒27°03'32 | ♓03°59'52 | ♈05°51 | ♓26°27 | ♌02°01 | ♊19°48 | ♓27°00 | ♉25°52 | ♈00°50 | ♒03°47 | ♓25°33 | ♓26°52 | ♏02°59 | ♈23°36 | **23** We |
| **24** Th | 14:09:07 | ♉04°04'04 | ♓11°03'01 | ♓18°12'28 | ♈06°54 | ♓26°49 | ♌02°27 | ♊19°59 | ♓27°07 | ♉25°55 | ♈00°52 | ♒03°47 | ♓25°30 | ♓26°53 | ♏03°06 | ♈23°39 | **24** Th |
| **25** Fr | 14:13:03 | ♉05°02'33 | ♓25°28'25 | ♈02°50'00 | ♈08°01 | ♓27°13 | ♌02°54 | ♊20°11 | ♓27°13 | ♉25°58 | ♈00°54 | ♒03°47 | ♓25°27 | ♓26°54 | ♏03°13 | ♈23°43 | **25** Fr |
| **26** Sa | 14:16:60 | ♉06°00'59 | ♈10°17'02 | ♈17°48'15 | ♈09°10 | ♓27°38 | ♌03°20 | ♊20°22 | ♓27°19 | ♉26°02 | ♈00°56 | ♒03°48 | ♓25°24 | ℞ 26°53 | ♏03°19 | ♈23°46 | **26** Sa |
| **27** Su | 14:20:56 | ♉06°59'24 | ♈25°23'06 | ♉02°59'57 | D 10°21 | ♓28°06 | ♌03°47 | ♊20°34 | ♓27°26 | ♉26°05 | ♈00°58 | ♒03°48 | ♓25°21 | ♓26°51 | ♏03°26 | ♈23°50 | **27** Su |
| **28** Mo | 14:24:53 | ♉07°57'47 | ♉10°38'02 | ♉18°15'32 | ♈11°35 | ♓28°34 | ♌04°13 | ♊20°46 | ♓27°32 | ♉26°08 | ♈01°00 | ♒03°48 | ♓25°18 | ♓26°47 | ♏03°33 | ♈23°53 | **28** Mo |
| **29** Tu | 14:28:49 | ♉08°56'08 | ♉25°51'34 | ♊03°24'23 | ♈12°51 | ♓29°04 | ♌04°40 | ♊20°58 | ♓27°38 | ♉26°12 | ♈01°02 | ♒03°48 | ♓25°14 | ♓26°41 | ♏03°40 | ♈23°57 | **29** Tu |
| **30** We | 14:32:46 | ♉09°54'27 | ♊10°53'16 | ♊18°16'44 | ♈14°10 | ♓29°36 | ♌05°08 | ♊21°10 | ♓27°44 | ♉26°15 | ♈01°03 | ♒03°48 | ♓25°11 | ♓26°34 | ♏03°46 | ♈24°00 | **30** We |
| **Δ Delta** | 01:54:20 | 28°23'34" | 383°29'42" | 383°27'15" | -15°25' | 2°04' | 11°32' | 5°11' | 3°15' | 1°30' | 1°00' | 0°15' | -1°32' | -0°47' | 3°13' | 1°42' | **Delta** |

Ephemeris tables and data provided by **Astro-Seek.com.** All times in UTC.

**APRIL 2025**

| S | M | T | W | T | F | S |
|---|---|---|---|---|---|---|
|   |   | 1 | 2 | 3 | 4 | 5 |
| 6 | 7 | 8 | 9 | 10 | 11 | 12 |
| 13 | 14 | 15 | 16 | 17 | 18 | 19 |
| 20 | 21 | 22 | 23 | 24 | 25 | 26 |
| 27 | 28 | 29 | 30 |   |   |   |

## MONTHLY INTENTION

## THIS MONTH I WILL...

4

**1** TUE

● ♉
♊ 4:26PM

---

**2** WED

● ♊

---

**3** THU

● ♊
♋ 6:50PM

---

**4** FRI

◐ ♋
Waxing Quarter moon in Cancer (10:14PM)
Mars-Saturn trine

---

**5** SAT

◐ ♋

**APRIL 2025**

| S | M | T | W | T | F | S |
|---|---|---|---|---|---|---|
|   |   | 1 | 2 | 3 | 4 | 5 |
| 6 | 7 | 8 | 9 | 10 | 11 | 12 |
| 13 | 14 | 15 | 16 | 17 | 18 | 19 |
| 20 | 21 | 22 | 23 | 24 | 25 | 26 |
| 27 | 28 | 29 | 30 |   |   |   |

## WEEKLY INTENTION

## TOP 3 TO-DOS

**4**

○

○

○

---

**6** SUN　　　　　　　　　　　　　　　　◐♋

♌ **12:34AM**
Venus-Mars trine (#2 of 2)

---

**7** MON　　　　　　　　　　　　　　　　○♌

Venus-Saturn meetup (#2 of 3)
Mercury retrograde ends (7:08AM)

**8** TUE

○♌
♍ 9:40AM

---

**9** WED

○♍

---

**10** THU

○♍
♎ 9:12PM

---

**11** FRI

○♎

---

**12** SAT

○♎
**FULL MOON IN LIBRA**
(8:22PM; 23°20′)
Venus retrograde ends (9:02PM)

**APRIL 2025**

| S | M | T | W | T | F | S |
|---|---|---|---|---|---|---|
|   |   | 1 | 2 | 3 | 4 | 5 |
| 6 | 7 | 8 | 9 | 10 | 11 | 12 |
| 13 | 14 | 15 | 16 | 17 | 18 | 19 |
| 20 | 21 | 22 | 23 | 24 | 25 | 26 |
| 27 | 28 | 29 | 30 |   |   |   |

## WEEKLY INTENTION

## TOP 3 TO-DOS

**4**

○

○

○

**13** SUN ○ ♎

♍ 9:54AM

**14** MON ○ ♍

**15** TUE

○ ♏︎
♐ 10:37PM

---

**16** WED

☽ ♐
Mercury in Aries until May 10 (2:25AM)

---

**17** THU

☽ ♐
Mercury-Neptune meetup

---

**18** FRI

☽ ♐
♑ 10:12AM
Mars in Leo until Jun 17 (12:21AM)

---

**19** SAT

☽ ♑
Sun enters Taurus (3:56PM)
Mars-Neptune trine

**TAURUS SEASON UNTIL MAY 20**

| S | M | T | W | T | F | S |
|---|---|---|---|---|---|---|
|   |   | 1 | 2 | 3 | 4 | 5 |
| 6 | 7 | 8 | 9 | 10 | 11 | 12 |
| 13 | 14 | 15 | 16 | 17 | 18 | 19 |
| 20 | 21 | 22 | 23 | 24 | 25 | 26 |
| 27 | 28 | 29 | 30 |   |   |   |

## WEEKLY INTENTION

## TOP 3 TO-DOS

○

○

○

**4**

---

**20** SUN

☾♑

♒ 7:22PM

Waning Quarter moon in Aquarius (9:35PM)
Sun-Mars square

---

**21** MON

☽♒

**22** TUE ◑ ♒

---

**23** WED ◑ ♒
### ♓ 1:07AM
Sun-Pluto square

---

**24** THU ◑ ♓
Venus-Saturn meetup #3 of 3

---

**25** FRI ◑ ♓
### ♈ 3:24AM

---

**26** SAT ● ♈
Mars-Pluto opposition

**APRIL 2025**

| S | M | T | W | T | F | S |
|---|---|---|---|---|---|---|
| | | 1 | 2 | 3 | 4 | 5 |
| 6 | 7 | 8 | 9 | 10 | 11 | 12 |
| 13 | 14 | 15 | 16 | 17 | 18 | 19 |
| 20 | 21 | 22 | 23 | 24 | 25 | 26 |
| 27 | 28 | 29 | 30 | | | |

## WEEKLY INTENTION

## TOP 3 TO-DOS

○

○

○

**4**

**27** SUN

● ♈

● ♉ 3:17AM

**NEW SUPERMOON IN TAURUS**
(3:31PM; 7°47')

**28** MON

● ♉

**29** TUE

●♉
♊ 2:34AM

---

**30** WED

●♊
Venus in Aries until Jun 6 (1:16PM)

---

## NOTES & THOUGHTS

# APRIL
## MONTHLY HOTSPOTS

4

APR 4

### MARS-SATURN TRINE

With Mars in Cancer joining forces with Saturn in Pisces, your intuition and emotional depth are your secret weapons. Mars in Cancer encourages you to protect what you cherish and advance with care, while Saturn in Pisces adds a layer of spiritual wisdom, urging you to trust your instincts. This cosmic combo allows you to tap into the subtle undercurrents of any situation. Instead of rushing forward, feel your way through the pros and cons, letting your intuition guide your next steps. Take a calculated risk that aligns with your emotional truth—you'll know when the timing feels just right.

### WAXING QUARTER MOON IN CANCER (10:14PM)

Feeling like your bedroom is more of a snore than a sanctuary? Tired of cooking up the same old soups and roasted root veggies? It's time to add some zest to your nest! The waxing quarter moon in cozy Cancer is here to awaken your inner Nate Berkus and inspire a mini home makeover. But before you start knocking down walls, remember that this lunar phase is too brief for major renovations. Instead, think small but impactful—like a fresh coat of paint, rearranging your living room, or tackling that overdue closet clean-out. If you're on the hunt for a new home, start scouring Zillow or exploring neighborhoods that catch your eye. Pay attention to the amenities and attractions that align with your optimal lifestyle. With la luna lighting the way, you might just stumble upon a listing that ticks all your boxes.

### APR 6 VENUS-MARS TRINE #2 OF 2

Set aside those attachment fears and open yourself up to deeper intimacy today, as the love planets canoodle in sensual water signs.

This is their second of three nostalgic trines while Mars is in Cancer and Venus is in Pisces, but there's a twist. When they last met this way on January 25, Mars was retrograde, which could have churned up some self-protective defenses. This time around it's Venus who's on a reverse commute, which may obscure the clear signals that you're attempting to send out. A surefire recipe for romantic success? Lean into nostalgia. Scroll through old photos, get tickets to see a band you've both always loved. If time permits, slip off for a couple nights to a place where you can both let your hair down and relax. If you're single and looking, you might feel brave enough to shoot your shot with a crush that never got off the ground.

APR 7

## VENUS-SATURN MEETUP #2 OF 3

For the second time this year, Venus falls under Saturn's stern command which could turn love into serious business. With the planet of romance in reverse, you may need to review agreements before you can launch ahead with any dating strategies or relationship goals. Under this strained alignment, old wounds may be scratched, especially since both planets are in sacrificial Pisces. You could find yourself hashing out that same old argument that was never fully resolved. Before you trot out a laundry list of complaints (including who's done more of the laundry), take a moment to find gratitude for the things that are actually going right between you. We're not suggesting you overlook your grievances. Just remember that the person standing in front of you, whether a lover or a friend, is someone you generally adore, not a monster trying to dump their responsibilities on you.

## MERCURY RETROGRADE ENDS

After a choppy three weeks, messenger Mercury wakes up from its befuddling three-week retrograde and powers forward through intuitive Pisces until April 16. With the messenger planet backstroking through the Fish's murky waters since March 29, emotions may have overtaken everyone's better senses—and let's not even talk about the rage cleaning you did while it was backing up through Aries from March 15 to 29. If you found yourself ugly crying, whether "inexplicably" or for a damn good reason, hopefully those tears were healing. But enough of this three-hanky drama! With Mercury back on track, the chronic misunderstandings that disrupted your early spring can pave the way to healing reconciliations. Contracts that were held up in red tape could finally move into the negotiation (and signing!) phase. But don't lose the important message Mercury retrograde taught about the pitfalls of skimming the surface instead of finding out what lies beneath. Even if you learned this in a tough love kind of way, you can spring forward with a new resolve to slow down, get every question answered and read the fine print.

## APR 12

### FULL MOON IN LIBRA (8:22PM; 23°20')

Birds of a feather might just stay together forever under the light of today's full moon in Libra, the sign of partnerships. If you're still searching for your perfect plus-one, cast a wider net. This full moon gets a buddy pass from global Jupiter (in Gemini), which could magnetize interest from a far-flung locale. Since Jupiter is the galactic gambler, you might as well make "nothing ventured, nothing gained" your mantra. Slide into the DMs of that deejay in Berlin who you've been following for months or invite your "will they, won't they" crush out on a proper Saturday night date. If you've been at odds with your person, these diplomatic moonbeams set the stage for a productive dialogue. The only catch? Feisty Mars in Cancer is squaring la luna, so go in softly to avoid riling up anyone's defense mechanisms or accidentally triggering their inner eight-year-old brat. Need to rebalance the load with a collaborator? Fair-minded Libra reminds us that an "even split" is different for everyone. Divvy up duties in a way that feels manageable for both of you and consider outsourcing things that you both hate doing.

### VENUS RETROGRADE ENDS

Cupid is back on the scene, bearing a freshly sharpened quiver of arrows. And after six weeks of misfires and mojo-dulling vibes, it's about damn time. Blame the delayed spring fever on romantic Venus who went retrograde on March 1. Here's hoping you made it out relatively unscathed, free from bad romances, bad haircuts and any other bad decisions in the interpersonal realm. As Venus corrects course today—and powers forward through poetic Pisces until April 30—get ready for a romantic uprising. Pull your most theatrical pieces to the front of your closet, especially those amazing shoes you tucked away for the winter. All the world's a fantasy novel while Venus floats through the sign of the spring-fevered Fish. While you're at it, spice up your social life with a spiritual element. A little woo goes a long way when it comes to forming lasting bonds.

## APRIL 16-MAY 10 MERCURY IN ARIES

Fear not, you haven't lost your edge! Today, spitfire Mercury swings back into Aries for its second pass, making up for the time it lost during its recent retrograde. While Mercury backtracked through fiery Aries from March 15 to 29, it prompted deep self-reflection and sparked some seriously stormy misunderstandings. Did you snap at someone close or worse, drag them to mutual friends? It's time to drop the excuses. Even if they did push all your buttons, the retrograde may have intensified your reactions. But with Mercury now moving direct, the fog lifts, and clarity returns. Capitalize on the next few weeks to smooth things over and try your absolute hardest to make amends. It's time to clear the air and move forward, one way or another.

## APR 17 MERCURY-NEPTUNE MEETUP

Okay, so this is awkward. For the first time since the late 1800s, intellectual Mercury teams up with subliminal Neptune in the abrasive field of Aries. Problems can be solved with both logic and intuition today, so don't ignore either input stream. Still, you may be hard-pressed to access the levels of sensitivity and compassion that you tapped so easily last month, when these planets teamed up in Pisces. A desire to experiment with new methodologies could overrun your ability to read the room. Slow down so you don't steamroll people who aren't up to speed on the latest and greatest technology. You may have to explain (and re-explain) those novel concepts before you get anyone on board for a test run.

## APRIL 18-JUNE 17 MARS IN LEO

Palace intrigue heats up again, as red-hot Mars struts back into Leo, escalating drama and elevating luxury. What's the fun of having all the toys unless you have people to play with? With Mars in this magnanimous realm, sharing is caring and spoiling the ones you love is even better. Life feels like a giant talent show now, with everyone vying for the trophy. Warning! Competition can get fierce during this transit, and if you aren't careful, it could devolve into a full-on game of thrones. Rather than go "House of Lannister" on potential allies, make an effort to recognize and uplift others. Even simple acts like remixing someone's post on social media can work wonders, making them feel valued and visible. No matter your relationship status, invite in a romantic renaissance by developing a more playful spirit. How can you pump up the passion with your love interest or get more direct results from digital dating? Doing the same thing over and over will only yield expected results. Daring Mars wants you to color outside those lines and give a new tactic a try.

## APR 19

### MARS-NEPTUNE TRINE

Mind blown! Another groundbreaking transit shakes up the month. For the first time since the 1800s, flamboyant Mars in Leo fistbumps dreamweaver Neptune in Aries, turning the world into an episode of Drag Race. "To thine own self be true" is the world's mantra while these boundary bashing and blurring planets link arms. There may be some highly entertaining ideas bandied about, coupled with stunning displays of ego. (Wow. Just. Wow.) Be mindful about who you hoist onto a pedestal. Loudmouthed "leaders" could be vaulted into power, creating chaos with their charismatic sideshows. While you may feel like pushing the envelope, think carefully before you post anything agitating under this celestial starmap. Is the controversy worth it? One impulsive rant or offensive photo could get you canceled or start a war in your personal life.

## SUN IN TAURUS (3:56PM) (APR 19-MAY 20)

Welcome to Taurus season! After four dynamic weeks of Aries' fiery energy, it's time to transition from fire to earth, focusing on stability and productivity. The passionate Aries spark has ignited your drive, and now Taurus, the steadfast Bull, is here to help you channel that energy into achieving your goals. It's time to refine those raw ideas and set the wheels in motion. Reminder! Taurus isn't all work and no play; this sign also has a taste for the finer things. So, while you're busy moving the needle, don't forget to sprinkle some luxury into your routine. The beauty of Taurus season is finding that balance between indulgence and practicality. Enjoying life's luxuries doesn't have to lead to extravagant spending. Take pleasure in nature, museum hop, or rediscover treasures in your own wardrobe. And if you're feeling inclined to splurge on a special treat, shop around and find the best deal you can.

## APR 20

## WANING QUARTER MOON IN AQUARIUS (9:35PM)

Last week's full moon in Libra got us all passionately fired up about partnerships. But in your eagerness to claim "two" as your magic number, did you get a little too zealous, even obsessive? Today's quarter moon in coolly objective Aquarius redirects your tunnel vision and helps you see things from a more levelheaded perspective. Take a 30,000-foot view of this connection and honestly weigh the potential pros and cons. You might have a surprising realization: You're trying to fit the relationship (or potential relationship) into the wrong box. Don't impose limits on the future by trying to force things to go a certain way. When you let go of control, you allow unexpected magic to flow in.

## SUN-MARS SQUARE

Watch for power struggles today, as the stalwart Taurus Sun clashes with headstrong Mars in Leo. A snarky retort could accidentally come across as a confrontation or insult. Big egos are at play, but beware the temptation to match someone's bloviating with your own simulated swagger. It's crucial to keep a level head and choose diplomacy over drama. Remember, asserting your viewpoint doesn't require overpowering the conversation. Finding common ground might be challenging, but it's the key to maintaining peace and making progress.

## APR 23 SUN-PLUTO SQUARE

Who's on top? During this intense biannual face-off between domineering Pluto and the ego-driven Sun, emotions can run high. It's natural to feel upset if you sense a power struggle brewing, but beware of knee-jerk reactions. Today, they're likely to do more harm than good. If standing up to a bully, demonstrate strength by maintaining your composure. But heed this caution: With both planets anchored in stubborn fixed signs (Pluto's in Aquarius and the Sun is in Taurus), no one will be in the mood to compromise. If a stalemate ensues and no one's willing to give even an inch, it might be wise to call a time-out and revisit the issue on another day.

## APR 24 VENUS-SATURN MEETUP #3 OF 3

Quit playing games with their hearts! Harmonizer Venus duets with no-nonsense Saturn for the third and final time this year. As they merge in gullible Pisces, it's time to stop making excuses and blow the whistle on the breadcrumbers, ghosters and garden variety players. Because Venus was retrograde on their last conjunction (April 7), a few deceptive types may have slid past your radar. Today, it becomes glaringly obvious who is worthy of your precious time and who needs to be kicked off the island. Creative compromises could emerge for couples who've been struggling to find equanimity. Don't soft-pedal issues that need to be brought out into the open. Time is precious, and you don't want to waste your life pining for someone who "isn't ready" to move in your desired direction, and may never be!

## APR 26 MARS-PLUTO OPPOSITION

Tempers, egos, and mind games, oh my! When fiery Mars in regal Leo opposes power-hungry Pluto in revolutionary Aquarius, the atmosphere could crackle with tension, teetering on the edge of a full-blown showdown. You might unwittingly wander into a psychological battlefield, where it's all too easy to snap and lose your cool. Staying composed won't just be your greatest asset today—it'll also be your biggest challenge. Keep your wits about you and don't take the bait, no matter how tempting it may be to react.

## APR 27 NEW MOON IN TAURUS (3:31PM; 7°47'; SUPERMOON)

Practical magic is in the air—no wand needed! Thanks to a potent supermoon in Taurus, you'll easily strike a balance between the sensual and the sensible. If life has felt unstable, this is your opportunity to reground yourself. Start by simplifying: Break down complex plans back to basics, draft blueprints, and streamline systems. To make sure all new developments are welcome, minimize uncertainties in crucial areas like time, money, and relationships. Taurus encourages a slow, steady approach to achieving your goals without sacrificing beauty or quality. Embrace eco-friendly and upcycled choices, supporting brands that respect our planet. Keeping a level head may take a little effort today, since the new moon gets caught in a three-way tug-of-war (a T-square) with stormy Pluto in Aquarius and feisty Mars in Leo. As you map out your trajectory, don't get caught up in the "compare and despair" trap with the cool kids. The only approval ratings that matter today are your own.

## APR 30-JUN 6 VENUS IN ARIES

Let's see some swag! As magnetic Venus zips back into fiery and self-determined Aries for the second time this year, you'll have ample opportunities to right any wrongs that disrupted your love life during the spring Venus retrograde. The first step might be this: reclaiming your self-sovereignty in relationships that have grown too close for comfort. While Venus was melting into a puddle of goo in Pisces, codependence may have crept into the healthiest bonds. Or maybe the cozy vibes have dulled the once-sexy sparks. Harness the autonomous energy of Aries and declare the next four weeks a personal reclamation. Get obsessed with a hobby and guard your "me time" like a hawk. The person who's been taking you for granted could swiftly wake up and realize your value.

# 5

# May
## MONTHLY HOROSCOPE

Creative inspiration streams in this May as the Taurus Sun continues shining in your fifth house of art, romance and self-expression until the 20th. Forget about following trends! This month, you'll lead the way with your inspired fashion sense and visionary ideas. This playful period casts you in the role of cultural activities director for your crew. Bring on the concerts, gallery openings, operas and more! On May 4, Pluto spins retrograde in Aquarius, backing through your second house of money and values until October 13. (Celebratory note: This is the first year since 2008 that stormy, triggering Pluto is NOT in your sign!) Review your financial strategy. Are your resources supporting the life you want to build? It may be time to rethink your approach to earning, saving and investing, or at least an aspect of it. Spring training, spring cleaning— you're ready for all of it starting May 20 when the Sun enters Gemini and your orderly sixth house. On May 24, your galactic guardian Saturn switches signs, temporarily moving into Aries and your fourth house of home and family. Saturn's disciplined energy can help you feel more rooted even if that means planting yourself in a new place over the course of this three-year cycle. Your new job? To lay a foundation that supports your long-term security and emotional well-being.

*Read your extended monthly forecast for*
*life, love, money and career! astrostyle.com*

# MAY
## Moon Phase Calendar

| SUN | MON | TUE | WED | THU | FRI | SAT |
|---|---|---|---|---|---|---|
| | | | | **1**<br>♊<br>♋ 3:23AM | **2**<br>♋ | **3**<br>♋<br>♌ 7:29AM |
| **4**<br>♌<br>2nd Quarter | **5**<br>♌<br>♍ 3:40PM | **6**<br>♍ | **7**<br>♍ | **8**<br>♍<br>♎ 3:06AM | **9**<br>♎ | **10**<br>♎<br>♏ 3:58PM |
| **11**<br>♏ | **12**<br>♏<br>Full Moon<br>12:56PM | **13**<br>♏<br>♐ 4:35AM | **14**<br>♐ | **15**<br>♐<br>♑ 3:58PM | **16**<br>♑ | **17**<br>♑ |
| **18**<br>♑<br>♒ 1:29AM | **19**<br>♒ | **20**<br>♒ 4th Quarter<br>♓ 8:28AM | **21**<br>♓ | **22**<br>♓<br>♈ 12:26PM | **23**<br>♈ | **24**<br>♈<br>♉ 1:38PM |
| **25**<br>♉ | **26**<br>♉→♊ 1:21PM<br>♊ New Moon<br>11:02PM | **27**<br>♊ | **28**<br>♊<br>♋ 1:33PM | **29**<br>♋ | **30**<br>♋<br>♌ 4:17PM | **31**<br>♌ |

*Times listed are Eastern US Time Zone*

MAY 12, 12:56PM

## full moon in
# Scorpio (22°13')

## SCORPIO FULL MOON CRYSTAL

### HEMATITE

This silvery stone is a great protection while under the spell of empathic, intuitive Scorpio. Hematite reflects and deflects any negative energy so you don't absorb it. With its high iron content, it also helps circulate Scorpio-ruled blood and wake you up for springtime.

*What's one thing you're celebrating under this full moon?*

## SCORPIO FULL MOON = CELEBRATE!

*Your loyal and caring spirit*

*Intense exchanges*

*The sexiest parts of yourself*

*The ways you've transformed your struggles into gold*

*True friendship*

*Resourcefulness and raw creative expression*

MAY 26, 11:02PM

# new moon in
# Gemini (6°06')

## GEMINI NEW MOON CRYSTAL

### PHANTOM QUARTZ

Shift your Gemini-ruled mindset with this protective, empowering stone. Phantom Quartz facilitates unexpected breakthroughs and promotes personal growth.

---

*What's one fresh intention you're ready to set under this new moon?*

---

## GEMINI NEW MOON = FOCUS

*Sharpen your communication style*

*Write and make media*

*Become active in your local community*

*Socialize with new people*

*Flirt and joke!*

*Pair up on short-term collaborations*

## May 2025

Longitude & Retrograde Ephemeris [00:00 UT]

| Day | Sid.time | ☉ | ☽ | +12h☽ | ☿ | ♀ | ♂ | ♃ | ♄ | ♅ | ♆ | ♇ | ☊ | ☊ | ⚸ | ⚷ | Day |
|---|---|---|---|---|---|---|---|---|---|---|---|---|---|---|---|---|---|
| 1 Th | 14:36:43 | ♉10°52'45 | ♊25°34'24 | ♋02°45'12 | ♈15°30 | ♈00°09 | ♌05°35 | ♊21°22 | ♓27°50 | ♉26°19 | ♈01°05 | ♒03°48 | ℞ 25°08 | ℞ 26°28 | ♏03°53 | ♈24°04 | 1 Th |
| 2 Fr | 14:40:39 | ♉11°51'01 | ♋09°49'09 | ♋16°45'37 | ♈16°53 | ♈00°43 | ♌06°03 | ♊21°34 | ♓27°56 | ♉26°22 | ♈01°07 | ♒03°49 | ♓25°05 | ♓26°23 | ♏04°00 | ♈24°07 | 2 Fr |
| 3 Sa | 14:44:36 | ♉12°49'14 | ♋23°35'01 | ♌00°17'03 | ♈18°18 | ♈01°19 | ♌06°31 | ♊21°46 | ♓28°02 | ♉26°25 | ♈01°09 | ♒03°49 | ♓25°02 | ♓26°19 | ♏04°06 | ♈24°11 | 3 Sa |
| 4 Su | 14:48:32 | ♉13°47'25 | ♌06°52'28 | ♌13°21'13 | ♈19°45 | ♈01°56 | ♌06°58 | ♊21°58 | ♓28°08 | ♉26°29 | ♈01°11 | ♒03°49 | ♓24°59 | ♓26°18 | ♏04°13 | ♈24°14 | 4 Su |
| 5 Mo | 14:52:29 | ♉14°45'35 | ♌19°44'12 | ♌26°01'35 | ♈21°14 | ♈02°33 | ♌07°27 | ♊22°10 | ♓28°14 | ♉26°32 | ♈01°12 | ℞ 03°49 | ♓24°55 | D 26°17 | ♏04°20 | ♈24°18 | 5 Mo |
| 6 Tu | 14:56:25 | ♉15°43'42 | ♍02°14'18 | ♍08°22'36 | ♈22°45 | ♈03°13 | ♌07°55 | ♊22°23 | ♓28°20 | ♉26°36 | ♈01°14 | ♒03°49 | ♓24°52 | ♓26°18 | ♏04°26 | ♈24°21 | 6 Tu |
| 7 We | 15:00:22 | ♉16°41'48 | ♍14°27'27 | ♍20°29'03 | ♈24°18 | ♈03°53 | ♌08°23 | ♊22°35 | ♓28°26 | ♉26°39 | ♈01°16 | ♒03°49 | ♓24°49 | ♓26°20 | ♏04°33 | ♈24°24 | 7 We |
| 8 Th | 15:04:18 | ♉17°39'51 | ♍26°28'21 | ♎02°25'32 | ♈25°52 | ♈04°34 | ♌08°52 | ♊22°47 | ♓28°32 | ♉26°43 | ♈01°18 | ♒03°48 | ♓24°46 | ℞ 26°20 | ♏04°40 | ♈24°28 | 8 Th |
| 9 Fr | 15:08:15 | ♉18°37'53 | ♎08°21'28 | ♎14°16'14 | ♈27°29 | ♈05°16 | ♌09°21 | ♊23°00 | ♓28°37 | ♉26°46 | ♈01°19 | ♒03°48 | ♓24°43 | ♓26°19 | ♏04°46 | ♈24°31 | 9 Fr |
| 10 Sa | 15:12:12 | ♉19°35'53 | ♎20°10'37 | ♎26°04'40 | ♈29°08 | ♈05°59 | ♌09°50 | ♊23°12 | ♓28°43 | ♉26°50 | ♈01°21 | ♒03°48 | ♓24°39 | ♓26°16 | ♏04°53 | ♈24°34 | 10 Sa |
| 11 Su | 15:16:08 | ♉20°33'51 | ♏01°59'05 | ♏07°53'46 | ♉00°49 | ♈06°44 | ♌10°19 | ♊23°25 | ♓28°48 | ♉26°53 | ♈01°23 | ♒03°48 | ♓24°36 | ♓26°11 | ♏05°00 | ♈24°38 | 11 Su |
| 12 Mo | 15:20:05 | ♉21°31'48 | ♏13°49'23 | ♏19°45'48 | ♉02°32 | ♈07°29 | ♌10°48 | ♊23°38 | ♓28°54 | ♉26°56 | ♈01°24 | ♒03°48 | ♓24°33 | ♓26°04 | ♏05°06 | ♈24°41 | 12 Mo |
| 13 Tu | 15:24:01 | ♉22°29'43 | ♏25°43'34 | ♐01°42'32 | ♉04°17 | ♈08°15 | ♌11°18 | ♊23°50 | ♓28°59 | ♉27°00 | ♈01°26 | ♒03°48 | ♓24°30 | ♓25°54 | ♏05°13 | ♈24°44 | 13 Tu |
| 14 We | 15:27:58 | ♉23°27'36 | ♐07°43'13 | ♐13°45'25 | ♉06°04 | ♈09°01 | ♌11°47 | ♊24°03 | ♓29°05 | ♉27°03 | ♈01°28 | ♒03°47 | ♓24°27 | ♓25°44 | ♏05°20 | ♈24°47 | 14 We |
| 15 Th | 15:31:54 | ♉24°25'28 | ♐19°49'41 | ♐25°55'49 | ♉07°52 | ♈09°49 | ♌12°17 | ♊24°16 | ♓29°10 | ♉27°07 | ♈01°29 | ♒03°47 | ♓24°24 | ♓25°33 | ♏05°26 | ♈24°51 | 15 Th |
| 16 Fr | 15:35:51 | ♉25°23'19 | ♑02°04'23 | ♑08°15'12 | ♉09°43 | ♈10°37 | ♌12°47 | ♊24°29 | ♓29°15 | ♉27°10 | ♈01°31 | ♒03°47 | ♓24°20 | ♓25°23 | ♏05°33 | ♈24°54 | 16 Fr |
| 17 Sa | 15:39:47 | ♉26°21'09 | ♑14°28'54 | ♑20°45'20 | ♉11°36 | ♈11°26 | ♌13°17 | ♊24°42 | ♓29°20 | ♉27°14 | ♈01°32 | ♒03°47 | ♓24°17 | ♓25°14 | ♏05°40 | ♈24°57 | 17 Sa |
| 18 Su | 15:43:44 | ♉27°18'57 | ♑27°05'13 | ♒03°28'26 | ♉13°31 | ♈12°16 | ♌13°47 | ♊24°55 | ♓29°25 | ♉27°17 | ♈01°34 | ♒03°46 | ♓24°14 | ♓25°08 | ♏05°46 | ♈25°00 | 18 Su |
| 19 Mo | 15:47:41 | ♉28°16'44 | ♒09°55'45 | ♒16°27'04 | ♉15°28 | ♈13°07 | ♌14°17 | ♊25°07 | ♓29°30 | ♉27°21 | ♈01°35 | ♒03°46 | ♓24°11 | ♓25°04 | ♏05°53 | ♈25°03 | 19 Mo |
| 20 Tu | 15:51:37 | ♉29°14'30 | ♒23°03'11 | ♒29°44'01 | ♉17°26 | ♈13°58 | ♌14°48 | ♊25°20 | ♓29°35 | ♉27°24 | ♈01°36 | ♒03°45 | ♓24°08 | ♓25°02 | ♏06°00 | ♈25°06 | 20 Tu |
| 21 We | 15:55:34 | ♊00°12'15 | ♓06°30'18 | ♓13°21'52 | ♉19°27 | ♈14°50 | ♌15°18 | ♊25°34 | ♓29°40 | ♉27°28 | ♈01°38 | ♒03°45 | ♓24°05 | D 25°02 | ♏06°06 | ♈25°09 | 21 We |
| 22 Th | 15:59:30 | ♊01°09'59 | ♓20°19'21 | ♓27°22'24 | ♉21°29 | ♈15°42 | ♌15°49 | ♊25°47 | ♓29°45 | ♉27°31 | ♈01°39 | ♒03°44 | ♓24°01 | ♓25°03 | ♏06°13 | ♈25°12 | 22 Th |
| 23 Fr | 16:03:27 | ♊02°07'41 | ♈04°31'26 | ♈11°45'48 | ♉23°33 | ♈16°35 | ♌16°20 | ♊26°00 | ♓29°50 | ♉27°35 | ♈01°41 | ♒03°44 | ♓23°58 | ℞ 25°03 | ♏06°20 | ♈25°16 | 23 Fr |
| 24 Sa | 16:07:23 | ♊03°05'23 | ♈19°05'39 | ♈26°29'57 | ♉25°39 | ♈17°29 | ♌16°51 | ♊26°13 | ♓29°54 | ♉27°38 | ♈01°42 | ♒03°43 | ♓23°55 | ♓25°01 | ♏06°26 | ♈25°19 | 24 Sa |
| 25 Su | 16:11:20 | ♊04°03'03 | ♉03°58'26 | ♉11°29'45 | ♉27°46 | ♈18°23 | ♌17°22 | ♊26°26 | ♓29°59 | ♉27°42 | ♈01°43 | ♒03°43 | ♓23°52 | ♓24°56 | ♏06°33 | ♈25°21 | 25 Su |
| 26 Mo | 16:15:16 | ♊05°00'43 | ♉19°03'16 | ♉26°37'19 | ♉29°54 | ♈19°17 | ♌17°53 | ♊26°39 | ♈00°03 | ♉27°45 | ♈01°44 | ♒03°42 | ♓23°49 | ♓24°49 | ♏06°40 | ♈25°24 | 26 Mo |
| 27 Tu | 16:19:13 | ♊05°58'22 | ♊04°11'07 | ♊11°42'53 | ♊02°04 | ♈20°13 | ♌18°25 | ♊26°53 | ♈00°08 | ♉27°49 | ♈01°46 | ♒03°42 | ♓23°45 | ♓24°40 | ♏06°47 | ♈25°27 | 27 Tu |
| 28 We | 16:23:10 | ♊06°55'59 | ♊19°11'49 | ♊26°36'18 | ♊04°14 | ♈21°08 | ♌18°56 | ♊27°06 | ♈00°12 | ♉27°52 | ♈01°47 | ♒03°41 | ♓23°42 | ♓24°30 | ♏06°53 | ♈25°30 | 28 We |
| 29 Th | 16:27:06 | ♊07°53'36 | ♋03°55'46 | ♋11°08'56 | ♊06°26 | ♈22°04 | ♌19°28 | ♊27°19 | ♈00°16 | ♉27°56 | ♈01°48 | ♒03°41 | ♓23°39 | ♓24°19 | ♏07°00 | ♈25°33 | 29 Th |
| 30 Fr | 16:31:03 | ♊08°51'11 | ♋18°15'37 | ♋25°14'58 | ♊08°38 | ♈23°01 | ♌19°59 | ♊27°33 | ♈00°21 | ♉27°59 | ♈01°49 | ♒03°40 | ♓23°36 | ♓24°10 | ♏07°07 | ♈25°36 | 30 Fr |
| 31 Sa | 16:34:59 | ♊09°48'44 | ♌02°07'14 | ♌08°51'56 | ♊10°50 | ♈23°58 | ♌20°31 | ♊27°46 | ♈00°25 | ♉28°03 | ♈01°50 | ♒03°39 | ♓23°33 | ♓24°03 | ♏07°13 | ♈25°39 | 31 Sa |
| Δ Delta | 01:58:16 | 28°55'59" | 396°32'49" | 396°06'44" | 55°19' | 23°48' | 14°55' | 6°24' | -2°34' | 1°44' | 0°45' | -0°09' | -1°35' | -2°24' | 3°20' | 1°34' | Delta |

Ephemeris tables and data provided by **Astro-Seek.com.** All times in UTC.

5

## MAY 2025

| S | M | T | W | T | F | S |
|---|---|---|---|---|---|---|
|   |   |   |   | 1 | 2 | 3 |
| 4 | 5 | 6 | 7 | 8 | 9 | 10 |
| 11 | 12 | 13 | 14 | 15 | 16 | 17 |
| 18 | 19 | 20 | 21 | 22 | 23 | 24 |
| 25 | 26 | 27 | 28 | 29 | 30 | 31 |

## MONTHLY INTENTION

## THIS MONTH I WILL...

**1** THU
◗ ♊
♋ 3:23AM

**2** FRI
◑ ♋
Venus-Neptune meetup #3 of 3

**3** SAT
◑ ♋
♌ 7:29AM

## MAY 2025

| S | M | T | W | T | F | S |
|---|---|---|---|---|---|---|
|   |   |   |   | 1 | 2 | 3 |
| 4 | 5 | 6 | 7 | 8 | 9 | 10 |
| 11 | 12 | 13 | 14 | 15 | 16 | 17 |
| 18 | 19 | 20 | 21 | 22 | 23 | 24 |
| 25 | 26 | 27 | 28 | 29 | 30 | 31 |

## WEEKLY INTENTION

## TOP 3 TO-DOS

○

○

○

**5**

---

**4** SUN
☽♌
Waxing quarter moon in Leo (9:52AM)
Pluto retrograde in Aquarius until Oct 13 (11:27AM)

---

**5** MON
☽♌
♍ 3:40PM

**6** TUE                                                    ☉ ♍

---

**7** WED                                              ☉ ♍

---

**8** THU                                              ☉ ♍
                                                         ♎ 3:06AM

---

**9** FRI                                                    ☉ ♎

---

**10** SAT                                             ☉ ♎
                                                     ♏ 3:58PM
Mercury in Taurus until May 25 (8:15AM)

| S | M | T | W | T | F | S |
|---|---|---|---|---|---|---|
|   |   |   |   | 1 | 2 | 3 |
| 4 | 5 | 6 | 7 | 8 | 9 | 10 |
| 11 | 12 | 13 | 14 | 15 | 16 | 17 |
| 18 | 19 | 20 | 21 | 22 | 23 | 24 |
| 25 | 26 | 27 | 28 | 29 | 30 | 31 |

## WEEKLY INTENTION

## TOP 3 TO-DOS

○

○

○

**11** SUN ☽ ♏

**12** MON ☽ ♏
**FULL MOON IN SCORPIO**
(12:56PM; 22°13')
Mercury-Pluto square

**13** TUE ○♏
♐ 4:35AM

**14** WED ○♐

**15** THU ○♐
♑ 3:58PM

**16** FRI ○♑

**17** SAT ○♑
Sun-Uranus meetup

| S | M | T | W | T | F | S |
|---|---|---|---|---|---|---|
|   |   |   |   | 1 | 2 | 3 |
| 4 | 5 | 6 | 7 | 8 | 9 | 10 |
| 11 | 12 | 13 | 14 | 15 | 16 | 17 |
| **18** | **19** | **20** | **21** | **22** | **23** | **24** |
| 25 | 26 | 27 | 28 | 29 | 30 | 31 |

## WEEKLY INTENTION

## TOP 3 TO-DOS

○

○

○

**5**

---

**18** SUN                                        ☽ ♑
                                                 ♒ 1:29AM
                                          Mercury-Mars square

---

**19** MON                                        ☽ ♒

**20** TUE

Waning quarter moon in Aquarius (7:59AM)

♓ **8:28AM**

Sun in Gemini (2:55PM)

**GEMINI SEASON UNTIL JUN 20**

---

**21** WED ◑♓

---

**22** THU ◑♓

♈ **12:26PM**

Venus-Mars trine

---

**23** FRI ●♈

---

**24** SAT ●♈

♉ **1:38PM**

Sun-Pluto trine

Mercury-Uranus meetup

Saturn in Aries until Sep 1 (11:35PM)

## MAY 2025

| S | M | T | W | T | F | S |
|---|---|---|---|---|---|---|
|   |   |   |   | 1 | 2 | 3 |
| 4 | 5 | 6 | 7 | 8 | 9 | 10 |
| 11 | 12 | 13 | 14 | 15 | 16 | 17 |
| 18 | 19 | 20 | 21 | 22 | 23 | 24 |
| 25 | 26 | 27 | 28 | 29 | 30 | 31 |

## WEEKLY INTENTION

## TOP 3 TO-DOS

○

○

○

**5**

---

**25** SUN ● ♉
Mercury in Gemini until Jun 8 (8:59PM)

---

**26** MON ● ♉
♊ 1:21PM
**NEW SUPERMOON IN GEMINI**
(11:02PM; 6°06')

190

**27** TUE

● ♊
Mercury-Pluto trine

---

**28** WED

● ♊
♋ 1:33PM

---

**29** THU

◐ ♋

---

**30** FRI

◐ ♋
♌ 4:17PM
Sun-Mercury meetup

---

**31** SAT

◐ ♌

# MAY
## MONTHLY HOTSPOTS

### MAY 2 VENUS-NEPTUNE MEETUP #3 OF 3

For the third and final time this year, Venus and Neptune co-star in a fairy-tale romance, uniting overhead in an exact conjunction. Their first two love scenes took place while both planets were in Pisces—on February 1 and again on March 27, while Venus was retrograde. No doubt those moments stirred up all sorts of feelings, from hope to desire to intense longing; yet, with both planets in passive Pisces, you may have been hesitant to act upon your urges. Now, as Venus and Neptune complete their trilogy in fearless Aries, the stage is set for you to shoot your shot. No vision of love is too idealistic today, whether you're sharing it aloud with friends or inviting someone to join you in a full-color fantasy.

### MAY 4

### WAXING QUARTER MOON IN LEO (9:52AM)

A pinch of passion can go a long way, as long as you sprinkle it mindfully. With today's waxing quarter moon in vibrant Leo, it's time to add some flair to your routine, especially if things have gotten a bit monotonous. Elevate presentations with artsy photos and plug your text into colorful templates. (Hello, Canva.) When inviting people to hang out, make it sound like the event of the season ("You won't believe the tickets I scored for Friday night!") instead of underselling it ("I'm going to a show, but I'm not sure this is your thing..."). While you don't have to go full Chappell Roan with your outfit choices, the Leo quarter moon loves a sequin and anything that falls into the "tasteful flair" camp. Today is about turning heads and leaving people wanting more.

## PLUTO RETROGRADE IN AQUARIUS (MAY 4-OCT 13)

Power struggles disrupt peaceful team efforts, as Pluto begins its annual five-month retrograde in Aquarius, the sign of collaborations. As this calculating planet goes into snooze mode, you might notice stagnation in the way your squad operates or how your goals are progressing. If you're feeling stuck or unable to gain traction, consider it a sign to pump the brakes, then, pop the hood. Is everyone aligned around the end game and the strategy for achieving it? This frustrating, five-month cycle can be a hidden blessing if you use it to strengthen your internal processes. In your zeal to change the world, did you bite off more than you can chew? Pluto is solidly in Aquarius until 2044, so release that pressure valve and try a phased approach. What could you achieve by the end of 2025 without tearing yourself (and your team) apart with stress in the process? Remember: One win builds upon the next.

## MAY 10-25 MERCURY IN TAURUS

Mental Mercury shifts into sensible Taurus, helping you think in a tactical way. No doubt some, "Wouldn't it be crazy if..." ideas got floated while Mercury was in Aries for the last few weeks. But do these concepts have legs? Run them through stress tests and see which ones have potential to go the distance—and ideally, be profitable. Then, get down to brass tacks. Crunch the numbers, plot a few action steps and carve out dedicated hours to methodically work through the details. This granular effort can feel agonizing in moments, but stick with it. You could save yourself hours of time, not to mention precious resources, by doing this advance planning.

## MAY 12

### FULL MOON IN SCORPIO (12:56PM; 22º13')

Intense attractions could become all-consuming as the year's only full moon in Scorpio charges the air with mystery and seduction. With experimental Uranus opposing la luna, peak erotic experiences await if you're willing to explore flavors beyond vanilla. Choose a safe word because trust and lust are mutually exclusive under these sensitive moonbeams. Watch out for jealousy and possessiveness, too, which could flare up under the slightest provocation. Maybe you're overreacting, maybe you're not, but either way, nothing gets resolved in the heat of anger. Do your best to deescalate, even if that means taking a timeout when emotions get hot. All sorts of joint ventures could be inked in the two weeks following this lunation, but make sure everyone's role is spelled out clearly to avoid power struggles. Financial abundance could flow your way in the form of royalties, inheritances or investment dollars from a funding source. Make sure you know the tax liabilities for anything you bring in.

## MERCURY-PLUTO SQUARE

Is someone secretly eyeing your spotlight? With Mercury in determined Taurus locking horns with secretive Pluto in Aquarius, it's wise to keep your big ideas under wraps for now. If you've been pouring your heart into a project, resist the urge to share it too soon. Not only might your hard work receive a lukewarm response, but there could also be opportunists lurking, ready to swipe your brilliance for themselves. However, there's a silver lining to these mixed signals; if a key stakeholder gives you a firm "no," you'll gain clarity on where to refine and strengthen your concept for a more compelling pitch. And if a promising offer comes your way, dig deep and do your homework before committing to anything.

## MAY 17 SUN-URANUS MEETUP

Change is the only constant today, as the Sun and revolutionary Uranus host their once-per-year summit in the skies. Even if there are no outside catalysts, you'll feel a strong urge to shake up any stagnant area of your life. Easy, though. With wrench-throwing Uranus in the mix, an unexpected plot twist could catch you off guard, and the Sun can give you a case of extreme overconfidence. Fortunately, both celestial bodies are in rock-steady Taurus, which can offset some of the chaos this yearly conjunction brings. Focus on finding a solution that's not only innovative but also sustainable in the long run. And as you do, don't let your mouth write a check that your a$$ can't cash.

## MAY 18 MERCURY-MARS SQUARE

Let your word be your bond today and make sure you're prepared to back up your claims with legit credentials. Grandstanding Mars is in Leo, making everyone prone to exaggeration. Nothing wrong with adding a few colorful details! But if you're bedazzling the truth with too many questionable assumptions, you could get called out, even canceled. Avoid the backlash and lean into no-nonsense Mercury in Taurus who is busy regulating every statement. On the other hand, are you flying too low under the radar? Stop wearing struggle like a merit badge. Support is all around you, but you have to ask for it!

## MAY 20

### WANING QUARTER MOON IN AQUARIUS (7:59AM)

About a week ago, the Scorpio full moon ignited your passion for a particular goal or desire, possibly pushing you into overdrive. But did that intensity spawn an obsession? Today's quarter moon in clear-sighted Aquarius is here to help you step back and gain a more balanced perspective. Nothing wrong with wanting to have creative control, but in the process, you may be alienating potential supporters and limiting your own expansion. Certain aspects of this mission could benefit from some outside input. Consider a team-oriented approach. The trick is to delegate to savvy, capable people, even if you have to train them on your specifications.

### SUN IN GEMINI (2:55PM) (MAY 20-JUN 20)

Unleash your journalistic curiosity as the Sun sashays into inquisitive Gemini for the next month. This buzzy, intellectual solar cycle makes us want to interact and know all the details about one another. Ask the questions, yes, even the nosy ones, in the name of getting to the bottom of who you're dealing with. The only catch? If you plan to pry, be prepared to have other people "in your business," too. Gemini, the sign of the Twins, unites kindred spirits. The best place to start searching for them is right in your own backyard. During Gemini season, the local scene usually buzzes with life. But if your neighborhood feels a little too placid, it might be time to stir things up. Collaborate with local venues to inject some fun into the community vibe. From mural painting to karaoke nights to outdoor concerts, it won't be hard to find willing playmates to help you bring events to life.

## MAY 22 VENUS-MARS TRINE

Cosmic lovebirds Venus and Mars dance a passionate tango as they flow into a "fire trine," which is a pulse-quickening 120-degree angle. Planning a date? Detour away from the usual places! Single? Steer clear of the usual suspects. With Venus in adventurous Aries and firecracker Mars in playful Leo, the new and unexplored will be a total turn-on. Need to have an honest chat about the state of your union? In these outspoken fire signs, Venus and Mars pull no punches. We'll all be a lot more unrestrained, which will certainly be exhilarating, but maybe not the best when it comes to setting boundaries. Couples can harness this energy to get started on a co-created project. From renovating the kitchen to starting a YouTube channel to planning a summer vacation with your friend group, put your heads together and start scheming.

## MAY 24

### SUN-PLUTO TRINE

Seduction is an art form today as the flirtatious Sun in Gemini and heady Pluto in Aquarius make eyes at each other in the sky. There's never a good reason to hide your light, but you don't need to turn it up to full wattage to grab attention. Play up your mystique in small ways. In love, a flash of skin, a suggestive comment, a quick glance—these are all things that can leave people wondering and wanting more. There are plenty of ways to be powerful without using force. With both planets in heady air signs, use your wit and intellect to get to the top.

### MERCURY-URANUS MEETUP

With clever Mercury and disruptor Uranus syncing up in Taurus, today could bring a breakthrough in your work or finances—if you're willing to think outside the box. Embrace a growth mindset and explore innovative ways to make your daily tasks more efficient, perhaps by experimenting with new technology or fresh strategies. This cosmic duo might also ignite a desire for a stylish refresh, whether it's revamping your home décor or updating your spring wardrobe. If you've been feeling stuck creatively, go on a sourcing mission. Window shopping, a walk through a gallery district, perhaps?

## SATURN IN ARIES (MAY 24-SEP 1)

Break new ground! Taskmaster Saturn starts fresh today, moving into Aries for the first time since 1998. This cycle supplies a powerful blend of discipline and drive, pushing you to take bold action while keeping a steady eye on long-term goals. Alas, this won't be a cake walk. Saturn is in "fall" in Aries, one of its least comfortable positions on the zodiac since its measured approach clashes with the restless impatience of Aries. For the next few months, you may struggle—but ultimately succeed—with channeling your passion into a productive effort. Step up as a leader, take responsibility for your actions, and lay the foundation for future achievements. This short-but-impactful cycle may end on September 1, but it picks up again next year, when Saturn begins its unbroken lap through Aries from February 13, 2026 to April 12, 2028.

## MAY 25-JUN 8 MERCURY IN GEMINI

Mic drops: incoming! Voluble Mercury throws a homecoming rager as it zooms into Gemini and pours a double shot of articulation! There's no time like the present to work on your memoir, record a podcast episode, or build your following with daily Instagram Lives. While Mercury hangs out in the sign of the Twins, it's dynamic duos for the win! Wordplay is foreplay during this cycle and you could woo some fascinating people by adding colorful adjectives and flowery metaphors to your everyday chatter. If you've hit a creative wall, gather your smartest friends. Brainstorms could turn into full-blown mental monsoons—but good luck staying focused for long during this distractible cycle!

## MAY 26 NEW MOON IN GEMINI (11:02PM; 6°06'; SUPERMOON)

Kindred spirits unite! The year's only new moon in Gemini—a potent supermoon—sparks exciting synergies with friends old and new.

Cooperative, communicative vibes are in the air, so ride the wave! When you join forces with people who share your enthusiasm, it feels like 1+1=3. Even better? Neptune and Saturn are at a friendly angle to la luna, guiding you toward collaborators who bring the rare mix of imagination and stability. And you'll have no trouble magnetizing them, thanks to supportive beams from seductive Pluto and friendly Mercury. Whatever words are rattling around in your head need to be articulated. Find a sounding board who will listen without judgment. This cathartic conversation could seed a meaningful media project that blossoms into something bigger over the coming six months.

## MAY 27 MERCURY-PLUTO TRINE

Stay on your tippy toes today. With clever Mercury and perceptive Pluto teaming up in sharp-minded air signs, the atmosphere is buzzing with quick wit and even quicker opinions. Someone could lob a question your way that requires an immediate, strategic response. Keep your answer concise and don't reveal too much. With Pluto in the mix, a touch of mystery can work to your advantage. Drop a hint, and let people ask if they want to know more. If you're trying to uncover someone's true intentions, focus on their body language just as much as their words. Sometimes, what's left unsaid speaks louder than anything.

## MAY 30 SUN-MERCURY MEETUP

Trust your instincts and speak your truth! There's zero room for hesitation today. With the bold Sun and articulate Mercury joining forces in chatty Gemini, your words carry extra weight, making others sit up and take notice. This is your moment to communicate with confidence and charisma, but here's a tip: Steer clear of overpromising or simply telling people what they want to hear. Instead, be genuine and straightforward, delivering your message with conviction. Remember, the best conversations are a two-way street, so be sure to listen as much as you talk to keep the dialogue flowing smoothly.

# June

## MONTHLY HOROSCOPE

**6**

June 2025 is a pivotal month for you, Capricorn, as the cosmos shift focus from career to connection. With the Sun in Gemini until June 20, you're all about efficiency and productivity, perfect for streamlining your day-to-day tasks and tackling those lingering projects. But the real headline arrives on June 9, when Jupiter moves into Cancer for the first time since 2014. This is huge—Jupiter will spend the next year in your relationship zone, expanding your partnerships and helping you form deeper, more meaningful, connections. Whether it's in business or love, expect opportunities to grow and strengthen key relationships. When the Sun joins Jupiter in Cancer at the solstice, it's time to prioritize collaboration over going it alone—lean on others and let teamwork take you further. Mid-month could bring some tension as Jupiter squares Saturn on June 15 and Neptune on June 18, highlighting the need to balance personal connections with your big-picture goals. Don't stress—just take a step back and reassess your priorities. Mars enters Virgo on June 17, giving you the motivation to focus on long-term growth and explore new ideas. By June 24, the Day of Miracles, the Sun and Jupiter align, offering a powerful moment to manifest relationship goals or seal a deal. Jupiter's here to help you build partnerships that last, Capricorn—don't be afraid to let others in!

*Read your extended monthly forecast for life, love, money and career! astrostyle.com*

# JUNE
## Moon Phase Calendar

| SUN | MON | TUE | WED | THU | FRI | SAT |
|---|---|---|---|---|---|---|
| 1<br>♌<br>♍ 11:00PM | 2<br>♍<br>2nd Quarter | 3<br>♍ | 4<br>♍<br>♎ 9:38AM | 5<br>♎ | 6<br>♎<br>♏ 10:23PM | 7<br>♏ |
| 8<br>♏ | 9<br>♏<br>♐ 10:56AM | 10<br>♐ | 11<br>♐ Full Moon<br>3:44AM<br>♐→♑ 9:55PM | 12<br>♑ | 13<br>♑ | 14<br>♑<br>♒ 7:00AM |
| 15<br>♒ | 16<br>♒<br>♓ 2:09PM | 17<br>♓ | 18<br>♓ 4th Quarter<br>♓→♈ 7:08PM | 19<br>♈ | 20<br>♈<br>♉ 9:53PM | 21<br>♉ |
| 22<br>♉<br>♊ 10:57PM | 23<br>♊ | 24<br>♊<br>♋ 11:44PM | 25<br>♋<br>New Moon<br>6:32AM | 26<br>♋ | 27<br>♋<br>♌ 2:05AM | 28<br>♌ |
| 29<br>♌<br>♍ 7:44AM | 30<br>♍ | | | | | |

*Times listed are Eastern US Time Zone*

| KEY | | | |
|---|---|---|---|
| ♈ ARIES | ♌ LEO | ♐ SAGITTARIUS | **FM** FULL MOON |
| ♉ TAURUS | ♍ VIRGO | ♑ CAPRICORN | **NM** NEW MOON |
| ♊ GEMINI | ♎ LIBRA | ♒ AQUARIUS | **LE** LUNAR ECLIPSE |
| ♋ CANCER | ♏ SCORPIO | ♓ PISCES | **SE** SOLAR ECLIPSE |

JUNE 11, 3:44AM
# full moon in
# Sagittarius (20°39')

## SAGITTARIUS FULL MOON CRYSTAL

### BLUE APATITE

This turquoise-hued crystal represents Sagittarian optimism and restores a positive, proactive approach to life. Blue Apatite activates the throat chakra and can help you speak your truth under this live-out-loud full moon.

---

*What's one thing you're celebrating under this full moon?*

---

## SAGITTARIUS FULL MOON = CELEBRATE!

*The spirit of wanderlust*

*Your unvarnished truths*

*Loved ones who live far away*

*The passport stamps you've collected or hope to one day*

*Visionary ideas that you're bringing to life*

*Diversity, inclusivity and cross-cultural connections*

JUNE 25, 6:32AM

# new moon in
# Cancer (4°08')

## CANCER NEW MOON CRYSTAL

### MOONSTONE
Like the moon-ruled sign of Cancer, this iridescent bluish-white stone is associated with the divine feminine and fertility. Moonstone supports with birthing new ideas and tuning in to your destiny.

**6**

*What's one fresh intention you're ready to set under this new moon?*

## CANCER NEW MOON = FOCUS

*Spend time near water*

*Connect to family*

*Get in touch with your emotions*

*Nourish yourself with good food and close friends*

*Spruce up your spaces so you feel at home everywhere*

## June 2025

Longitude & Retrograde Ephemeris [00:00 UT]

| Day | Sid.time | ☉ | ☽ | +12h☽ | ☿ | ♀ | ♂ | ♃ | ♄ | ♅ | ♆ | ♇ | ☊ | ☊ | ⚸ | ⚷ | Day |
|---|---|---|---|---|---|---|---|---|---|---|---|---|---|---|---|---|---|
| **1** Su | 16:38:56 | ♊10°46'17 | ♌15°29'42 | ♌22°00'24 | ♊13°02 | ♈24°55 | ♌21°03 | ♊27°59 | ♈00°29 | ♉28°06 | ♈01°51 | ℞03°39 | ℞23°30 | ℞23°59 | ♏07°20 | ♈25°41 | **1** Su |
| **2** Mo | 16:42:52 | ♊11°43'48 | ♌28°24'54 | ♍04°43'19 | ♊15°13 | ♈25°53 | ♌21°35 | ♊28°13 | ♈00°33 | ♉28°09 | ♈01°52 | ♒03°38 | ♓23°26 | ♓23°57 | ♏07°27 | ♈25°44 | **2** Mo |
| **3** Tu | 16:46:49 | ♊12°41'17 | ♍10°56'38 | ♍17°05'06 | ♊17°24 | ♈26°51 | ♌22°07 | ♊28°26 | ♈00°36 | ♉28°13 | ♈01°54 | ♒03°37 | ♓23°23 | ♓23°56 | ♏07°33 | ♈25°47 | **3** Tu |
| **4** We | 16:50:46 | ♊13°38'45 | ♍23°09'46 | ♍29°10'55 | ♊19°35 | ♈27°50 | ♌22°39 | ♊28°40 | ♈00°40 | ♉28°16 | ♈01°55 | ♒03°36 | ♓23°20 | D 23°56 | ♏07°40 | ♈25°49 | **4** We |
| **5** Th | 16:54:42 | ♊14°36'12 | ♎05°09'36 | ♎11°06'06 | ♊21°44 | ♈28°49 | ♌23°12 | ♊28°53 | ♈00°44 | ♉28°20 | ♈01°55 | ♒03°35 | ♓23°17 | ℞23°56 | ♏07°47 | ♈25°52 | **5** Th |
| **6** Fr | 16:58:39 | ♊15°33'38 | ♎17°01'23 | ♎22°55'41 | ♊23°51 | ♈29°48 | ♌23°44 | ♊29°07 | ♈00°48 | ♉28°23 | ♈01°56 | ♒03°35 | ♓23°14 | ♓23°54 | ♏07°53 | ♈25°55 | **6** Fr |
| **7** Sa | 17:02:35 | ♊16°31'03 | ♎28°49'54 | ♏04°44'10 | ♊25°58 | ♉00°47 | ♌24°17 | ♊29°20 | ♈00°51 | ♉28°26 | ♈01°57 | ♒03°34 | ♓23°11 | ♓23°50 | ♏08°00 | ♈25°57 | **7** Sa |
| **8** Su | 17:06:32 | ♊17°28'27 | ♏10°39'19 | ♏16°35'20 | ♊28°02 | ♉01°47 | ♌24°49 | ♊29°34 | ♈00°54 | ♉28°30 | ♈01°58 | ♒03°33 | ♓23°07 | ♓23°43 | ♏08°07 | ♈26°00 | **8** Su |
| **9** Mo | 17:10:28 | ♊18°25'50 | ♏22°32'58 | ♏28°32'07 | ♋00°05 | ♉02°48 | ♌25°22 | ♊29°48 | ♈00°58 | ♉28°33 | ♈01°59 | ♒03°32 | ♓23°04 | ♓23°34 | ♏08°13 | ♈26°02 | **9** Mo |
| **10** Tu | 17:14:25 | ♊19°23'12 | ♐04°33'24 | ♐10°36'37 | ♋02°05 | ♉03°48 | ♌25°55 | ♋00°01 | ♈01°01 | ♉28°36 | ♈02°00 | ♒03°31 | ♓23°01 | ♓23°22 | ♏08°20 | ♈26°05 | **10** Tu |
| **11** We | 17:18:21 | ♊20°20'33 | ♐16°42'19 | ♐22°50'13 | ♋04°04 | ♉04°49 | ♌26°28 | ♋00°15 | ♈01°04 | ♉28°40 | ♈02°01 | ♒03°30 | ♓22°58 | ♓23°09 | ♏08°27 | ♈26°07 | **11** We |
| **12** Th | 17:22:18 | ♊21°17'53 | ♐29°00'47 | ♑05°13'41 | ♋06°00 | ♉05°50 | ♌27°01 | ♋00°28 | ♈01°07 | ♉28°43 | ♈02°01 | ♒03°29 | ♓22°55 | ♓22°55 | ♏08°33 | ♈26°09 | **12** Th |
| **13** Fr | 17:26:15 | ♊22°15'12 | ♑11°29'22 | ♑17°47'29 | ♋07°54 | ♉06°52 | ♌27°34 | ♋00°42 | ♈01°10 | ♉28°46 | ♈02°02 | ♒03°28 | ♓22°51 | ♓22°43 | ♏08°40 | ♈26°12 | **13** Fr |
| **14** Sa | 17:30:11 | ♊23°12'32 | ♑24°08'28 | ♒00°32'00 | ♋09°46 | ♉07°54 | ♌28°07 | ♋00°56 | ♈01°13 | ♉28°50 | ♈02°03 | ♒03°27 | ♓22°48 | ♓22°32 | ♏08°47 | ♈26°14 | **14** Sa |
| **15** Su | 17:34:08 | ♊24°09'50 | ♒06°58'34 | ♒13°27'52 | ♋11°35 | ♉08°56 | ♌28°41 | ♋01°09 | ♈01°16 | ♉28°53 | ♈02°04 | ♒03°26 | ♓22°45 | ♓22°24 | ♏08°54 | ♈26°16 | **15** Su |
| **16** Mo | 17:38:04 | ♊25°07'08 | ♒20°00'28 | ♒26°36'05 | ♋13°22 | ♉09°58 | ♌29°14 | ♋01°23 | ♈01°19 | ♉28°56 | ♈02°04 | ♒03°25 | ♓22°42 | ♓22°19 | ♏09°00 | ♈26°18 | **16** Mo |
| **17** Tu | 17:42:01 | ♊26°04'26 | ♓03°15'22 | ♓09°58'04 | ♋15°07 | ♉11°01 | ♌29°47 | ♋01°37 | ♈01°21 | ♉28°59 | ♈02°05 | ♒03°24 | ♓22°39 | ♓22°16 | ♏09°07 | ♈26°21 | **17** Tu |
| **18** We | 17:45:57 | ♊27°01'42 | ♓16°44'48 | ♓23°35'20 | ♋16°49 | ♉12°03 | ♍00°21 | ♋01°50 | ♈01°24 | ♉29°03 | ♈02°05 | ♒03°23 | ♓22°36 | ♓22°15 | ♏09°14 | ♈26°23 | **18** We |
| **19** Th | 17:49:54 | ♊27°58'59 | ♈00°30'16 | ♈07°29'16 | ♋18°28 | ♉13°06 | ♍00°55 | ♋02°04 | ♈01°26 | ♉29°06 | ♈02°06 | ♒03°22 | ♓22°32 | ♓22°15 | ♏09°20 | ♈26°25 | **19** Th |
| **20** Fr | 17:53:50 | ♊28°56'16 | ♈14°32'48 | ♈21°40'20 | ♋20°05 | ♉14°10 | ♍01°29 | ♋02°18 | ♈01°29 | ♉29°09 | ♈02°06 | ♒03°21 | ♓22°29 | ♓22°15 | ♏09°27 | ♈26°27 | **20** Fr |
| **21** Sa | 17:57:47 | ♊29°53'33 | ♈28°52'09 | ♉06°07'29 | ♋21°40 | ♉15°13 | ♍02°02 | ♋02°31 | ♈01°31 | ♉29°12 | ♈02°07 | ♒03°20 | ♓22°26 | ♓22°12 | ♏09°34 | ♈26°29 | **21** Sa |
| **22** Su | 18:01:44 | ♋00°50'49 | ♉13°26'18 | ♉20°47'31 | ♋23°12 | ♉16°17 | ♍02°36 | ♋02°45 | ♈01°33 | ♉29°15 | ♈02°07 | ♒03°19 | ♓22°23 | ♓22°08 | ♏09°40 | ♈26°31 | **22** Su |
| **23** Mo | 18:05:40 | ♋01°48'06 | ♉28°10'51 | ♊05°34'57 | ♋24°42 | ♉17°21 | ♍03°10 | ♋02°59 | ♈01°35 | ♉29°18 | ♈02°08 | ♒03°18 | ♓22°20 | ♓22°01 | ♏09°47 | ♈26°33 | **23** Mo |
| **24** Tu | 18:09:37 | ♋02°45'22 | ♊12°59'16 | ♊20°22'19 | ♋26°09 | ♉18°25 | ♍03°44 | ♋03°13 | ♈01°37 | ♉29°21 | ♈02°08 | ♒03°16 | ♓22°17 | ♓21°51 | ♏09°54 | ♈26°35 | **24** Tu |
| **25** We | 18:13:33 | ♋03°42'38 | ♊27°43'30 | ♋05°01'19 | ♋27°34 | ♉19°29 | ♍04°19 | ♋03°26 | ♈01°39 | ♉29°24 | ♈02°08 | ♒03°15 | ♓22°13 | ♓21°40 | ♏10°00 | ♈26°36 | **25** We |
| **26** Th | 18:17:30 | ♋04°39'54 | ♋12°15'17 | ♋19°24'07 | ♋28°56 | ♉20°34 | ♍04°53 | ♋03°40 | ♈01°41 | ♉29°27 | ♈02°09 | ♒03°14 | ♓22°10 | ♓21°29 | ♏10°07 | ♈26°38 | **26** Th |
| **27** Fr | 18:21:26 | ♋05°37'09 | ♋26°27'37 | ♌03°24'47 | ♌00°15 | ♉21°39 | ♍05°27 | ♋03°54 | ♈01°42 | ♉29°30 | ♈02°09 | ♒03°13 | ♓22°07 | ♓21°20 | ♏10°14 | ♈26°40 | **27** Fr |
| **28** Sa | 18:25:23 | ♋06°34'24 | ♌10°15'45 | ♌16°59'55 | ♌01°32 | ♉22°44 | ♍06°02 | ♋04°07 | ♈01°44 | ♉29°33 | ♈02°09 | ♒03°12 | ♓22°04 | ♓21°12 | ♏10°20 | ♈26°42 | **28** Sa |
| **29** Su | 18:29:19 | ♋07°31'38 | ♌23°37'43 | ♍00°08'53 | ♌02°46 | ♉23°49 | ♍06°36 | ♋04°21 | ♈01°45 | ♉29°36 | ♈02°09 | ♒03°10 | ♓22°01 | ♓21°07 | ♏10°27 | ♈26°43 | **29** Su |
| **30** Mo | 18:33:16 | ♋08°28'52 | ♍06°34'09 | ♍12°53'29 | ♌03°57 | ♉24°54 | ♍07°11 | ♋04°35 | ♈01°47 | ♉29°39 | ♈02°10 | ♒03°09 | ♓21°57 | ♓21°04 | ♏10°34 | ♈26°45 | **30** Mo |
| **Δ Delta** | 01:54:20 | 27°42'35" | 381°04'27" | 380°53'04" | 50°55' | 29°58' | 16°07' | 6°35' | 1°18' | 1°33' | 0°18' | -0°29' | -1°32' | -2°54' | 3°13' | 1°03' | **Delta** |

Ephemeris tables and data provided by **Astro-Seek.com.** All times in UTC.

**JUNE 2025**

| S | M | T | W | T | F | S |
|---|---|---|---|---|---|---|
| 1 | 2 | 3 | 4 | 5 | 6 | 7 |
| 8 | 9 | 10 | 11 | 12 | 13 | 14 |
| 15 | 16 | 17 | 18 | 19 | 20 | 21 |
| 22 | 23 | 24 | 25 | 26 | 27 | 28 |
| 29 | 30 | | | | | |

## MONTHLY INTENTION

## THIS MONTH I WILL...

**6**

**1** SUN

☽♌

♍ 11:00PM

**2** MON

☽♍

Waxing quarter moon in Virgo (11:41PM)

**3** TUE ◑ ♍

---

**4** WED ◑ ♍
♎ **9:38AM**

---

**5** THU ◑ ♎

---

**6** FRI ◑ ♎
♏ **10:23PM**
Venus in Taurus until Jul 4 (12:43AM)

---

**7** SAT ◑ ♏

**JUNE 2025**

| S | M | T | W | T | F | S |
|---|---|---|---|---|---|---|
| 1 | 2 | 3 | 4 | 5 | 6 | 7 |
| 8 | 9 | 10 | 11 | 12 | 13 | 14 |
| 15 | 16 | 17 | 18 | 19 | 20 | 21 |
| 22 | 23 | 24 | 25 | 26 | 27 | 28 |
| 29 | 30 | | | | | |

## WEEKLY INTENTION

## TOP 3 TO-DOS

○

○

○

6

---

**8** SUN ○ ♏

Mercury-Jupiter meetup
Mercury in Cancer until Jun 26 (6:58PM)

---

**9** MON ○ ♏

♐ **10:56AM**
Mercury-Saturn square
Venus-Pluto square
Jupiter in Cancer until Jun 30, 2026 (5:02PM)
Mercury-Neptune square

**10** TUE ○♐

---

**11** WED ○♐
**FULL MOON IN SAGITTARIUS**
**(3:44AM; 20°39′)**
**♑9:55PM**

---

**12** THU ○♑

---

**13** FRI ○♑

---

**14** SAT ○♑
**♒7:00AM**

## JUNE 2025

| S | M | T | W | T | F | S |
|---|---|---|---|---|---|---|
| 1 | 2 | 3 | 4 | 5 | 6 | 7 |
| 8 | 9 | 10 | 11 | 12 | 13 | 14 |
| **15** | **16** | **17** | **18** | **19** | **20** | **21** |
| 22 | 23 | 24 | 25 | 26 | 27 | 28 |
| 29 | 30 | | | | | |

## WEEKLY INTENTION

## TOP 3 TO-DOS

○

○

○

**6**

**15** SUN ◗♒︎

Mars-Uranus square
Jupiter-Saturn square

**16** MON ◗♒︎

♓ 2:09PM

**17** TUE ◐♓

Mars in Virgo until Aug 6 (4:35AM)

---

**18** WED ◐♓

Waning quarter moon in Pisces (3:19PM)
**♈ 7:08PM**
Jupiter-Neptune square

---

**19** THU ◐♈

---

**20** FRI ◐♈
**♉ 9:53PM**
Sun in Cancer (10:42PM)

**CANCER SEASON UNTIL JUL 22**

---

**21** SAT ◐♉

| S | M | T | W | T | F | S |
|---|---|---|---|---|---|---|
| 1 | 2 | 3 | 4 | 5 | 6 | 7 |
| 8 | 9 | 10 | 11 | 12 | 13 | 14 |
| 15 | 16 | 17 | 18 | 19 | 20 | 21 |
| 22 | 23 | 24 | 25 | 26 | 27 | 28 |
| 29 | 30 | | | | | |

## WEEKLY INTENTION

## TOP 3 TO-DOS

◯

◯

◯

**6**

---

**22** SUN                                    ●♉

♊ 10:57PM
Sun-Saturn square

---

**23** MON                                    ●♊

Sun-Neptune square

**24** TUE

●♊
♋ 11:44PM
Sun-Jupiter meetup
The Day of Miracles

---

**25** WED

●♋
## NEW MOON IN CANCER
(6:31AM;4°08')

---

**26** THU

●♋
Mercury in Leo until Sep 2 (3:09PM)

---

**27** FRI

●♋
♌ 2:05AM
Mercury-Saturn trine

---

**28** SAT

●♌
Mercury-Neptune trine

**JUNE 2025**

| S | M | T | W | T | F | S |
|---|---|---|---|---|---|---|
| 1 | 2 | 3 | 4 | 5 | 6 | 7 |
| 8 | 9 | 10 | 11 | 12 | 13 | 14 |
| 15 | 16 | 17 | 18 | 19 | 20 | 21 |
| 22 | 23 | 24 | 25 | 26 | 27 | 28 |
| 29 | 30 | | | | | |

## WEEKLY INTENTION

## TOP 3 TO-DOS

○

○

○

**29** SUN

◑♌

♍ 7:44AM

Mercury-Pluto opposition

**30** MON

◑♍

**6**

# JUNE
## MONTHLY HOTSPOTS

### JUN 2 WAXING QUARTER MOON IN VIRGO (11:40PM)
Grab the magnifying glass and take a closer look. With the waxing quarter moon in discerning Virgo, every flaw and imperfection that might have slipped past you earlier is now coming into focus. Last week's Gemini new moon may have sparked a flurry of new ideas, but now it's time to back them up with a practical plan. Fine-tune your strategy and put a step-by-step strategy in place. Before you finalize anything, take the time to carefully review your work and ensure it's polished to perfection. Since Virgo also rules health and wellness, it's the perfect moment to start integrating clean and green habits into your summer routine. Let this cosmic energy support your journey to a healthier, more organized lifestyle.

### JUN 6-JUL 4 VENUS IN TAURUS
Sweet sensuality is in the air! Affectionate Venus returns to her cozy home in tactile Taurus, awakening our senses and whetting our appetites for all things luxurious. This is the time to indulge in life's earthy luxuries, from a plant-based meal to the vivid hues of seasonal flowers. Pamper yourself and spoil those you love, because "too much of a good thing" feels just right under Taurus's influence. Relationships can also deepen and become more serious during this stabilizing transit, as Taurus's traditional energy encourages lasting connections and grounded commitments.

## JUN 8

### MERCURY-JUPITER MEETUP

The cosmic muse is coming through the loudspeaker today
as communicator Mercury teams up with expansive Jupiter in
curious Gemini. With these two effervescent planets joining
forces, your words will flow effortlessly, making it a breeze to get
conversations started. Ask plenty of thoughtful questions and be
sure to open up and share what's on your mind. You never know
where a kindred spirit connection might lead. Skip the small talk
and dive into broad, intellectual conversations. You're in for a
meeting of the minds that could spark something truly special.

### MERCURY IN CANCER (JUN 8-26)

Clarify your boundaries and keep personal intel under wraps. With
communicator Mercury nesting in sentimental Cancer for the next few
weeks, extreme privacy is the best policy. Take time to create a solid
emotional bond with people before revealing your innermost thoughts.
If you've been pondering a social media break, consider taking the
month of June off from scrolling and posting. (Your meals will still be
memorable even if you don't share them with the world!) Channel
your energy into zhushing your space to make it both streamlined and
cozy. Make a gallery wall of cherished family photos, update to smart
gadgets, liven up rooms with verdant houseplants and colorful textiles.

## JUN 9

### MERCURY-SATURN SQUARE

Defensive much? You could lash out at the slightest provocation
under today's thin-skinned square between Mercury in Cancer
and Saturn in prickly Aries. Don't jump to conclusions about other
people's motives. Even if their actions appear inconsiderate, there
could be more to the story than you initially realize. Knee-jerk
reactions could come back to bite you. When you find yourself
resisting something "on principle," take a look at what that might
really be about. Are you afraid of losing control or being exposed

as not having all the answers? Keep the imposter syndrome in
check but do make sure you've done all your homework.

## VENUS-PLUTO SQUARE

Watch out for power struggles and emotional battles as sensual Venus in
Taurus squares off with icy Pluto in Aquarius. While it's tempting to push
back against someone's domineering behavior, think twice. Matching
their aggression will only add fuel to the fire, deepening any rifts.
Instead, try to uncover the root issue driving this friction. Spoiler alert: It
might just trace back to an old childhood wound (doesn't it always?).
You might find yourself obsessing over someone who's wronged you,
which could lead to impulsive behavior like firing off a heated text or
trolling their social media. If you're in a solid relationship, you might feel
the urge to push bae's buttons just keep things "exciting." Be sure you
know what you're getting into before you awaken any sleeping giants.

## JUPITER IN CANCER (JUN 9-JUN 30, 2026)

Surf's up! Big-hearted, philosophical Jupiter sets sail on nurturing
Cancer's emotion ocean—its first visit to this sign since 2014! As the
red-spotted planet sounds a global call for empathy, kindness and
compassion are en vogue again. Home and family ties take center
stage during this yearlong transit. Now's the time to create a sanctuary
that nurtures you soul, but that doesn't mean you'll be stuck inside
the same four walls. Reconnect to long-distance relatives or take a
life-changing trip to your ancestral homeland. Jupiter is "exalted" in
Cancer, making this its most powerful position in the zodiac. Jupiter
in domestic Cancer can heat up the residential real estate market
while also creating greater opportunities for first-time home buyers.
Fiscal security is also highlighted, so start tucking away more funds
in your investment accounts. Need to make more bank? Home-
based businesses are blessed by enterprising Jupiter in Cancer.

## MERCURY-NEPTUNE SQUARE

Your logical left brain battles your intuitive right brain as analytical
Mercury in Cancer squares off with subliminal Neptune in Aries. This
clash could leave you torn between following standard operating

procedures or scrapping the safe route to go follow your gut instincts. And with both planets in take-charge cardinal signs, your ego might be having too loud of a say. To cut through the confusion, think about how your choice will impact your life in ten minutes, ten months, and ten years. You might be surprised by the clarity it brings!

## JUN 11 FULL MOON IN SAGITTARIUS (3:44AM; 20°39')

Modesty, schmodesty. There's almost no way to be "too much" under the supersizing influence of the year's only full moon in Sagittarius. Stretch beyond the limits of what's safe and familiar. With daredevil Mars fistbumping the full moon, this could bring untold rewards over the coming two weeks. (Just make sure you know the difference between a "savvy risk" and a "foolish gamble.") If you have the time and means, pack your bags for an epic getaway. Otherwise, broaden your horizons through summer classes, personal growth work and diverse experiences that push you into inspiring new terrain. Nothing ventured, nothing gained!

## JUN 15

### MARS-URANUS SQUARE

Negotiate? Not today! As unruly Uranus in stubborn Taurus battles fiery Mars in proud Leo, tensions are bound to escalate. The battle lines are drawn, and neither side seems eager to wave the white flag. Do your best to stay mindful and avoid burning any bridges you might need to cross later. Patience will be your saving grace today!

### JUPITER-SATURN SQUARE

Your ego is not your amigo, but good luck remembering that today! As hypersensitive Jupiter in Cancer combats authoritative Saturn in Aries, pride steers the ship and people can be downright petty. Don't waste time trying to reason with narcissists, especially when adulting is a distant dream. Better to let everyone sulk (or fume!) in their corners. You can approach the topic again—or not!—once the storm clears. While you wait for molehills to stop looking like mountains, see if you can find a common cause. While you may have very different approaches for achieving an end goal, do you actually want the same thing? Focusing on that may be the saving grace today—especially with someone you consider "family."

## JUN 17-AUG 6 MARS IN VIRGO

Order in the court! As action-oriented Mars charges into detail-driven Virgo, the next month and a half is optimized for efficiency. Turn your lofty ideas into actionable plans, complete with budgets and schedules. This health-focused, fix-it-fast transit motivates you to improve every aspect of your life, from your eating habits to your workflow. There's no better time to push a wellness routine in place as Mars supplies the motivation and Virgo helps you track results and stick to a regimen. Expect a surge in productive energy, but be mindful of how you come across when doling out advice. You might sound more critical than you mean to, especially since Mars in Virgo can make us all especially judgmental. Keep this in mind: You'll attract more flies with honey than with your "helpful hints."

## JUN 18

### WANING QUARTER MOON IN PISCES (3:19PM)

Stuck in a creative logjam? Today's imaginative quarter moon in Pisces gets inspiration flowing. Before you start sourcing ideas from art and fashion feeds, put down your phone and fully immerse yourself in every sensation around you. Under this meditative transit, you need less input and more quiet time. If you're looking to turn dreams into reality, Pisces' manifesting energy is on your side. A supportive person may be just a text (or a thought!) away. Don't be surprised if someone crosses your mind and then you bump into them shortly after—this is a day made for serendipity. If burnout is creeping in, book a healing treatment or head home early to recharge.

### JUPITER-NEPTUNE SQUARE

What's the big idea? As visionary Jupiter plays tug-of-war with spiritual Neptune, it breaks our thinking out of the box. Fresh possibilities could become tangible realities at an accelerated pace. But tap the sensitivity of Neptune and weigh it against the gung-ho momentum of Jupiter. It's great to blaze trails, but how will new developments affect the ecosystem of your life? If you forgot to consider feelings or ask for consent, you may need to revise plans. But that's not the same as people-pleasing! If you're hiding your truth because you don't want to make people "feel bad," play with being self-authorized and making a bold move.

### JUN 20-JUL 22 SUN IN CANCER (10:42PM)

Happy Solstice! The Sun reaches its highest point in the northern hemisphere, signaling the start of Cancer season each year. For the next month, we'll all radiate feelings of warmth, connection and nourishment that are hallmarks of this water sign. Home is where the heart is now, so get your space set up for both nesting and guesting. Has it been a while since you've visited beloved relatives and your oldest, dearest friends? Tap the nostalgic vibes of Cancer season and meet up for picnics, beach days or longer visits to your hometown. Tender emotions may surface regularly but don't keep them in. Cathartic Marco Polos with your besties can keep you sane when everyone else is spiraling.

### JUN 22 SUN-SATURN SQUARE

If your stomach is in knots, don't reflexively reach for the probiotics. It's Cancer season and your symptoms may be a reflection of what's happening in your emotional life. Have you been biting your tongue and keeping your opinions to yourself? Perhaps you've been swallowing your feelings when the going gets tough. Today's remedy: Stop and listen to your own internal dialogue, the way a nurturing parent would soothe a child. Something needs to change here, but first, give yourself permission to be (privately) annoyed, frustrated or irritated without feeling guilty. After that, Saturn in Aries helps you get proactive. The goal is to implement changes in a wise, mature and measured way.

### JUN 23 SUN-NEPTUNE SQUARE

Martyr alert! As the Sun in compassionate Cancer gets snared by sacrificial Neptune in Aries, everyone's doing the most. Do your best to NOT get sucked in. This "competitive caretaking" could leave you feeling put upon, exhausted and unappreciated for all your genuine efforts.

Do an internal audit: Are you asking too much of people? (Even if they "owe" you.) Keeping score? Perhaps it's time to slow down a little, take a break, and stop trying to accomplish everything at warp speed. If you start operating at a more human pace, you might find that others are happy to get on board and help.

## JUN 24 SUN-JUPITER MEETUP, THE DAY OF MIRACLES
Energy and optimism reign as the magnanimous Sun and generous Jupiter align for their once-per-year cazimi meetup. For the first time in over a decade, they're joining forces in nurturing Cancer, shining lucky rays on home, family and personal finances. If you've been searching for a new place to call home, the perfect listing could appear or maybe you'll finally bury the hatchet with a beloved relative. On this "Day of Miracles," the Sun and Jupiter cast a rosy, can-do glow over all endeavors. Embrace this positive momentum and find new ways to uplift others and share your light with the world.

## JUN 25 NEW MOON IN CANCER (6:32AM; 4°08')
Serve it up, family-style! The year's only new moon in Cancer sets the stage for close-knit bonding. If you're the type who's "never met a stranger," you may want to tighten up the radius of your inner circle so you can devote quality attention to the unwavering supporters in your life. Over the next two weeks, find ways to sing their praises and make sure they get the VIP treatment from you. Spending time near water will be especially rejuvenating now, so reply "yes" to those pool parties and beach weekends! On the home front, this nurturing new moon might reveal a dreamy real estate opportunity or inspire an interior design makeover. Whether you're cleaning out your storage spaces or doing a soul-soothing house-blessing ritual, now's the perfect time for a midyear energy cleanse to refresh your most sacred spaces. Just be careful not to bite off more than you can chew! This new moon aligns with maximizer Jupiter and clashes with Saturn and Neptune in impulsive Aries, which can give your projects "scope creep" or set the stage for unrealistic expectations.

## JUN 26-SEP 2 MERCURY IN LEO

Curtains up! Social Mercury struts into playful and passionate Leo, turning up the heat on your summer fun. If your calendar suddenly fills with beach parties and your creativity skyrockets, you can thank Mercury's lively jaunt through this colorful sign's terrain. For the first part of this cycle, express yourself with warmth, excitement, and maybe even a touch of theatrical flair. But here's a head's up: From July 18 to August 11, Mercury will spin into a summer retrograde through Leo, marking three weeks where dialing DOWN the drama will be imperative. Try to resolve any brewing tension before then. If you're pitching an idea or giving a presentation, lean into storytelling and bold visuals to drive your message home.

## JUN 27 MERCURY-SATURN TRINE

Speak with conviction and you'll be unstoppable! As communicator Mercury in Leo dances into a potent fire trine with disciplined Saturn in Aries, present yourself with authority and confidence. This is your chance to back up your words with action and prove to your peers that you're someone who delivers. By coming through with the complete package, you could secure a sought-after opportunity, or at the very least, earn the respect of the MVPs.

## JUN 28 MERCURY-NEPTUNE TRINE

Mercury in Leo and Neptune in Aries form a powerful fire trine today, fueling your creativity and intuition with bold, assertive energy. This dynamic alignment pushes you to step up and take charge, using both confidence and insight to make an impact. While setting boundaries might feel secondary, harness this strong-willed energy to be both a commanding presence and a supportive listener. Rather than jumping in with solutions, let others speak their truth, showing them that you're fully engaged. To sharpen your own divine connection, try a moving meditation like yoga or a quiet hike. As you do, ask your guides for unmistakable signs that will propel you toward your highest path.

# 6

## JUN 29 MERCURY-PLUTO OPPOSITION

What's really going on here? Today's triggering cosmic energy could push all your buttons, as people attempt to play mental chess and veil their true intentions. With calculating Pluto opposing communicator Mercury, it's best to keep things close to the vest and avoid making assumptions. Even if your observational skills are sharp, the full story might be more complicated than it appears. Even the most basic exchanges could be riddled with suggestive tones and innuendoes. Instead of trying to decode what someone's really saying, just ask, "What do you mean?" and let them do the explaining. If a power struggle starts to simmer, bow out gracefully before things get heated.

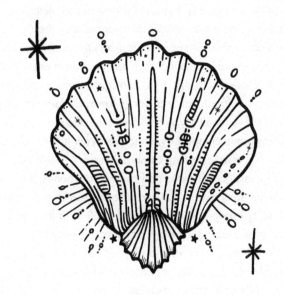

# July

## MONTHLY HOROSCOPE

Make it a double! While the Sun copilots alongside expansive Jupiter in Cancer until the 22nd, some of your most meaningful progress will happen through close, one-on-one interactions. Seek out powerful allies from the boardroom to the bedroom. You're building something that needs a strong foundation, and collaboration will be key. On July 7, unpredictable Uranus shifts into Gemini and your sixth house of work, wellness, and daily routines, where it will remain until November 7. Prepare for some shake-ups in your day-to-day life. This six-month preview is just a taste of the larger cycle of change that Uranus will bring starting in April 2026. During this innovative cycle, you may find yourself drawn to completely new methods of working or adopting unconventional approaches to health and wellness. A little chaos can create the space for radical improvements. Adding to the introspective energy of the month, Neptune, Saturn and Chiron all turn retrograde in Aries—on the 4th, 13th, and 30th, respectively—focusing their energy in your fourth house of home, family and emotional security. Over these next five months, you could reconnect to your roots while also navigating some complex dynamics with your inner circle. Set clear boundaries while also remaining compassionate. That will be the key to healing any generational trauma and childhood wounds. You're on the prowl for soulful, sexy exchanges once Leo Season begins on the 22nd. But with Mercury retrograde, also in Leo, from July 18 to August 11, your eighth house of secrets, power plays and erotic energy is getting a bit of a shakeup. Wires may cross around shared finances or deeply personal matters. Double-check the fine print and even lawyer up if you need to sign anything. Mercury retrograde is also notorious for bringing back old flames. Careful not to rekindle anything that was once toxic. The "excitement" isn't worth the price.

*Read your extended monthly forecast for life, love, money and career! astrostyle.com*

# JULY
## Moon Phase Calendar

| SUN | MON | TUE | WED | THU | FRI | SAT |
|-----|-----|-----|-----|-----|-----|-----|
| | | **1** ♍ 5:16PM | **2** ♎ 2nd Quarter | **3** ♎ | **4** ♏ 5:33AM | **5** ♏ |
| **6** ♏ 6:06PM | **7** ♐ | **8** ♐ | **9** ♐ 4:55AM | **10** ♑ Full Moon 4:37PM | **11** ♒ 1:21PM | **12** ♒ |
| **13** ♒ 7:45PM | **14** ♓ | **15** ♓ | **16** ♓ ♈ 12:32AM | **17** ♈ 4th Quarter | **18** ♈ ♉ 3:59AM | **19** ♉ |
| **20** ♉ ♊ 6:22AM | **21** ♊ | **22** ♊ ♋ 8:26AM | **23** ♋ | **24** ♋→♌ 11:28AM ♌ New Moon 3:11PM | **25** ♌ | **26** ♌ ♍ 4:55PM |
| **27** ♍ | **28** ♍ | **29** ♍ ♎ 1:43AM | **30** ♎ | **31** ♎ ♏ 1:25PM | | |

*Times listed are Eastern US Time Zone*

## KEY

| | | | | | |
|---|---|---|---|---|---|
| ♈ ARIES | ♌ LEO | ♐ SAGITTARIUS | **FM** FULL MOON | | |
| ♉ TAURUS | ♍ VIRGO | ♑ CAPRICORN | **NM** NEW MOON | | |
| ♊ GEMINI | ♎ LIBRA | ♒ AQUARIUS | **LE** LUNAR ECLIPSE | | |
| ♋ CANCER | ♏ SCORPIO | ♓ PISCES | **SE** SOLAR ECLIPSE | | |

JULY 10, 4:37PM
# full moon in
# Capricorn (18°50')

## CAPRICORN FULL MOON CRYSTAL

### AZURITE
This pebbled blue and green stone is excellent for supporting concentration and getting you motivated for those Capricorn-fueled missions. Azurite clears your mind of distractions, sharpens mental powers and increases access to your innate wisdom.

**What's one thing you're celebrating under this full moon?**

## CAPRICORN FULL MOON = CELEBRATE!

*Your current milestones and wins*

*Your competitive edge*

*Perseverance*

*Time outdoors and in nature*

*The people who champion you and help you grow*

*The places where you feel confident taking charge and leading the troops*

*Diversity, inclusivity and cross-cultural connections*

JULY 24, 3:11 PM

# new moon in
# Leo (2°08′)

## LEO
## NEW MOON
## CRYSTAL

### CITRINE
Golden Citrine glows with the regal, joy-inducing hue of Leo! This stone boosts ambition and self-esteem while helping you attract abundance during one of the most creative seasons of the year.

**What's one fresh intention you're ready to set under this new moon?**

## LEO NEW MOON = FOCUS

*Find your place to shine*

*Spend time with kids*

*Take a leadership role*

*Host and attend glamorous parties*

*Enjoy romance and playtime*

**July 2025**

Longitude & Retrograde Ephemeris [00:00 UT]

| Day | Sid.time | ☉ | ☽ | +12h☽ | ☿ | ♀ | ♂ | ♃ | ♄ | ♅ | ♆ | ♇ | ☊ | ☊ | ⚸ | ⚷ | Day |
|---|---|---|---|---|---|---|---|---|---|---|---|---|---|---|---|---|---|
| **1** Tu | 18:37:13 | ♋09°26'06 | ♍19°07'48 | ♍25°17'15 | ℞s 05°06 | ♉26°00 | ♍07°46 | ♋04°48 | ♈01°48 | ♉29°42 | ♈02°10 | ℞ 03°08 | ℞ 21°54 | ℞ 21°03 | ♏10°41 | ♈26°46 | **1** Tu |
| **2** We | 18:41:09 | ♋10°23'19 | ♎01°22'50 | ♎07°24'50 | ♌06°11 | ♉27°05 | ♍08°20 | ♋05°02 | ♈01°49 | ♉29°45 | ♈02°10 | ♒03°07 | ♓21°51 | D 21°03 | ♏10°47 | ♈26°48 | **2** We |
| **3** Th | 18:45:06 | ♋11°20'32 | ♎13°24'18 | ♎19°21'29 | ♌07°14 | ♉28°11 | ♍08°55 | ♋05°16 | ♈01°50 | ♉29°48 | ♈02°10 | ♒03°05 | ♓21°48 | ℞ 21°04 | ♏10°54 | ♈26°49 | **3** Th |
| **4** Fr | 18:49:02 | ♋12°17'44 | ♎25°17'27 | ♏01°12'29 | ♌08°13 | ♉29°17 | ♍09°30 | ♋05°29 | ♈01°51 | ♉29°50 | ♈02°10 | ♒03°04 | ♓21°45 | ♓21°03 | ♏11°01 | ♈26°51 | **4** Fr |
| **5** Sa | 18:52:59 | ♋13°14'56 | ♏07°07'33 | ♏13°02'53 | ♌09°09 | ♊00°23 | ♍10°05 | ♋05°43 | ♈01°52 | ♉29°53 | ℞ 02°10 | ♒03°03 | ♓21°42 | ♓21°00 | ♏11°07 | ♈26°52 | **5** Sa |
| **6** Su | 18:56:55 | ♋14°12'08 | ♏18°59'24 | ♏24°57'12 | ♌10°02 | ♊01°29 | ♍10°40 | ♋05°57 | ♈01°53 | ♉29°56 | ♈02°10 | ♒03°02 | ♓21°38 | ♓20°55 | ♏11°14 | ♈26°53 | **6** Su |
| **7** Mo | 19:00:52 | ♋15°09'20 | ♐00°57'07 | ♐06°59'11 | ♌10°52 | ♊02°36 | ♍11°15 | ♋06°10 | ♈01°54 | ♉29°59 | ♈02°10 | ♒03°00 | ♓21°35 | ♓20°48 | ♏11°21 | ♈26°55 | **7** Mo |
| **8** Tu | 19:04:48 | ♋16°06'32 | ♐13°04'04 | ♐19°11'41 | ♌11°38 | ♊03°42 | ♍11°51 | ♋06°24 | ♈01°54 | ♊00°01 | ♈02°10 | ♒02°59 | ♓21°32 | ♓20°38 | ♏11°27 | ♈26°56 | **8** Tu |
| **9** We | 19:08:45 | ♋17°03'44 | ♐25°22'36 | ♑01°36'34 | ♌12°20 | ♊04°49 | ♍12°26 | ♋06°37 | ♈01°55 | ♊00°04 | ♈02°10 | ♒02°58 | ♓21°29 | ♓20°28 | ♏11°34 | ♈26°57 | **9** We |
| **10** Th | 19:12:42 | ♋18°00'55 | ♑07°54'03 | ♑14°14'43 | ♌12°59 | ♊05°56 | ♍13°01 | ♋06°51 | ♈01°55 | ♊00°07 | ♈02°10 | ♒02°56 | ♓21°26 | ♓20°17 | ♏11°41 | ♈26°58 | **10** Th |
| **11** Fr | 19:16:38 | ♋18°58'07 | ♑20°38'53 | ♑27°06'09 | ♌13°33 | ♊07°03 | ♍13°37 | ♋07°05 | ♈01°55 | ♊00°09 | ♈02°09 | ♒02°55 | ♓21°23 | ♓20°06 | ♏11°47 | ♈26°59 | **11** Fr |
| **12** Sa | 19:20:35 | ♋19°55'19 | ♒03°36'47 | ♒10°10'18 | ♌14°04 | ♊08°10 | ♍14°12 | ♋07°18 | ♈01°55 | ♊00°12 | ♈02°09 | ♒02°53 | ♓21°19 | ♓19°57 | ♏11°54 | ♈27°00 | **12** Sa |
| **13** Su | 19:24:31 | ♋20°52'32 | ♒16°46'59 | ♒23°26'19 | ♌14°30 | ♊09°17 | ♍14°48 | ♋07°32 | ♈01°56 | ♊00°14 | ♈02°09 | ♒02°52 | ♓21°16 | ♓19°51 | ♏12°01 | ♈27°01 | **13** Su |
| **14** Mo | 19:28:28 | ♋21°49'44 | ♓00°08'37 | ♓06°53'21 | ♌14°52 | ♊10°24 | ♍15°24 | ♋07°45 | ℞ 01°56 | ♊00°17 | ♈02°09 | ♒02°51 | ♓21°13 | ♓19°47 | ♏12°08 | ♈27°02 | **14** Mo |
| **15** Tu | 19:32:24 | ♋22°46'57 | ♓13°40'55 | ♓20°30'48 | ♌15°09 | ♊11°32 | ♍15°59 | ♋07°58 | ♈01°55 | ♊00°19 | ♈02°08 | ♒02°49 | ♓21°10 | ♓19°45 | ♏12°14 | ♈27°03 | **15** Tu |
| **16** We | 19:36:21 | ♋23°44'11 | ♓27°23'26 | ♈04°18'20 | ♌15°22 | ♊12°39 | ♍16°35 | ♋08°12 | ♈01°55 | ♊00°22 | ♈02°08 | ♒02°48 | ♓21°07 | D 19°45 | ♏12°21 | ♈27°04 | **16** We |
| **17** Th | 19:40:18 | ♋24°41'25 | ♈11°15'56 | ♈18°15'44 | ♌15°31 | ♊13°47 | ♍17°11 | ♋08°25 | ♈01°55 | ♊00°24 | ♈02°08 | ♒02°47 | ♓21°03 | ♓19°46 | ♏12°28 | ♈27°04 | **17** Th |
| **18** Fr | 19:44:14 | ♋25°38'40 | ♈25°18'07 | ♉02°22'33 | ♌15°34 | ♊14°55 | ♍17°47 | ♋08°39 | ♈01°54 | ♊00°26 | ♈02°07 | ♒02°45 | ♓21°00 | ♓19°47 | ♏12°34 | ♈27°05 | **18** Fr |
| **19** Sa | 19:48:11 | ♋26°35'55 | ♉09°29'18 | ♉16°37'41 | ℞ 15°32 | ♊16°03 | ♍18°23 | ♋08°52 | ♈01°54 | ♊00°29 | ♈02°07 | ♒02°44 | ♓20°57 | ℞ 19°46 | ♏12°41 | ♈27°06 | **19** Sa |
| **20** Su | 19:52:07 | ♋27°33'12 | ♉23°47'50 | ♊00°58'54 | ♌15°26 | ♊17°11 | ♍18°59 | ♋09°05 | ♈01°53 | ♊00°31 | ♈02°06 | ♒02°42 | ♓20°54 | ♓19°43 | ♏12°48 | ♈27°06 | **20** Su |
| **21** Mo | 19:56:04 | ♋28°30'29 | ♊08°10'52 | ♊15°22'42 | ♌15°15 | ♊18°20 | ♍19°35 | ♋09°19 | ♈01°52 | ♊00°33 | ♈02°06 | ♒02°41 | ♓20°51 | ♓19°39 | ♏12°54 | ♈27°07 | **21** Mo |
| **22** Tu | 20:00:00 | ♋29°27'47 | ♊22°34'15 | ♊29°44'22 | ♌14°59 | ♊19°28 | ♍20°11 | ♋09°32 | ♈01°52 | ♊00°35 | ♈02°05 | ♒02°40 | ♓20°48 | ♓19°32 | ♏13°01 | ♈27°07 | **22** Tu |
| **23** We | 20:03:57 | ♌00°25'06 | ♋06°52'49 | ♋13°58'27 | ♌14°38 | ♊20°36 | ♍20°48 | ♋09°45 | ♈01°51 | ♊00°37 | ♈02°05 | ♒02°38 | ♓20°44 | ♓19°25 | ♏13°08 | ♈27°08 | **23** We |
| **24** Th | 20:07:53 | ♌01°22'26 | ♋21°01'04 | ♋27°59'36 | ♌14°13 | ♊21°45 | ♍21°24 | ♋09°58 | ♈01°50 | ♊00°39 | ♈02°04 | ♒02°37 | ♓20°41 | ♓19°17 | ♏13°14 | ♈27°08 | **24** Th |
| **25** Fr | 20:11:50 | ♌02°19'45 | ♌04°53'59 | ♌11°43'21 | ♌13°44 | ♊22°54 | ♍22°00 | ♋10°11 | ♈01°49 | ♊00°42 | ♈02°04 | ♒02°35 | ♓20°38 | ♓19°10 | ♏13°21 | ♈27°08 | **25** Fr |
| **26** Sa | 20:15:47 | ♌03°17'06 | ♌18°27'48 | ♌25°06'44 | ♌13°10 | ♊24°03 | ♍22°37 | ♋10°24 | ♈01°47 | ♊00°44 | ♈02°03 | ♒02°34 | ♓20°35 | ♓19°05 | ♏13°28 | ♈27°09 | **26** Sa |
| **27** Su | 20:19:43 | ♌04°14'27 | ♍01°40'29 | ♍08°08'41 | ♌12°34 | ♊25°11 | ♍23°14 | ♋10°38 | ♈01°46 | ♊00°46 | ♈02°02 | ♒02°32 | ♓20°32 | ♓19°01 | ♏13°35 | ♈27°09 | **27** Su |
| **28** Mo | 20:23:40 | ♌05°11'49 | ♍14°31'53 | ♍20°49'57 | ♌11°54 | ♊26°20 | ♍23°50 | ♋10°51 | ♈01°45 | ♊00°47 | ♈02°02 | ♒02°31 | ♓20°29 | ♓19°00 | ♏13°41 | ♈27°09 | **28** Mo |
| **29** Tu | 20:27:36 | ♌06°09'11 | ♍27°03'37 | ♎03°12'54 | ♌11°12 | ♊27°30 | ♍24°27 | ♋11°04 | ♈01°43 | ♊00°49 | ♈02°01 | ♒02°30 | ♓20°25 | D 19°00 | ♏13°48 | ♈27°09 | **29** Tu |
| **30** We | 20:31:33 | ♌07°06'34 | ♎09°18'40 | ♎15°21'05 | ♌10°29 | ♊28°39 | ♍25°04 | ♋11°16 | ♈01°41 | ♊00°51 | ♈02°00 | ♒02°28 | ♓20°22 | ♓19°01 | ♏13°55 | ♈27°09 | **30** We |
| **31** Th | 20:35:29 | ♌08°03'57 | ♎21°21'05 | ♎27°18'55 | ♌09°44 | ♊29°48 | ♍25°41 | ♋11°29 | ♈01°40 | ♊00°53 | ♈01°59 | ♒02°27 | ♓20°19 | ♓19°03 | ♏14°01 | ℞ 27°09 | **31** Th |
| **Δ Delta** | 01:58:15 | 28°37'51" | 392°13'17" | 392°01'40" | 4°38' | 33°48' | 17°55' | 6°40' | -0°08' | 1°11' | -0°10' | -0°41' | -1°35' | -2°00' | 3°20' | 0°22' | **Delta** |

Ephemeris tables and data provided by **Astro-Seek.com.** All times in UTC.

7

# NOTES & THOUGHTS

**JULY 2025**

| S | M | T | W | T | F | S |
|---|---|---|---|---|---|---|
|   |   | 1 | 2 | 3 | 4 | 5 |
| 6 | 7 | 8 | 9 | 10 | 11 | 12 |
| 13 | 14 | 15 | 16 | 17 | 18 | 19 |
| 20 | 21 | 22 | 23 | 24 | 25 | 26 |
| 27 | 28 | 29 | 30 | 31 |   |   |

## MONTHLY INTENTION

## THIS MONTH I WILL...

7

**1** TUE

◐ ♍︎
♎︎ 5:16PM

---

**2** WED

◑ ♎︎
Waxing quarter moon in Libra (3:30PM)

---

**3** THU

◑ ♎︎

---

**4** FRI

◑ ♎︎
♏︎ 5:33AM
Venus-Uranus meetup
Venus in Gemini until Jul 30 (11:31AM)
Neptune retrograde in Aries until Oct 22 (5:34PM)

---

**5** SAT

○ ♏︎

| S | M | T | W | T | F | S |
|---|---|---|---|---|---|---|
| | | 1 | 2 | 3 | 4 | 5 |
| 6 | 7 | 8 | 9 | 10 | 11 | 12 |
| 13 | 14 | 15 | 16 | 17 | 18 | 19 |
| 20 | 21 | 22 | 23 | 24 | 25 | 26 |
| 27 | 28 | 29 | 30 | 31 | | |

## WEEKLY INTENTION

## TOP 3 TO-DOS

○

○

○

**7**

**6** SUN

○ ♏
⚹ 6:06PM

---

**7** MON

○ ♐
Uranus in Gemini until Nov 7 (3:45AM)
Venus-Pluto trine

**8** TUE ○♐

---

**9** WED ○♐
♑ 4:55AM

---

**10** THU ○♑
**FULL MOON IN CAPRICORN**
(4:37PM; 18°50′)

---

**11** FRI ○♑
♒ 1:21PM

---

**12** SAT ○♒

| S | M | T | W | T | F | S |
|---|---|---|---|---|---|---|
|   |   | 1 | 2 | 3 | 4 | 5 |
| 6 | 7 | 8 | 9 | 10 | 11 | 12 |
| **13** | **14** | **15** | **16** | **17** | **18** | **19** |
| 20 | 21 | 22 | 23 | 24 | 25 | 26 |
| 27 | 28 | 29 | 30 | 31 |   |   |

## WEEKLY INTENTION

## TOP 3 TO-DOS

○

○

○

**7**

**13** SUN ○♒

♓ 7:45PM

Saturn retrograde in Aries until Sep 1 (12:07AM)

**14** MON ○♓

**15** TUE ☽ ♓

---

**16** WED ☽ ♓
♈ 12:32AM

---

**17** THU ☽ ♈
Waning quarter moon in Aries (8:38PM)

---

**18** FRI ☽ ♈
♉ 3:59AM
Mercury retrograde in Leo until Aug 11 (12:45AM)

---

**19** SAT ☽ ♉

## JULY 2025

| S | M | T | W | T | F | S |
|---|---|---|---|---|---|---|
|   |   | 1 | 2 | 3 | 4 | 5 |
| 6 | 7 | 8 | 9 | 10 | 11 | 12 |
| 13 | 14 | 15 | 16 | 17 | 18 | 19 |
| 20 | 21 | 22 | 23 | 24 | 25 | 26 |
| 27 | 28 | 29 | 30 | 31 |   |   |

## WEEKLY INTENTION

## TOP 3 TO-DOS

○

○

○

**7**

**20** SUN ☽♉
♊ 6:22AM

**21** MON ☽♊

**22** TUE

● ♊
♋ 8:26AM
Sun in Leo (9:29AM)

**LEO SEASON UNTIL AUG 22**

---

**23** WED

● ♋
Venus-Mars square

---

**24** THU

● ♋
Sun-Saturn trine
♌ 11:28AM
Sun-Neptune trine
**New Moon in Leo**
(3:11PM; 2°08')

---

**25** FRI

● ♌
Sun-Pluto opposition

---

**26** SAT

● ♌
♍ 4:55PM

**JULY 2025**

| S | M | T | W | T | F | S |
|---|---|---|---|---|---|---|
| | | 1 | 2 | 3 | 4 | 5 |
| 6 | 7 | 8 | 9 | 10 | 11 | 12 |
| 13 | 14 | 15 | 16 | 17 | 18 | 19 |
| 20 | 21 | 22 | 23 | 24 | 25 | 26 |
| 27 | 28 | 29 | 30 | 31 | | |

## WEEKLY INTENTION

## TOP 3 TO-DOS

○

○

○

**27** SUN ●♍

**28** MON ◐♍

**29** TUE

● ♍
♎ 1:43AM

---

**30** WED

◐ ♎
Venus in Cancer until Aug 25 (11:57PM)
Chiron Retrograde until Jan 2, 2026 (10:42AM)

---

**31** THU

◐ ♎
♏ 1:25PM
Sun-Mercury retrograde meetup

---

## NOTES & THOUGHTS

# 7

# JULY
## MONTHLY HOTSPOTS

### JUL 2 WAXING QUARTER MOON IN LIBRA (3:30PM)

No more sweeping that conflict under the rug. It's time to face the music and hopefully drum up a harmonious solution for all. Today's waxing quarter moon is in Libra, the most balanced and strategic of the signs. This can help you navigate any speedbumps on the path to peace. Take a deep breath, because you may have to weather some unpleasant conversations before you can make strides forward. Try not to let your feelings cloud the facts. Be open to other perspectives and don't be afraid to apologize if the fault lies with you. Without shaming or blaming, hold people accountable for their part in the matter. Creative solutions can emerge if you stay focused on finding win-wins.

7

### JUL 4

#### VENUS-URANUS MEETUP

This Independence Day comes with an extra round of fireworks as seductive Venus sets off sparks with renegade Uranus. This free-spirited planetary mashup could inspire you to do something wildly unexpected, especially when it comes to your love life. It's all fun and games until someone crosses a line, so get consent before making any moves. Single and looking? Sparks could ignite with someone who might not normally turn your head. With both planets in sensual earth signs, the spark might begin with a physical attraction that stops you in your tracks.

## VENUS IN GEMINI (11:31AM) (JUL 4-30)

Wordplay is foreplay, as Venus logs into articulate Gemini. Clever conversations and tantalizing text threads can get pulses racing, but don't get stuck in the superficial, flirty zone. During this sapiosexual spell, deep and intellectual exchanges might feel better than (or at least as good as) sex. Feel like pushing boundaries? Go ahead— dive into taboo topics or challenge outdated norms that don't resonate with you. With Venus in this curious sign, the desire to explore new territory is irresistible. Just be mindful of mixed signals, as they're bound to surface during this silver-tongued transit.

## NEPTUNE RETROGRADE (JUL 4-DEC 10)

Peel back the layers of your psyche, as Neptune slips into its annual, five-month retrograde. For the first time since 1875, Neptune spins back through fiery Aries, creating an added sense of urgency around self-care and soul-searching. During this part of the retrograde, which lasts until October 22, confront issues around identity, self-assertion, and how you wield your personal power. You may address impulsive behaviors or reactions that have been masking deeper wounds. When Neptune shifts back into Pisces on October 22— it's last retrograde lap through this sign in our lifetimes—lingering emotional wounds could demand attention. Keep an eye out for energy vampires and codependent dynamics during this boundary-blurring phase through Pisces, which lasts until December 10.

## JULY 7

## URANUS IN GEMINI (JUL 7-NOV 7)

Welcome to the innovation station! For the first time since 1941-49, zany Uranus plugs into Gemini's grid, bringing a thrilling mix of excitement and unpredictability to our lives. During this dynamic transit, everything's up for grabs. Uranus in Gemini shakes up daily routines and supercharges minds with groundbreaking ideas. Expect the unexpected—whether it's through a radical shift in how you communicate, a sudden change in your social circles, or an intense fascination with cutting-edge technology. Life may feel like a sci-fi movie some days, with the costumes and gadgets to match. This four-month period is a preview of a longer cycle that begins again from April 25, 2026 to May 22, 2033. Collectively, we are breaking free from a static, singular way of doing things and embracing a "both/and" mindset rather than one focused on "either/or." This game-changing planet's purpose is to disrupt the status quo. Stay flexible and ready to pivot at a moment's notice. Uranus in Gemini is here to revolutionize the way you think, connect, and engage with the world. The more open you are to change, the more exciting and rewarding this transit will be!

## VENUS-PLUTO TRINE

Charisma is an aphrodisiac today as seductive Venus aligns with smoldering Pluto in communicative air signs, Gemini and Aquarius. Watching someone move confidently and command a room will send your pulse racing. You might find yourself drawn to a well-connected VIP or meet someone intriguing through a mutual acquaintance. Say "yes" to that exclusive invite or ticketed event where you can mingle with the who's who—or team up with a partner to make a powerful impact for a cause close to your heart. This is the perfect day to work your influence and connect with others who share your ambitious drive!

## JUL 10 FULL MOON IN CAPRICORN (4:37PM; 18°50')

Time for a mid-year assessment. What have you accomplished since the beginning of 2025? Do you even remember your New Year's resolutions? Consider how relevant they still are as the year's unfolded. Today's full moon in goal-getter Capricorn is here to shine a light on your progress—or lack thereof. With an energizing trine to motivator Mars in Virgo, it's the perfect moment to review, revamp, and recalibrate your plans. Capricorn is all about ambition and high achievement, but don't forget to celebrate the wins you've already scored. Remember, there's no gold star for burning out in the name of productivity. Take a moment to acknowledge your progress and show gratitude to those who've supported your journey. It's all about balancing the hustle with a little self-love!

## JUL 13-NOV 27 SATURN RETROGRADE

Are you pushing forward with purpose or charging ahead without a clear plan? Cosmic inspector Saturn begins its annual four-and-a-half-month retrograde today. For the first time since the late 90s, it's backing up through "me first" Aries, prompting you to take a closer look at how you assert your ambitions, personal power, and leadership. While the ringed taskmaster reverses through this sign until September 1, you might reevaluate your personal brand. A solo project could hit a speedbump, or you could intentionally slow down your timeline for quality's sake. From September 1 until November 27, Saturn backspins into imaginative Pisces, where the lines between reality and dreams can blur. If you've been swept up in a pipe dream, Saturn's reversal will deliver the reality check you need. But don't dismiss your dreams entirely—this is also a time to cultivate any spiritual or artistic talents you've been exploring. Use this retrograde to master the basics, refine your skills, and lay a solid foundation before taking things to the next level.

## JULY 17 WANING QUARTER MOON IN ARIES (8:38PM)

It's not enough to simply speak up for yourself under today's waning quarter moon in assertive Aries. If you're looking for support, you'll need to capture people's interest without overwhelming them or applying too much pressure. Even if there's a bit of tension brewing, make sure to present your requests with confidence and composure. Approach every conversation with a can-do attitude, because when enthusiastic Aries is in the spotlight, people are eager to be part of the winning team! Keep things positive, and you'll rally the troops in no time.

## JUL 18-AUG 11 MERCURY RETROGRADE IN LEO

Roll up the red carpet! As Mercury pivots into a three-week retrograde in glamorous, flamboyant Leo, it's better to fly under the radar than risk getting overexposed. Scrambled romantic signals, celebrity breakups and flagrant fashion faux pas will interrupt your summer program. Hold off on bold style choices and save any risky cosmetic procedures until after August 11. Exes might resurface, and lovers' quarrels could ignite out of nowhere. With Mercury's backspin in Leo, however, there's a risk of being too lowkey. Don't let opportunities slip by out of fear or insecurity. Conflict resolution will be challenging, and blame-shifting could backfire. The best way to navigate this turbulent phase is to stay humble and keep your heart open—without being overly trusting, too soon. Leo rules our "kings and queens," and this retrograde could reveal some fascinating (and perhaps disturbing) information about those in power. Before stepping into a leadership role, make sure you know what you're getting into. Heavy is the head that wears the crown—at least until August 11.

## JUL 22-AUG 22 SUN IN LEO

Passion, playtime and power couples—oh my! The Sun struts into regal, romantic Leo for its annual four-week run, bringing out the exhibitionists in us all. This solar cycle turns up the volume on our actions, but here's the twist—Mercury is retrograde for the first few weeks of Leo season, adding a reflective layer to the mix until August 11. Dust off those neglected talents and start rehearsing your act. The retrograde period is perfect for fine-tuning your vision and positioning your personal "brand" for its ascent. If you've got a product to promote, give it one last high-gloss polish during the retrograde and plan your big reveal once Mercury goes direct. Confidence is your best accessory now, as long as you aren't faking it 'til you make it.

## JUL 23 VENUS-MARS SQUARE

Communications could hit a rough patch today, under a challenging dust-up between cosmic lovebirds Venus as Mars. Venus is tossing up a word salad in Gemini, turning even the simplest conversations into mind boggling debates. With Mars in critical, detail-oriented Virgo, it's crucial to focus on solutions rather than zeroing in on your other people's "flaws." This could be tricky with these planets at odds. If you've hit a romantic plateau, this Mars-Venus square is your cue to shake things up. Single? Spark up a conversation with someone new. With both planets in mutable signs, it's the perfect moment to step outside your comfort zone and reignite that spark!

## SUN-SATURN TRINE

Turn your passion into action! For the first time since the late 1800s, the courageous Leo Sun forms a royal flush with can-do Saturn in Aries, pumping you up with purposeful intention. With both of these authoritative planets in fire signs, there's an opportunity to dream big. If you've been scattering your focus, rein it in. Take time to visualize what the business world calls your BHAG—your "big, hairy, audacious goal." Picture yourself at the finish line of an accomplishment that feels challenging, even out of reach. Then, start thinking about the first step you can take in that direction. Micro moves can catalyze major results over time. Leaders and decision-makers, this transit reminds you that with great power comes great responsibility. Use this energy wisely to build something that lasts, and don't shy away from putting in the effort. The universe is giving you the green light to make a lasting impact. Don't hide your shine!

## SUN-NEPTUNE TRINE

Declare your boldest dreams—the universe is ready to respond with fiery enthusiasm! Today, the radiant Sun in Leo teams up with visionary Neptune in Aries, urging you to speak your desires into existence with confidence and passion. Miracles could arrive in the form of sudden flashes of inspiration or spontaneous opportunities that ignite your spirit. Don't reflexively pass on invitations that feel out of your comfort zone, especially if they involve travel or adrenaline-pumping activities. They might be the sparks that light your way to a new, fulfilling path. For example, joining a new friend for whitewater rafting or going camping at a music festival could lead to a thrilling and perfectly-timed breakthrough. As you call on the universe for support, ask for these blessings to arrive with a motivating surge of energy, fueling your drive to conquer whatever comes your way.

## NEW MOON IN LEO (3:11PM; 2°08')

Cupid fires off a fresh quiver of arrows today, as the new moon in Leo marks an annual romantic reset. This proactive lunar lift wants you back in the driver's seat (and on the throne) in your love life. If you've stopped articulating your desires or sharing your feelings, that ends today. With Mercury retrograde in Leo—and the new moon connecting to serious Saturn and mysterious Neptune and Pluto—it's ultra-important to send out clear signals to the people who matter in your life. Speak up when you have something to contribute to the conversation—and ask questions when you want to know more. This new moon is a powerful starting block for creative projects. How can you develop your talents over the next six months? Block off time and search out the support you need, whether a coach, teacher or art supplies.

## JUL 25 SUN-PLUTO OPPOSITION

Power plays could disrupt your normally smooth interactions today as the commanding Sun clashes with intense Pluto. Stay alert for subtle intimidation tactics and be wary of people who attempt to ply you with charm and flattery. With Pluto in persuasive Aquarius and the Sun in proud Leo, someone might try to slip past your defenses by appealing to your vanity. Don't give people access to your inner sanctum—of your intellectual property—until you're sure of their true intentions. (Even then, you might have them sign an NDA.) At the same time, consider whether you're being too guarded with someone who actually HAS earned your trust. Are old fears clouding your judgment? It might be hard to see clearly today. If your instincts are raising red flags, don't brush it off. Stall on decision-making and conduct an independent investigation to get the full story.

## JUL 30

### VENUS IN CANCER

The nostalgic is romantic starting today, as love planet Venus sails out of Gemini's cerebral port and into Cancer's sentimental waters. After three weeks of overthinking every move, surrender and let your emotions take the wheel. During this warm-fuzzy phase, you may find yourself craving nurturing and comfort. Stay in rather than booking every spare moment with social activities. Private, relaxed moments allow you to connect to friends, lovers or your S.O. in the intimate style that Cancer prefers. Couples could find a shared focus turning to domestic matters, whether you're exchanging keys, pondering a renovation or shopping for an apartment (all things best done after Mercury turns direct on August 11). Be mindful not to bring too much caretaking into your romantic connections if you don't want to go from "hot mama" to "mother hen" in your partner's eyes.

## CHIRON RETROGRADE IN ARIES (JUL 30–JAN 1, 2026)

Got battle scars? Emotional turbulence has been rough out there since "wounded healer" asteroid Chiron moved into Aries in 2018, pushing anger, combat and revolution into the zeitgeist. This transit, which lasts until 2027, emphasizes self-sovereignty. Who are we as individuals and what do we stand for within the whole of humanity? During the retrograde, you could revisit old hurts or unhealed rage that may be stalling personal growth. Aries energy is fiery and independent. If you've been struggling with issues like self-worth and assertiveness, Chiron's backspin invites you to do deep healing work to push past those blocks. Instead of burying hurt or pretending it doesn't exist, integrate tender spots and let them guide you through a personal transformation. Do the work and by the time Chiron moves forward in January, you may emerge with a renewed sense of self, stronger and more at peace with your raw vulnerabilities.

## JUL 31 SUN-MERCURY RETROGRADE MEETUP

Say what? As the Leo Sun bangs into Mercury retrograde in Leo, pride and egos are on full display, which could turn even the most basic communication into an epic power struggle. ("Did that junior exec seriously just ask me to get him a coffee?") Hold off on making any pitches if you can, but if that's not an option, run a thorough LinkedIn and Google search on the people you're presenting to, noting who's in charge of what. Green lights could turn red fast if you threaten people's authority or make them feel "less than" in any way.

# August

## MONTHLY HOROSCOPE

**8**

Your urge to merge may be verging on insatiable as August kicks off with the Leo Sun prowling through your seductive, mysterious eighth house until August 22. Whether you're signing a business deal or coordinating a rendezvous with a lover (or something equally scintillating), revel in the power of your allure. But don't be TOO hard to get. Mercury remains in a signal-jamming retrograde through the 11th, which could throw the right person off your trail if you don't give a few direct hints. Fortunately, gracious Venus is sweetening the deal, hanging out in Cancer and your seventh house of parity and partnership until August 25. Cultivate relationships that bring out the best in you and make sure to give the people who have already earned your trust plenty of acknowledgement. Career goals (your favorite!) get a giant tailwind starting August 6 as momentous Mars blazes into Libra and your tenth house of success and recognition for six weeks. A leadership role is calling your name, so take charge without apology. It's the Capricorn way! Once Virgo season kicks off on August 22, you'll be ready for a vacation—the further from home the better. With your globetrotting ninth house lit up, you might even tie this trip to a secondary purpose, like a personal growth seminar or business meeting. The very next day, August 23, brings the first of two rare, back-to-back new moons in Virgo, providing another push outside your comfort zone. Use this fresh-start energy to pave the way for an even bigger leap when the solar (new moon) eclipse in Virgo arrives on September 21. The world is your oyster, filled with pearls of wisdom that you're ready to discover and incorporate into your view of life.

*Read your extended monthly forecast for life, love, money and career! astrostyle.com*

# AUGUST
## Moon Phase Calendar

| SUN | MON | TUE | WED | THU | FRI | SAT |
|---|---|---|---|---|---|---|
| | | | | | **1** ♏ 2nd Quarter | **2** ♏ |
| **3** ♏ ♐ 2:00AM | **4** ♐ | **5** ♐ ♑ 1:04PM | **6** ♑ | **7** ♑ ♒ 9:18PM | **8** ♒ | **9** ♒ Full Moon 3:55AM |
| **10** ♓ 2:50AM | **11** ♓ | **12** ♓ ♈ 6:33AM | **13** ♈ | **14** ♈ ♉ 9:22AM | **15** ♉ | **16** ♉ 4th Quarter ♉→♊ 12:01PM |
| **17** ♊ | **18** ♊ ♋ 3:05PM | **19** ♋ | **20** ♋ ♌ 7:17PM | **21** ♌ | **22** ♌ | **23** ♌→♍ 1:24AM ♍ New Moon 2:07AM |
| **24** ♍ | **25** ♍ ♎ 10:08AM | **26** ♎ | **27** ♎ ♏ 9:27PM | **28** ♏ | **29** ♏ | **30** ♏ ♐ 10:04AM |
| **31** ♐ 2nd Quarter | | | | | | |

*Times listed are Eastern US Time Zone*

### KEY

| | | | | | |
|---|---|---|---|---|---|
| ♈ ARIES | ♌ LEO | ♐ SAGITTARIUS | **FM** | FULL MOON |
| ♉ TAURUS | ♍ VIRGO | ♑ CAPRICORN | **NM** | NEW MOON |
| ♊ GEMINI | ♎ LIBRA | ♒ AQUARIUS | **LE** | LUNAR ECLIPSE |
| ♋ CANCER | ♏ SCORPIO | ♓ PISCES | **SE** | SOLAR ECLIPSE |

AUGUST 9, 3:55AM

# full moon in
# Aquarius (17°00')

## AQUARIUS FULL MOON CRYSTAL

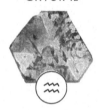

### LABRADORITE

Rainbow-hued labradorite looks different from every angle, reflecting the diversity and originality that Aquarius celebrates. An "illusion-buster," this stone protects us from over-serving others. Labradorite enables big-picture thinking and is powerful for meditation and insight.

*What's one thing you're celebrating under this full moon?*

**8**

## AQUARIUS FULL MOON = CELEBRATE!

*Your most inventive ideas*

*Teams and communities where you feel seen and embraced*

*Your sharing and accepting spirit*

*Technology that keeps you connected*

*Hopes and dreams for the future*

*Your idealistic nature that refuses to give up on humanity*

AUGUST 23, 2:07AM

new moon in
## Virgo #1 (0°23')

## VIRGO NEW MOON CRYSTAL

### LEPIDOLITE

This soothing stone is also called the "grandmother stone" or "peace stone." Use it to calm your nerves and ease the worrying tendency that Virgo can stir up. Lepidolite encourages us to quiet inner criticism and embrace self-love and compassion.

*What's one fresh intention you're ready to set under this new moon?*

## VIRGO NEW MOON = FOCUS

*Adopt (or cuddle) a pet*

*Work out and eat clean*

*Hire service providers and assistants*

*Practice random acts of kindness*

*Embrace healthy routines*

*Implement efficient systems*

*Break projects into actionable steps*

**August 2025**

Longitude & Retrograde Ephemeris [00:00 UT]

| Day | Sid.time | ☉ | ☽ | +12h☽ | ☿ | ♀ | ♂ | ♃ | ♄ | ♅ | ♆ | ♇ | ☊ | ☊ | ⚸ | ⚷ | Day |
|---|---|---|---|---|---|---|---|---|---|---|---|---|---|---|---|---|---|
| **1** Fr | 20:39:26 | ♌09°01'21 | ♏03°15'34 | ♏09°11'17 | ℞ 09°00Ω | ♋00°57 | ♍26°18 | ♋11°42 | ℞ 01°38 | ♊00°55 | ℞ 01°58 | ℞ 02°25 | ℞ 20°16 | ♓19°04 | ♏14°08 | ℞ 27°09 | **1** Fr |
| **2** Sa | 20:43:22 | ♌09°58'45 | ♏15°07'05 | ♏21°03'11 | ♌08°16 | ♋02°07 | ♍26°55 | ♋11°55 | ♈01°36 | ♊00°57 | ♈01°58 | ♒02°24 | ♓20°13 | ℞ 19°04 | ♏14°15 | ♈27°09 | **2** Sa |
| **3** Su | 20:47:19 | ♌10°56'11 | ♏27°00'36 | ♐02°59'29 | ♌07°33 | ♋03°17 | ♍27°32 | ♋12°08 | ♈01°34 | ♊00°58 | ♈01°57 | ♒02°23 | ♓20°09 | ♓19°02 | ♏14°21 | ♈27°09 | **3** Su |
| **4** Mo | 20:51:16 | ♌11°53'36 | ♐09°00'47 | ♐15°04'36 | ♌06°53 | ♋04°26 | ♍28°09 | ♋12°21 | ♈01°32 | ♊01°00 | ♈01°56 | ♒02°21 | ♓20°06 | ♓18°59 | ♏14°28 | ♈27°09 | **4** Mo |
| **5** Tu | 20:55:12 | ♌12°51'03 | ♐21°11'47 | ♐27°22'18 | ♌06°16 | ♋05°36 | ♍28°46 | ♋12°33 | ♈01°30 | ♊01°01 | ♈01°55 | ♒02°20 | ♓20°03 | ♓18°55 | ♏14°35 | ♈27°09 | **5** Tu |
| **6** We | 20:59:09 | ♌13°48'30 | ♑03°36'53 | ♑09°55'23 | ♌05°43 | ♋06°46 | ♍29°23 | ♋12°46 | ♈01°27 | ♊01°03 | ♈01°54 | ♒02°18 | ♓20°00 | ♓18°50 | ♏14°42 | ♈27°08 | **6** We |
| **7** Th | 21:03:05 | ♌14°45'58 | ♑16°18'24 | ♑22°45'35 | ♌05°14 | ♋07°56 | ♎00°00 | ♋12°58 | ♈01°25 | ♊01°04 | ♈01°53 | ♒02°17 | ♓19°57 | ♓18°44 | ♏14°48 | ♈27°08 | **7** Th |
| **8** Fr | 21:07:02 | ♌15°43'27 | ♑29°17'24 | ♒05°53'20 | ♌04°50 | ♋09°06 | ♎00°38 | ♋13°11 | ♈01°23 | ♊01°06 | ♈01°52 | ♒02°16 | ♓19°54 | ♓18°39 | ♏14°55 | ♈27°07 | **8** Fr |
| **9** Sa | 21:10:58 | ♌16°40'57 | ♒12°33'43 | ♒19°17'53 | ♌04°32 | ♋10°16 | ♎01°15 | ♋13°23 | ♈01°20 | ♊01°07 | ♈01°51 | ♒02°14 | ♓19°50 | ♓18°34 | ♏15°02 | ♈27°07 | **9** Sa |
| **10** Su | 21:14:55 | ♌17°38'28 | ♒26°06'03 | ♓02°57'27 | ♌04°20 | ♋11°26 | ♎01°53 | ♋13°36 | ♈01°17 | ♊01°09 | ♈01°50 | ♒02°13 | ♓19°47 | ♓18°31 | ♏15°08 | ♈27°06 | **10** Su |
| **11** Mo | 21:18:51 | ♌18°36'00 | ♓09°52'12 | ♓16°49'29 | ♌04°15 | ♋12°37 | ♎02°30 | ♋13°48 | ♈01°15 | ♊01°10 | ♈01°49 | ♒02°12 | ♓19°44 | ♓18°29 | ♏15°15 | ♈27°06 | **11** Mo |
| **12** Tu | 21:22:48 | ♌19°33'33 | ♓23°49'23 | ♈00°51'05 | D♌04°16 | ♋13°47 | ♎03°08 | ♋14°00 | ♈01°12 | ♊01°11 | ♈01°48 | ♒02°10 | ♓19°41 | D 18°29 | ♏15°22 | ♈27°05 | **12** Tu |
| **13** We | 21:26:45 | ♌20°31'07 | ♈07°54'40 | ♈14°59'19 | ♌04°24 | ♋14°58 | ♎03°46 | ♋14°13 | ♈01°09 | ♊01°13 | ♈01°47 | ♒02°09 | ♓19°38 | ♓18°30 | ♏15°28 | ♈27°05 | **13** We |
| **14** Th | 21:30:41 | ♌21°28'43 | ♈22°05'10 | ♈29°11'27 | ♌04°40 | ♋16°08 | ♎04°23 | ♋14°25 | ♈01°06 | ♊01°14 | ♈01°45 | ♒02°08 | ♓19°35 | ♓18°32 | ♏15°35 | ♈27°04 | **14** Th |
| **15** Fr | 21:34:38 | ♌22°26'21 | ♉06°18'19 | ♉13°25'01 | ♌05°02 | ♋17°19 | ♎05°01 | ♋14°37 | ♈01°03 | ♊01°15 | ♈01°44 | ♒02°06 | ♓19°31 | ♓18°33 | ♏15°42 | ♈27°03 | **15** Fr |
| **16** Sa | 21:38:34 | ♌23°24'00 | ♉20°31'45 | ♉27°37'46 | ♌05°32 | ♋18°30 | ♎05°39 | ♋14°49 | ♈01°00 | ♊01°16 | ♈01°43 | ♒02°05 | ♓19°28 | ♓18°34 | ♏15°49 | ♈27°02 | **16** Sa |
| **17** Su | 21:42:31 | ♌24°21'40 | ♊04°43'17 | ♊11°47'31 | ♌06°09 | ♋19°41 | ♎06°17 | ♋15°01 | ♈00°57 | ♊01°17 | ♈01°42 | ♒02°04 | ♓19°25 | ℞ 18°33 | ♏15°55 | ♈27°01 | **17** Su |
| **18** Mo | 21:46:27 | ♌25°19'22 | ♊18°50'42 | ♊25°52'02 | ♌06°53 | ♋20°52 | ♎06°55 | ♋15°13 | ♈00°54 | ♊01°18 | ♈01°41 | ♒02°02 | ♓19°22 | ♓18°32 | ♏16°02 | ♈27°00 | **18** Mo |
| **19** Tu | 21:50:24 | ♌26°17'06 | ♋02°51'41 | ♋09°48'54 | ♌07°44 | ♋22°03 | ♎07°33 | ♋15°25 | ♈00°50 | ♊01°19 | ♈01°39 | ♒02°01 | ♓19°19 | ♓18°30 | ♏16°09 | ♈26°59 | **19** Tu |
| **20** We | 21:54:20 | ♌27°14'52 | ♋16°43'48 | ♋23°35'40 | ♌08°41 | ♋23°14 | ♎08°11 | ♋15°37 | ♈00°47 | ♊01°20 | ♈01°38 | ♒02°00 | ♓19°15 | ♓18°27 | ♏16°15 | ♈26°58 | **20** We |
| **21** Th | 21:58:17 | ♌28°12'39 | ♌00°24'37 | ♌07°09'59 | ♌09°45 | ♋24°25 | ♎08°50 | ♋15°48 | ♈00°43 | ♊01°21 | ♈01°37 | ♒01°59 | ♓19°12 | ♓18°24 | ♏16°22 | ♈26°57 | **21** Th |
| **22** Fr | 22:02:14 | ♌29°10'27 | ♌13°51'56 | ♌20°29'52 | ♌10°56 | ♋25°36 | ♎09°28 | ♋16°00 | ♈00°40 | ♊01°21 | ♈01°35 | ♒01°58 | ♓19°09 | ♓18°21 | ♏16°29 | ♈26°56 | **22** Fr |
| **23** Sa | 22:06:10 | ♍00°08'17 | ♌27°04'03 | ♍03°33'58 | ♌12°12 | ♋26°48 | ♎10°06 | ♋16°11 | ♈00°36 | ♊01°22 | ♈01°34 | ♒01°56 | ♓19°06 | ♓18°19 | ♏16°35 | ♈26°55 | **23** Sa |
| **24** Su | 22:10:07 | ♍01°06'08 | ♍10°00'00 | ♍16°21'47 | ♌13°34 | ♋27°59 | ♎10°45 | ♋16°23 | ♈00°32 | ♊01°23 | ♈01°33 | ♒01°55 | ♓19°03 | ♓18°18 | ♏16°42 | ♈26°54 | **24** Su |
| **25** Mo | 22:14:03 | ♍02°04'01 | ♍22°39'47 | ♍28°53'47 | ♌15°02 | ♋29°10 | ♎11°23 | ♋16°34 | ♈00°29 | ♊01°24 | ♈01°31 | ♒01°54 | ♓19°00 | D 18°18 | ♏16°49 | ♈26°53 | **25** Mo |
| **26** Tu | 22:17:60 | ♍03°01'55 | ♎05°04'23 | ♎11°11'27 | ♌16°34 | ♌00°22 | ♎12°02 | ♋16°46 | ♈00°25 | ♊01°24 | ♈01°30 | ♒01°53 | ♓18°56 | ♓18°19 | ♏16°56 | ♈26°51 | **26** Tu |
| **27** We | 22:21:56 | ♍03°59'50 | ♎17°15'44 | ♎23°17'12 | ♌18°10 | ♌01°34 | ♎12°40 | ♋16°57 | ♈00°21 | ♊01°25 | ♈01°29 | ♒01°52 | ♓18°53 | ♓18°20 | ♏17°02 | ♈26°50 | **27** We |
| **28** Th | 22:25:53 | ♍04°57'47 | ♎29°16'41 | ♏05°14'16 | ♌19°51 | ♌02°45 | ♎13°19 | ♋17°08 | ♈00°17 | ♊01°25 | ♈01°27 | ♒01°50 | ♓18°50 | ♓18°21 | ♏17°09 | ♈26°48 | **28** Th |
| **29** Fr | 22:29:49 | ♍05°55'45 | ♏11°10'50 | ♏17°06'32 | ♌21°35 | ♌03°57 | ♎13°58 | ♋17°19 | ♈00°13 | ♊01°26 | ♈01°26 | ♒01°49 | ♓18°47 | ♓18°22 | ♏17°16 | ♈26°47 | **29** Fr |
| **30** Sa | 22:33:46 | ♍06°53'44 | ♏23°02'19 | ♏28°58'22 | ♌23°21 | ♌05°09 | ♎14°37 | ♋17°30 | ♈00°09 | ♊01°26 | ♈01°24 | ♒01°48 | ♓18°44 | ♓18°23 | ♏17°22 | ♈26°45 | **30** Sa |
| **31** Su | 22:37:43 | ♍07°51'45 | ♐04°55'39 | ♐10°54'22 | ♌25°11 | ♌06°21 | ♎15°15 | ♋17°41 | ♈00°05 | ♊01°26 | ♈01°23 | ♒01°47 | ♓18°41 | ♓18°23 | ♏17°29 | ♈26°44 | **31** Su |
| **Δ Delta** | 01:58:17 | 28°50'24" | 391°40'04" | 391°43'04" | 16°11' | 35°23' | 18°57' | 5°58' | -1°32' | 0°31' | -0°35' | -0°38' | -1°35' | -0°40' | 3°20' | -0°25' | **Delta** |

Ephemeris tables and data provided by **Astro-Seek.com.** All times in UTC.

## AUGUST 2025

| S | M | T | W | T | F | S |
|---|---|---|---|---|---|---|
|   |   |   |   |   | 1 | 2 |
| 3 | 4 | 5 | 6 | 7 | 8 | 9 |
| 10 | 11 | 12 | 13 | 14 | 15 | 16 |
| 17 | 18 | 19 | 20 | 21 | 22 | 23 |
| 24 | 25 | 26 | 27 | 28 | 29 | 30 |
| 31 |   |   |   |   |   |   |

## MONTHLY INTENTION

**1** FRI ☽ ♏

Waxing quarter moon in Scorpio (8:41AM)
Venus-Saturn square
Venus-Neptune square

**2** SAT ☽ ♏

**AUGUST 2025**

| S | M | T | W | T | F | S |
|---|---|---|---|---|---|---|
|   |   |   |   |   | 1 | 2 |
| 3 | 4 | 5 | 6 | 7 | 8 | 9 |
| 10 | 11 | 12 | 13 | 14 | 15 | 16 |
| 17 | 18 | 19 | 20 | 21 | 22 | 23 |
| 24 | 25 | 26 | 27 | 28 | 29 | 30 |
| 31 |   |   |   |   |   |   |

## WEEKLY INTENTION

## TOP 3 TO-DOS

○

○

○

**3** SUN ☽♍
♐ 2:00AM

**4** MON ☽♐

8

**5** TUE

○♐
♑ 1:04PM

---

**6** WED

○♑
Mars in Libra until Sep 22 (7:23PM)

---

**7** THU

○♑
♒ 9:18PM

---

**8** FRI

○♒
Mars-Uranus trine
Mars-Saturn opposition

---

**9** SAT

○♒
**FULL MOON IN AQUARIUS**
(3:55AM; 17°00′)
Mars-Neptune opposition

### AUGUST 2025

| S | M | T | W | T | F | S |
|---|---|---|---|---|---|---|
|   |   |   |   |   | 1 | 2 |
| 3 | 4 | 5 | 6 | 7 | 8 | 9 |
| 10 | 11 | 12 | 13 | 14 | 15 | 16 |
| 17 | 18 | 19 | 20 | 21 | 22 | 23 |
| 24 | 25 | 26 | 27 | 28 | 29 | 30 |
| 31 |   |   |   |   |   |   |

## WEEKLY INTENTION

## TOP 3 TO-DOS

○

○

○

**8**

**10** SUN                                        ○♒
                                            ♓ 2:50AM
                                      Mars-Pluto trine

**11** MON                                       ○♓
                          Mercury retrograde ends (3:30AM)

**12** TUE

○♓
♈ 6:33AM
Venus-Jupiter meetup

---

**13** WED

○♈

---

**14** THU

○♈
♉ 9:22AM

---

**15** FRI

◑♉

---

**16** SAT

◑♉
Waning Quarter moon in Taurus (1:12AM)
♊ 12:01PM

## AUGUST 2025

| S | M | T | W | T | F | S |
|---|---|---|---|---|---|---|
|   |   |   |   |   | 1 | 2 |
| 3 | 4 | 5 | 6 | 7 | 8 | 9 |
| 10 | 11 | 12 | 13 | 14 | 15 | 16 |
| **17** | **18** | **19** | **20** | **21** | **22** | **23** |
| 24 | 25 | 26 | 27 | 28 | 29 | 30 |
| 31 |   |   |   |   |   |   |

## WEEKLY INTENTION

## TOP 3 TO-DOS

◯

◯

◯

**17** SUN ◗♊

**18** MON ◖♊
♋3:05PM

**19** TUE ◑ ♋

---

**20** WED ◑ ♋
♌ 7:17PM

---

**21** THU ◑ ♌

---

**22** FRI ● ♌
Sun in Virgo (4:34PM)

**VIRGO SEASON UNTIL SEP 22**

---

**23** SAT ● ♌
♍ 1:24AM
**NEW MOON IN VIRGO**
**(2:07AM; 0º23') #1 OF 2**

**AUGUST 2025**

| S | M | T | W | T | F | S |
|---|---|---|---|---|---|---|
| | | | | | 1 | 2 |
| 3 | 4 | 5 | 6 | 7 | 8 | 9 |
| 10 | 11 | 12 | 13 | 14 | 15 | 16 |
| 17 | 18 | 19 | 20 | 21 | 22 | 23 |
| 24 | 25 | 26 | 27 | 28 | 29 | 30 |
| 31 | | | | | | |

## WEEKLY INTENTION

## TOP 3 TO-DOS

◯

◯

◯

**24** SUN　　●♍
Sun-Uranus square

**25** MON　　●♍
♎ 10:08AM
Venus in Leo until Sep 19 (12:27PM)
Venus-Saturn trine

**26** TUE

● ♎︎
Venus-Neptune trine

---

**27** WED

● ♎︎
♏︎ 9:27PM
Venus-Pluto opposition

---

**28** THU

◐ ♏︎

---

**29** FRI

◐ ♏︎

---

**30** SAT

◑ ♏︎
♐︎ 10:04AM

## AUGUST 2025

| S | M | T | W | T | F | S |
|---|---|---|---|---|---|---|
|   |   |   |   |   | 1 | 2 |
| 3 | 4 | 5 | 6 | 7 | 8 | 9 |
| 10 | 11 | 12 | 13 | 14 | 15 | 16 |
| 17 | 18 | 19 | 20 | 21 | 22 | 23 |
| 24 | 25 | 26 | 27 | 28 | 29 | 30 |
| 31 |   |   |   |   |   |   |

## WEEKLY INTENTION

## TOP 3 TO-DOS

○

○

○

**31** SUN ◐♐

Waxing quarter moon in Sagittarius (2:25AM)

## NOTES & THOUGHTS

8

# AUGUST
## MONTHLY HOTSPOTS

8

### AUG 1

#### WAXING QUARTER MOON IN SCORPIO (8:41AM)

To share or not to share? Today's balancing Scorpio quarter moon helps you figure out what's worth revealing and what's better left unsaid. If you're too cryptic, it might frustrate people who are trying to get a clear read on you—and that, in turn, can make you seem harder to trust. On the flip side, you don't want to flood people by oversharing. Try to strike a balance between coming across as approachable and discerning. Let people earn your confidence gradually, but don't be so guarded that it feels like they need to jump through hoops to get close!

#### VENUS-SATURN SQUARE

Avoid riding on assumptions today. As Venus in sensitive Cancer clashes with authoritative Saturn in feisty Aries any attempts to read between the lines will only leave you feeling confused and upset. Whether it's romantic or business-related, take stock: Are you both on the same page about where you're heading together? If one of you feels burdened with doing all the emotional (or literal) heavy lifting, don't move forward without addressing it first. It's crucial that both parties feel heard and supported but ease into any tense discussions. The frustration you've been carrying could be breaking news to the other person who thought everything was "fine." If you want to clear the air, make sure to extend the benefit of the doubt.

## VENUS-NEPTUNE SQUARE

Mixed signals and muddled messages could also be part of today's already-complex forecast. Venus in nurturing Cancer forms her second square of the day, this time with hazy Neptune in headstrong Aries. Attempts to launch a charm offensive could backfire, causing people to feel like you're giving them a hard sell. If you're seeking advice, make sure you're asking opinions from people with actual experience. The cacophony of hot takes could be downright overwhelming. Here's a thought: Keep some things to yourself and let them marinate. Remember, feelings are fleeting and usually aren't the whole story.

## AUG 6-SEP 22 MARS IN LIBRA

Summer flings could turn serious over the next seven weeks, as lusty Mars blazes into Libra and amps up everyone's urge to merge for the rest of the season. Easy though! It's tempting to romanticize when Mars blasts into this "love and marriage" sign every other year. As the impatient red planet accelerates the action, you could get locked into a serious situation before you REALLY know what (and who) you're dealing with. If it's longevity you're after, what's the rush? That goes for all sorts of partnerships, from pleasure to business. Lean into Libra's languorous vibes and make the courtship process the exciting part. For couples, Mars in Libra adds a dash of spice, but it can also stir up passive-aggressive bickering, especially if one of you is pulling an unequal share of the load. Mars is in "detriment" in Libra, meaning it's an uncomfortable place. And it makes sense: Mars is the god of war, while Libra is all about peace, love and harmony. It will take extra effort to maintain your emotional equilibrium now.

## AUG 8

## MARS-URANUS TRINE

It's all about who you know! Networking efforts shift into fifth gear as driven Mars in Libra connects the dots with team-spirited Uranus in Gemini. With these overachieving planets in social air signs, this is one of the best days of the year for assembling a supergroup. If you've already formed your soul squad, put your heads together. Genius ideas could sprout promising (and profitable!) wings under this air-sign trine. Struggling to find a meeting time that works for everyone? Start a group on Marco Polo or Slack to get the ball rolling in the meanwhile.

## MARS-SATURN OPPOSITION

We'd never tell you to give up on a dream, but if you're hitting roadblocks, pull over and recalibrate your plan. Today, assertive Mars locks horns with restrictive Saturn, but here's where things get wonky. With Mars in patient Libra and Saturn in impulsive Aries, everything could feel wildly out of balance. Hitting the gas when the direction is confusing could take you on a senseless detour. So, chill. This speedbump could be a blessing in disguise. Bake in time to test your ideas, gather crucial feedback and make sure your actions are aligned with your core values. Once you've fine-tuned the details, you'll be primed for a powerful comeback!

# AUG 9

## FULL MOON IN AQUARIUS (3:55AM; 17°00')

There's strength in numbers today, as the year's only full moon in collaborative, forward-thinking Aquarius lights up the skies. If you've been struggling to get ahead, here's your cue to reach out to community. Surround yourself with people who fuel your mission and give you the courage to speak out. Just remember to give credit where it's due. What goes around, comes around. Feeling too blessed to be stressed? Share your good fortune with people who could use a leg up. Aquarius is the sign of activism, so dive in and make a difference! Rally behind a cause you're passionate about or raise your voice against injustice. While teamwork is the theme, here's a cosmic reminder: Blending in doesn't mean losing yourself. This full moon wants you to let individuality shine.

## MARS-NEPTUNE OPPOSITION

Know thy limits! With relentless Mars in Libra facing off against boundary-blurring Neptune in Aries, finding the "stop" button could feel impossible. It's easy to lose track of how much might be considered "overboard" under this exhausting cosmic clash. But if you push too hard, burnout is practically guaranteed. Mars in genial Libra wants to keep everyone happy, while Neptune in dreamy Aries urges you to give it your all—even when you're running on fumes. Generosity may surge, but be mindful of your energy reserves. Instead of soldiering through, build in essential breaks to avoid crashing.

## AUG 10 MARS-PLUTO TRINE

Forget brainstorms. Today's intellectual air trine between potent Mars and Pluto could deliver mental monsoons! Everyone's genius will be firing on all cylinders. See what happens when you team up with other great minds. Mars fuels your boldness while Pluto gives you the strategic savvy to unpack a problem that's been vexing you. If you hit on a groundbreaking solution, let the decision-makers in on it. But first, make sure you've adequately stamped your name on any ideas you want credit for. Both Mars and Pluto are known for being cutthroat, and even while in sociable air signs (Mars in Libra, Pluto in Aquarius), they still caution against being overly trusting.

## AUG 11 MERCURY RETROGRADE ENDS

If a feral cat got hold of your tongue over the past few weeks, you might be shy about letting out so much as a "mew." Blame it on mouthy Mercury, who's been on a retrograde stalk through Leo's jungle since July 18. There's nothing healthy about holding in emotions forever, and fortunately, you won't have to. This dramatic arc takes a turn for the positive as Mercury shifts back into direct motion today. Better still? The silver-tongued celestial flirt roams happily through Leo's jungle until September 2. What felt like a Greek tragedy earlier this month might not become a comedy overnight (or ever). But maybe you'll finally be able to laugh about it...a little...or glean the golden lesson from the experience. Have you noticed any glaring gaps in leadership since July 18? Don't ignore the call of the crown if you're supposed to take charge around here. And if you're trying to get a clear read on a love interest, signals become way more obvious starting today.

## AUG 12 VENUS-JUPITER MEETUP

Naughty by nurture? As bawdy Jupiter aligns with loving Venus in the tender sign of Cancer, the stage is set for a love story steeped in TLC and devotion. It's been more than a decade since Venus and Jupiter met in the Crab's compassionate realm making this a banner day for sweet, soulful affection. Focus on relationships that are truly reciprocal. If that means casting your net into new waters, so be it. Worldly, adventurous Jupiter invites you to expand your romantic boundaries. As you do, let superficial flings dissolve and half-hearted entanglements fade away. Even if no one good is on your radar today, start making space for authentic, heartfelt connections in your life. Couples could benefit from a change of scenery over the coming week, ideally in a cozy, intimate setting. Even if you're tucked away at home, try to find minutes to screen out the rest of the world and relax in each other's company.

## AUG 16 WANING QUARTER MOON IN TAURUS (1:12AM)

Stop, drop and reprioritize. Today's grounding quarter moon in sensible yet sensual Taurus reconnects you with your deepest values. Assess your priorities and principles, ensuring you're firmly anchored in them before making any significant choices. If you feel your focus drifting, trip back to the essentials and eliminate the excess. Less is more as long as you don't veer into extreme austerity. Trim back on areas where you might be overindulging, and consider how you can reintroduce little luxuries in more sustainable ways. Taurus energy loves to splurge but also respects resourcefulness, allowing you to enjoy the best of both worlds. If your spending is starting to exceed your budget or if a project is expanding beyond its initial scope, plan a "money date." Choose a cozy cafe, bring your budgets, and review them in a setting that makes the task feel like a treat rather than a chore.

## AUG 22–SEP 22 SUN IN VIRGO (4:34PM)

Back to basics! As the Sun waves goodbye to the high-drama of Leo and enters meticulous Virgo, it casts a healthy glow on our late-summer affairs. Clean living is the new flex, especially after a month of Leo's indulgent hedonism. In preparation for September's back-to-everything bustle, lean into this earth sign's efficiency to get life organized and systematized. Whether it's decluttering your space or fine-tuning your digital tools, give every corner of your life a thorough once-over. Don't spend ALL your time folding laundry and wiping down surfaces. Outdoorsy Virgo season beckons you into sunshine for bike rides to the beach, yoga in the park and sunset pickleball tournaments. Virgo's green ethos inspires conscious consumerism. Look for brands that are environmentally focused, sustainably sourced and have fair labor practices. Savor the harvest of fresh, locally sourced produce, each bite packed with vitality-boosting nutrients.

## AUG 23 NEW MOON IN VIRGO (2:07AM; 0°23') #1 OF 2

Bless this mess? Absolutely not. Today's new moon in Virgo—the first of a rare, back-to-back pair in 2025—sends us into efficiency overload. It's time to sort, file, organize, systematize—and energize. Reduce space by decluttering both your physical and virtual environments. Those distracting piles and unchecked messages take up a lot of psychic energy, even when you're worrying about when to get them done. Chip away at them by devoting a daily block of time for clearing the slate. With this new moon squaring Gemini, you may need to pull back from distractions in order to get the job done. If that means temporarily hiding a few apps and muting threads, so be it. Since wellness is Virgo's domain use this lunar launch to get a fitness routine in motion. Could your meals be healthier, your sleep more sanctified? Feather your nest with everything you need to keep your body humming like a well-oiled machine—from a fridge full of fresh produce, snacks like raw almonds in the pantry and an essential oil diffuser on your nightstand.

## AUG 24 SUN-URANUS SQUARE

Do your very best to remain solution-oriented today. As the Sun in meticulous Virgo squares off with wrench-throwing Uranus in Gemini, control issues may flare while rebellious actions could escalate tensions. This biannual clash tends to heighten ego battles and power struggles, prompting quick, unconsidered reactions. With Uranus playing devil's advocate in Gemini, contrarian attitudes can make it impossible to align around anything. Thanks to the flaw-finding Virgo Sun, nitpicking can intensify, leading to standoffs. Aim to be a problem solver in the face of any discord. If that's not possible, call a timeout until tomorrow when the skies are more agreeable.

## AUG 25

### VENUS IN LEO (AUG 25-SEP 19)

Romantic Venus restores her sultry roar as she shimmies into the lion's den until September 19. If you've had trouble tapping into your fierceness over the past few weeks, the tide turns now. This glamorous, amorous cycle calls for high-fashion 'fits, eight-course dinners and full-on PDA. This is a powerful time to initiate creative projects, dive back into the dating pool, or rev up romance, either with a new interest or long-term love. Work on your personal branding to make sure your front-facing presentation is a proper reflection of the genius within. With Mercury fully out of retrograde, the coast is clear to hire a stylist, set up a photo shoot or work with a professional designer. When it comes to love, this Venus cycle holds nothing back. Hire the skywriter, gush like a hopeful on The Bachelor ("I am so ready to take this journey with you..."), swipe right like it was your second job. But don't forget legendary Leo Whitney Houston's words: Learning to love yourself is the greatest love of all.

### VENUS-SATURN TRINE

Love goals take a more solid shape today as romantic Venus in Leo swings into a harmonizing fire trine with structured Saturn in Aries. With both planets in outspoken fire signs, it won't be hard to bring up the subject of "us" or start a conversation (with anyone, anywhere) about your ideal vision for your romantic life. With future-focused Saturn involved, couples can discuss ways to support each other's ambitions. How can you make time for the relationship while cheering on one another's independent growth? Stuck in a situationship? If you're ready for more than the other person has to give, thank them for the experience and gracefully move forward. And if you're the one who doesn't see a long-term future, be mature and set them free instead of keeping them hanging on.

## AUG 26 VENUS-NEPTUNE TRINE

Take the guardrails off your imagination as passionate Venus in Leo fist-bumps inspirational Neptune in Aries. This energizing fire trine turns up the heat on emotions, melting barriers and fostering deep connections. However, that surge of openness and warmth could also leave you vulnerable to a charming raconteur. Sharpen your discernment to ensure that only the truly deserving gain access to your inner circle. If you're typically reserved or tend to keep a stiff upper lip, today offers a beautiful opportunity to soften those defenses. Embrace the courage to connect authentically and allow your heart to lead the way. It's an optimal day for heartfelt exchanges. Embrace the spirit of boldness and spontaneity in your relationships.

## AUG 27 VENUS-PLUTO OPPOSITION

Trust issues could flare up as Venus in dramatic Leo locks horns with calculating Pluto in cool Aquarius. If you experience yourself having a knee-jerk reaction to a perceived betrayal—or even the slightest feeling of neglect—try to remember that appearances can be deceiving. While it's wise to flag suspicious behavior, do your detective work before flinging accusations. Even if you find evidence, you're not likely to get any answers by intensely grilling the "suspect." If you're just getting to know someone, pay attention to red flags and leave any situation where you feel unsafe or uncomfortable. Did someone's profile raise suspicion on an app? Don't ignore your intuition. Report and block anyone who seems outright inappropriate.

## AUG 31 WAXING QUARTER MOON IN SAGITTARIUS (2:25AM)

Feeling bogged down by the minutiae and missing your spark? Today's balancing quarter moon in expansive Sagittarius reignites your visionary zeal. Take time to evaluate areas where you've become inflexible and open up to alternative viewpoints. Remember, exploring new ideas doesn't commit you to them. Sagittarius, the philosopher of the zodiac, encourages you to consider broader implications. Are your efforts inclusive enough? Scrutinize your approach and make a few adjustments. Results may already manifest with next week's full moon!

# September

## MONTHLY HOROSCOPE

**9**

How wide can you cast your net? With the Sun in Virgo lighting up your ninth house of exploration, travel and higher learning until September 22, there's no limiting your wingspan. But don't sleep on the neighborhood scene. On the 1st, your ruler, structured Saturn, retrogrades back into Pisces and your third house of hometown happenings. You could make a solid name for yourself by simply taking on a local initiative. That goes triple on the 7th, when the Pisces lunar (full moon) eclipse brings surprising opportunities to network, study or stir up excitement in your own backyard. If there's been a miscommunication or lingering tension with a sibling, coworker or neighbor, this eclipse can bring it to a head. Push for resolution, whether that means walking away or hashing out a win-win. On September 21, the closing solar eclipse arrives with the new moon in Virgo—which is also the second in a rare, back-to-back pair to hit this sign. News could come from afar or you could get the nudge you need to take a big risk like enrolling in a degree program, moving to a new city or starting your own business. Capricorn media makers could get a surprising offer near this date. Not that you need to wait around for it. Take-charge Mars continues to ignite your tenth house of career (Libra) until September 22, pushing you to be proactive about professional matters. You're ready to lead, but keep your secret autocrat in check. You need allies, even when you're at the top! The 22nd is the equinox and the start of Libra season, as the Sun picks up the baton from Mars and keeps your ambitious energy flowing. Don't try to shoulder it all alone. Teamwork makes a few of those dreams work once Mars heads into Scorpio and your communal eleventh house from September 22 to November 4. You'll feel a surge of energy for collaborative projects and social causes, making this the perfect time to rally your network and work together for a greater goal. Geek is chic, so don't shy away from AI or other tech tools that can make your life easier.

*Read your extended monthly forecast for*
*life, love, money and career! astrostyle.com*

# SEPTEMBER
## Moon Phase Calendar

| SUN | MON | TUE | WED | THU | FRI | SAT |
|-----|-----|-----|-----|-----|-----|-----|
| | **1**<br>♐ 9:45PM | **2**<br>♑ | **3**<br>♑ | **4**<br>♑<br>♒ 6:32AM | **5**<br>♒ | **6**<br>♒<br>♓ 11:54AM |
| **7**<br>♓ Full Moon<br>& Lunar Eclipse<br>2:09PM | **8**<br>♓<br>♈ 2:37PM | **9**<br>♈ | **10**<br>♈<br>♉ 4:03PM | **11**<br>♉ | **12**<br>♉<br>♊ 5:38PM | **13**<br>♊ |
| **14**<br>♊ 4th Quarter<br>♊→♋ 8:30PM | **15**<br>♋ | **16**<br>♋ | **17**<br>♋<br>♌ 1:20AM | **18**<br>♌ | **19**<br>♌<br>♍ 8:23AM | **20**<br>♍ |
| **21**<br>♍ New Moon<br>& Solar Eclipse<br>3:54PM<br>♍→♎ 5:41PM | **22**<br>♎ | **23**<br>♎ | **24**<br>♎<br>♏ 5:00AM | **25**<br>♏ | **26**<br>♏<br>♐ 5:37PM | **27**<br>♐ |
| **28**<br>♐ | **29**<br>♐→♑ 5:55AM<br>♑ 2nd Quarter | **30**<br>♑ | | | | |

*Times listed are Eastern US Time Zone*

## KEY

| | | | |
|---|---|---|---|
| ♈ ARIES | ♌ LEO | ♐ SAGITTARIUS | **FM** FULL MOON |
| ♉ TAURUS | ♍ VIRGO | ♑ CAPRICORN | **NM** NEW MOON |
| ♊ GEMINI | ♎ LIBRA | ♒ AQUARIUS | **LE** LUNAR ECLIPSE |
| ♋ CANCER | ♏ SCORPIO | ♓ PISCES | **SE** SOLAR ECLIPSE |

# full moon in
# Pisces (15°23')

## PISCES FULL MOON CRYSTAL

### ANGELITE

This pale blue stone activates the Pisces-ruled upper chakras (throat, third-eye and crown), allowing your mind to download messages from your angels, guides and your higher self. Angelite can dissolve emotional or energetic boundaries that may be holding you back from progress.

---

*What's one thing you're celebrating under this full moon?*

---

## PISCES FULL MOON = CELEBRATE!

*Your secret fantasies*

*Your creative spirit*

*Messages from your dreams*

*People who inspire you to think beyond current limitations*

*Compassion and empathy*

*Blurry lines that don't need to be sharpened*

*The beauty in "ugly" things*

new moon in

# Virgo #2 (29°05')

## VIRGO NEW MOON CRYSTAL

### LEPIDOLITE

This soothing stone is also called the "grandmother stone" or "peace stone." Use it to calm your nerves and ease the worrying tendency that Virgo can stir up. Lepidolite encourages us to quiet inner criticism and embrace self-love and compassion.

---

**What's one fresh intention you're ready to set under this new moon?**

---

**9**

## VIRGO NEW MOON = FOCUS

*Adopt (or cuddle) a pet*

*Work out and eat clean*

*Hire service providers and assistants*

*Practice random acts of kindness*

*Embrace healthy routines*

*Implement efficient systems*

*Break projects into actionable steps*

## September 2025

Longitude & Retrograde Ephemeris [00:00 UT]

| Day | Sid.time | ☉ | ☽ | +12h☽ | ☿ | ♀ | ♂ | ♃ | ♄ | ♅ | ♆ | ♇ | ☊ | ☊ | ⚸ | ⚷ | Day |
|---|---|---|---|---|---|---|---|---|---|---|---|---|---|---|---|---|---|
| **1** Mo | 22:41:39 | ♍08°49'47 | ♐16°55'30 | ♐22°59'13 | ♌27°03 | ♌07°33 | ♎15°54 | ♋17°52 | ℞ 00°01 | ♊01°27 | ℞ 01°21 | ℞ 01°46 | ℞ 18°37 | ℞ 18°23 | ♏17°36 | ℞ 26°42 | **1** Mo |
| **2** Tu | 22:45:36 | ♍09°47'51 | ♐29°06'28 | ♑05°17'20 | ♌28°56 | ♌08°45 | ♎16°33 | ♋18°03 | ♓29°57 | ♊01°27 | ♈01°20 | ♒01°45 | ♓18°34 | ♓18°23 | ♏17°42 | ♈26°41 | **2** Tu |
| **3** We | 22:49:32 | ♍10°45'56 | ♑11°32'43 | ♑17°52'37 | ♍00°50 | ♌09°57 | ♎17°12 | ♋18°13 | ♓29°52 | ♊01°27 | ♈01°18 | ♒01°44 | ♓18°31 | ♓18°22 | ♏17°49 | ♈26°39 | **3** We |
| **4** Th | 22:53:29 | ♍11°44'02 | ♑24°17'46 | ♒00°48'02 | ♍02°46 | ♌11°09 | ♎17°51 | ♋18°24 | ♓29°48 | ♊01°27 | ♈01°17 | ♒01°43 | ♓18°28 | ♓18°21 | ♏17°56 | ♈26°37 | **4** Th |
| **5** Fr | 22:57:25 | ♍12°42'10 | ♒07°24'01 | ♒14°05'21 | ♍04°42 | ♌12°22 | ♎18°31 | ♋18°34 | ♓29°44 | ♊01°27 | ♈01°15 | ♒01°42 | ♓18°25 | ♓18°20 | ♏18°03 | ♈26°35 | **5** Fr |
| **6** Sa | 23:01:22 | ♍13°40'19 | ♒20°52'26 | ♒27°44'42 | ♍06°38 | ♌13°34 | ♎19°10 | ♋18°45 | ♓29°40 | ♊01°27 | ♈01°14 | ♒01°41 | ♓18°21 | ♓18°20 | ♏18°09 | ♈26°34 | **6** Sa |
| **7** Su | 23:05:18 | ♍14°38'30 | ♓04°42'19 | ♓11°44'29 | ♍08°34 | ♌14°47 | ♎19°49 | ♋18°55 | ♓29°35 | ℞ 01°27 | ♈01°12 | ♒01°40 | ♓18°18 | ♓18°20 | ♏18°16 | ♈26°32 | **7** Su |
| **8** Mo | 23:09:15 | ♍15°36'43 | ♓18°51'09 | ♓26°01'18 | ♍10°31 | ♌15°59 | ♎20°29 | ♋19°05 | ♓29°31 | ♊01°27 | ♈01°10 | ♒01°39 | ♓18°15 | D 18°19 | ♏18°23 | ♈26°30 | **8** Mo |
| **9** Tu | 23:13:12 | ♍16°34'57 | ♈03°14'44 | ♈10°30'18 | ♍12°26 | ♌17°12 | ♎21°08 | ♋19°15 | ♓29°26 | ♊01°27 | ♈01°09 | ♒01°38 | ♓18°12 | ♓18°20 | ♏18°29 | ♈26°28 | **9** Tu |
| **10** We | 23:17:08 | ♍17°33'13 | ♈17°47'43 | ♈25°05'45 | ♍14°22 | ♌18°24 | ♎21°47 | ♋19°25 | ♓29°22 | ♊01°27 | ♈01°07 | ♒01°37 | ♓18°09 | ♓18°20 | ♏18°36 | ♈26°26 | **10** We |
| **11** Th | 23:21:05 | ♍18°31'31 | ♉02°24'09 | ♉09°41'42 | ♍16°16 | ♌19°37 | ♎22°27 | ♋19°35 | ♓29°17 | ♊01°27 | ♈01°06 | ♒01°36 | ♓18°06 | ℞ 18°20 | ♏18°43 | ♈26°24 | **11** Th |
| **12** Fr | 23:25:01 | ♍19°29'51 | ♉16°58'13 | ♉24°12'39 | ♍18°10 | ♌20°50 | ♎23°07 | ♋19°45 | ♓29°13 | ♊01°26 | ♈01°04 | ♒01°36 | ♓18°02 | ♓18°20 | ♏18°49 | ♈26°22 | **12** Fr |
| **13** Sa | 23:28:58 | ♍20°28'14 | ♊01°24'57 | ♊08°34'13 | ♍20°03 | ♌22°03 | ♎23°46 | ♋19°54 | ♓29°08 | ♊01°26 | ♈01°02 | ♒01°35 | ♓17°59 | ♓18°19 | ♏18°56 | ♈26°20 | **13** Sa |
| **14** Su | 23:32:54 | ♍21°26'38 | ♊15°40'33 | ♊22°43'15 | ♍21°55 | ♌23°15 | ♎24°26 | ♋20°04 | ♓29°04 | ♊01°26 | ♈01°01 | ♒01°34 | ♓17°56 | ♓18°19 | ♏19°03 | ♈26°18 | **14** Su |
| **15** Mo | 23:36:51 | ♍22°25'05 | ♊29°42'35 | ♋06°37'58 | ♍23°47 | ♌24°28 | ♎25°06 | ♋20°13 | ♓28°59 | ♊01°25 | ♈00°59 | ♒01°33 | ♓17°53 | D 18°19 | ♏19°10 | ♈26°16 | **15** Mo |
| **16** Tu | 23:40:47 | ♍23°23'34 | ♋13°29'46 | ♋20°17'33 | ♍25°37 | ♌25°41 | ♎25°46 | ♋20°22 | ♓28°54 | ♊01°25 | ♈00°57 | ♒01°32 | ♓17°50 | ♓18°20 | ♏19°16 | ♈26°13 | **16** Tu |
| **17** We | 23:44:44 | ♍24°22'05 | ♋27°01'45 | ♌03°42'01 | ♍27°26 | ♌26°55 | ♎26°26 | ♋20°32 | ♓28°50 | ♊01°24 | ♈00°56 | ♒01°32 | ♓17°47 | ♓18°20 | ♏19°23 | ♈26°11 | **17** We |
| **18** Th | 23:48:41 | ♍25°20'38 | ♌10°18'49 | ♌16°51'49 | ♍29°14 | ♌28°08 | ♎27°06 | ♋20°41 | ♓28°45 | ♊01°24 | ♈00°54 | ♒01°31 | ♓17°43 | ♓18°21 | ♏19°30 | ♈26°09 | **18** Th |
| **19** Fr | 23:52:37 | ♍26°19'13 | ♌23°21'32 | ♌29°47'39 | ♎01°01 | ♌29°21 | ♎27°46 | ♋20°50 | ♓28°41 | ♊01°23 | ♈00°52 | ♒01°30 | ♓17°40 | ♓18°21 | ♏19°36 | ♈26°07 | **19** Fr |
| **20** Sa | 23:56:34 | ♍27°17'50 | ♍06°10'40 | ♍12°30'18 | ♎02°48 | ♍00°34 | ♎28°26 | ♋20°59 | ♓28°36 | ♊01°23 | ♈00°51 | ♒01°30 | ♓17°37 | ♓18°22 | ♏19°43 | ♈26°04 | **20** Sa |
| **21** Su | 00:00:30 | ♍28°16'30 | ♍18°47'02 | ♍25°00'38 | ♎04°33 | ♍01°47 | ♎29°06 | ♋21°07 | ♓28°31 | ♊01°22 | ♈00°49 | ♒01°29 | ♓17°34 | ℞ 18°22 | ♏19°50 | ♈26°02 | **21** Su |
| **22** Mo | 00:04:27 | ♍29°15'11 | ♎01°11'36 | ♎07°19'42 | ♎06°17 | ♍03°01 | ♎29°46 | ♋21°16 | ♓28°27 | ♊01°21 | ♈00°48 | ♒01°28 | ♓17°31 | ♓18°22 | ♏19°57 | ♈26°00 | **22** Mo |
| **23** Tu | 00:08:23 | ♎00°13'54 | ♎13°25'29 | ♎19°28'47 | ♎08°00 | ♍04°14 | ♏00°27 | ♋21°24 | ♓28°22 | ♊01°20 | ♈00°46 | ♒01°28 | ♓17°27 | ♓18°21 | ♏20°03 | ♈25°57 | **23** Tu |
| **24** We | 00:12:20 | ♎01°12'39 | ♎25°30'11 | ♏01°29'33 | ♎09°42 | ♍05°28 | ♏01°07 | ♋21°33 | ♓28°17 | ♊01°19 | ♈00°44 | ♒01°27 | ♓17°24 | ♓18°19 | ♏20°10 | ♈25°55 | **24** We |
| **25** Th | 00:16:16 | ♎02°11'26 | ♏07°27'33 | ♏13°24'09 | ♎11°23 | ♍06°41 | ♏01°47 | ♋21°41 | ♓28°13 | ♊01°18 | ♈00°43 | ♒01°27 | ♓17°21 | ♓18°17 | ♏20°17 | ♈25°52 | **25** Th |
| **26** Fr | 00:20:13 | ♎03°10'14 | ♏19°20'03 | ♏25°15'16 | ♎13°03 | ♍07°55 | ♏02°28 | ♋21°49 | ♓28°08 | ♊01°18 | ♈00°41 | ♒01°26 | ♓17°18 | ♓18°15 | ♏20°23 | ♈25°50 | **26** Fr |
| **27** Sa | 00:24:09 | ♎04°09'05 | ♐01°10'39 | ♐07°06'13 | ♎14°43 | ♍09°09 | ♏03°08 | ♋21°57 | ♓28°03 | ♊01°17 | ♈00°39 | ♒01°26 | ♓17°15 | ♓18°13 | ♏20°30 | ♈25°47 | **27** Sa |
| **28** Su | 00:28:06 | ♎05°07'57 | ♐13°02'53 | ♐19°00'46 | ♎16°21 | ♍10°22 | ♏03°49 | ♋22°05 | ♓27°59 | ♊01°15 | ♈00°38 | ♒01°25 | ♓17°12 | ♓18°11 | ♏20°37 | ♈25°45 | **28** Su |
| **29** Mo | 00:32:03 | ♎06°06'52 | ♐25°00'48 | ♑01°03'09 | ♎17°58 | ♍11°36 | ♏04°30 | ♋22°12 | ♓27°54 | ♊01°14 | ♈00°36 | ♒01°25 | ♓17°08 | ♓18°10 | ♏20°43 | ♈25°42 | **29** Mo |
| **30** Tu | 00:35:59 | ♎07°05'48 | ♑07°08'47 | ♑13°17'53 | ♎19°35 | ♍12°50 | ♏05°11 | ♋22°20 | ♓27°50 | ♊01°13 | ♈00°34 | ♒01°24 | ♓17°05 | D 18°09 | ♏20°50 | ♈25°40 | **30** Tu |
| **Δ Delta** | 01:54:19 | 28°16'00" | 380°13'17" | 380°18'40" | 52°32' | 35°16' | 19°16' | 4°28' | 2°11' | -0°13' | -0°46' | -0°21' | -1°32' | -0°13' | 3°14' | -1°02' | **Delta** |

Ephemeris tables and data provided by **Astro-Seek.com.** All times in UTC.

**SEPTEMBER 2025**

| S | M | T | W | T | F | S |
|---|---|---|---|---|---|---|
|   | 1 | 2 | 3 | 4 | 5 | 6 |
| 7 | 8 | 9 | 10 | 11 | 12 | 13 |
| 14 | 15 | 16 | 17 | 18 | 19 | 20 |
| 21 | 22 | 23 | 24 | 25 | 26 | 27 |
| 28 | 29 | 30 |   |   |   |   |

# MONTHLY INTENTION

## TOP 3 TO-DOS

◯

◯

◯

## THIS MONTH I WILL...

**9**

---

**1** MON

☾♐
♑ 9:45PM
Saturn retrograde in Pisces until Nov 27 (4:07AM)

**2** TUE ☉♐

Mercury In Virgo until Sep 18 (9:23AM)

---

**3** WED ☉♐

Mercury-Uranus square

---

**4** THU ☉♐
♒ **6:32AM**

Mars-Jupiter square

---

**5** FRI ☉♒

---

**6** SAT ☉♒
♓ **11:54AM**

Uranus Retrograde in Gemini until Nov 7 (12:51AM)

**SEPTEMBER 2025**

| S | M | T | W | T | F | S |
|---|---|---|---|---|---|---|
| | 1 | 2 | 3 | 4 | 5 | 6 |
| 7 | 8 | 9 | 10 | 11 | 12 | 13 |
| 14 | 15 | 16 | 17 | 18 | 19 | 20 |
| 21 | 22 | 23 | 24 | 25 | 26 | 27 |
| 28 | 29 | 30 | | | | |

## WEEKLY INTENTION

## TOP 3 TO-DOS

○

○

○

**7** SUN

○♓
**FULL MOON IN PISCES
& TOTAL LUNAR ECLIPSE**
(2:09PM; 15°23')

**8** MON

○♓
♈ 2:37PM

9

**9** TUE ○♈

---

**10** WED ○♈
♉ 4:03PM

---

**11** THU ○♉

---

**12** FRI ○♉
♊ 5:38PM

---

**13** SAT ☽♊
Sun-Mercury meetup in Virgo

## SEPTEMBER 2025

| S | M | T | W | T | F | S |
|---|---|---|---|---|---|---|
|   | 1 | 2 | 3 | 4 | 5 | 6 |
| 7 | 8 | 9 | 10 | 11 | 12 | 13 |
| 14 | 15 | 16 | 17 | 18 | 19 | 20 |
| 21 | 22 | 23 | 24 | 25 | 26 | 27 |
| 28 | 29 | 30 |   |   |   |   |

## WEEKLY INTENTION

## TOP 3 TO-DOS

○

○

○

**14** SUN ◗ ♊
Waning Quarter moon in Gemini (6:33AM)
♋ 8:30PM

**15** MON ◗ ♋

**16** TUE

---

**17** WED
♌ 1:20AM
Mercury-Saturn opposition

---

**18** THU
Mercury in Libra until Oct 6 (6:06AM)
Mercury-Neptune opposition

---

**19** FRI
♍ 8:23AM
Mercury-Uranus trine
Mercury-Pluto trine
Venus in Virgo until Oct 13 (8:39AM)

---

**20** SAT ●♍
Venus-Uranus square

## SEPTEMBER 2025

| S | M | T | W | T | F | S |
|---|---|---|---|---|---|---|
|   | 1 | 2 | 3 | 4 | 5 | 6 |
| 7 | 8 | 9 | 10 | 11 | 12 | 13 |
| 14 | 15 | 16 | 17 | 18 | 19 | 20 |
| 21 | 22 | 23 | 24 | 25 | 26 | 27 |
| 28 | 29 | 30 |   |   |   |   |

## WEEKLY INTENTION

## TOP 3 TO-DOS

○

○

○

**21** SUN ● ♍

### NEW MOON IN VIRGO #2
### & PARTIAL SOLAR ECLIPSE
(3:54PM; 29°05')
Sun-Saturn opposition
♎ 5:41PM

**22** MON ● ♎

Mars in Scorpio until Nov 4 (3:54AM)
Sun in Libra (2:19PM)

## LIBRA SEASON UNTIL OCT 22

**9**

**23** TUE

● ♎
Sun-Neptune opposition
Sun-Uranus trine

**24** WED

● ♎
♏ **5:00AM**
Sun-Pluto trine
Mars-Pluto square

**25** THU

● ♏

**26** FRI

● ♏
♐ **5:37PM**

**27** SAT

◑ ♐

| S | M | T | W | T | F | S |
|---|---|---|---|---|---|---|
|   | 1 | 2 | 3 | 4 | 5 | 6 |
| 7 | 8 | 9 | 10 | 11 | 12 | 13 |
| 14 | 15 | 16 | 17 | 18 | 19 | 20 |
| 21 | 22 | 23 | 24 | 25 | 26 | 27 |
| **28** | **29** | **30** | | | | |

## WEEKLY INTENTION

## TOP 3 TO-DOS

○

○

○

**28** SUN ◐♐

**9**

**29** MON ◐♐
♑ 5:55AM
Waxing Quarter moon in Capricorn (7:54PM)

---

## NOTES & THOUGHTS

# SEPTEMBER
## MONTHLY HOTSPOTS

### SEP 1–NOV 27 SATURN RETROGRADE IN PISCES

Inspect to protect! Cosmic auditor Saturn, who's been retrograde in Aries since July 13, slips back into Pisces, the sign of soulful and subconscious healing. For the remaining three months of its backspin (until November 27), the taskmaster planet puts the kibosh on escapism and brings a healthy dose of reality checks to match your fantasies. If you put the cart before the horse while Saturn was in Aries, you may need to backtrack and make sure you have proper support for your mission. During this part of the retrograde, take time to master the basics or polish your core skills before hanging your shingle.

### SEP 2-18 MERCURY IN VIRGO

Embrace the minimalist ethos as strategic Mercury buzzes into its home sign of Virgo and directs you to streamline and simplify. Fling open cupboards, closets and storage spaces and give the contents an unflinching review. Donate, swap and say farewell to things that are no longer your vibe. More importantly, don't race to replace them. Having fewer, but more treasured, objects can be preferable to stuffing every square inch of your home with "stuff." Wellness is earthy Virgo's domain. Since Mercury loves to monitor data, a fitness tracker could become your ultimate fall accessory. Speaking of monitoring, watch a tendency to be nosy and critical over the next few weeks. This opinionated Mercury cycle turns everyone into a life coach, but if your advice wasn't asked for, think twice before offering it. Instead, turn the focus to making your own life better.

## SEP 3 MERCURY-URANUS SQUARE

Can you put your money where your mouth is? Mercury in detail-oriented Virgo spins into a testy square with Uranus in quick-witted Gemini. This could serve up a stark reality check, prompting a necessary shift in your game plan. While "faking it till you make it" has its moments, that approach won't cut it now. Your brilliant ideas risk remaining unrealized if you're caught overpromising and underdelivering. This misstep could chip away at your credibility, painting you more as an unreliable dreamer than the pioneering innovator you aim to be. To avoid this pitfall, streamline your master plan into manageable phases. Celebrate a small milestone rather than rushing toward a premature victory lap. Remember, those incremental achievements are what actually build substantial success.

## SEPT 4 MARS-JUPITER SQUARE

Familiarity can breed contempt today, so look out! As Mars in Libra locks into a tense square with maximizer Jupiter in Cancer, you may feel pressured, manipulated or otherwise guilt-tripped by the people closest to you. (And all they did was ask you how you wanted them to prepare your coffee!) It's not about a lack of appreciation, but rather a growing sense of obligation that is making it hard for you—or the other person involved—to say "no." If you're the egregious over-functioner, take this as your cue to pause and pull back. With a little time and space, the other person is bound to pick up the reins. First, they might need to miss you a little—excruciating as that pause in the action can be. Maybe it's you who needs a longer lapse in between heartfelt huddles. Be honest but kind, making sure to reassure loved ones that you're not abandoning them—and that yes, you WILL be back. Is a romantic relationship wilting from neglect as you tend to family and close friends? Unless it's truly an emergency, don't cancel your coffee date (or ignore your buzzing app) to go dry a sister's tears. Send an empowering "You've got this" text, then follow Cupid's arrows to your bliss.

## SEP 6–FEB 3, 2026 URANUS RETROGRADE

Did someone hit the mute button on your rebel yell? Renegade Uranus spins into its annual, five-month retrograde, and for the first time since the 1940s, its backspin begins in motormouthed Gemini. On November 7, the side-spinning planet paddles back through money-minded Taurus for the remainder of its retrograde, until February 3, 2026. Starting today, begin a period of reevaluation and innovation in how you communicate, think, and connect. Question old beliefs and explore new ideas, especially in the Gemini-ruled realms of technology, education, and media. As Uranus retraces its steps, be prepared for unexpected revelations that challenge conventional thinking. When Uranus reverses into Taurus on November 7, it takes its final trip through the Bull's pen in our lifetimes. This will be a chance to crystallize all the hard-won economic lessons you've learned since this cycle began in 2018. Values—and what you consider valuable—may have evolved in ways you never expected. Take stock.

## SEP 7 FULL MOON IN PISCES (2:09PM; 15°23') (TOTAL LUNAR ECLIPSE IN PISCES)

Surrender to a soulful, spiritual groove—you might not have any other choice as the annual full moon in Pisces arrives as a total lunar eclipse. At its best, this full moon can be enchanted and poetic, helping you voice your dreams and deeply held desires. Let down your walls and boundaries a bit. A willingness to be open—and to just try new experiences—could bring major life shifts as the full moon trines worldly, adventurous Jupiter. But that's no excuse for casting good sense aside. Because this full moon is also a shadowy lunar eclipse, you may romanticize to the point of delusion. Careful not to put a rose-tinted filter over your eclipse glasses. There's good and bad to everything (and everyone) but it's essential to look at the full picture, especially since analytical Mercury opposes the full moon. A snake who's been lurking in the grass could be exposed within 2-4 weeks of this full moon. No more excuses! As the twelfth and final sign of the zodiac, Pisces helps us let it go. Farewell, toxic frenemies and energy vampires!

**9**

Hello, to all that is good, true and beautiful—traits that go WAY beyond surface appearances.

## SEP 13 SUN-MERCURY MEETUP IN VIRGO

As the Sun and congenial Mercury sync up in service-oriented Virgo, look for ways to contribute, no matter how small. Show up with an extra coffee in hand, help a friend make a few last-minute Canva graphics for a presentation, offer a relative a ride to a doctor's appointment. And if you find yourself at your desk (which is likely), don't just plow ahead on the most stressful task. Instead, make "working smarter not harder" your operating principle. Use apps and trackers to keep organized, and if the load gets too heavy, ask for support. Got some advice to offer? Don't mince words, but follow persnickety Virgo's directive to be clear and make every syllable count.

## SEP 14 WANING QUARTER MOON IN GEMINI (6:33AM)

Feeling out of sorts or just not quite connected? It's time to open up and talk it out! Today's waning quarter moon in communicative Gemini is perfect for dissecting, digesting, and discussing recent developments, especially any revelations sparked by last week's Pisces full moon. If concepts or situations seem too vague, this lunar phase helps you articulate them clearly and straightforwardly. A creative idea is always stimulating, but it truly begins to sparkle when paired with a concrete plan. If your enthusiasm for a recent passion has cooled, give yourself permission to shift directions. It's all part of the process of finding what truly resonates with you.

## SEP 17 MERCURY-SATURN OPPOSITION

Analysis paralysis alert! Today could have you stuck in a cycle of overthinking as detail-oriented Mercury in meticulous Virgo opposes exacting Saturn in dreamy Pisces. Nothing wrong with using your imagination, but if you've ventured too far from the tried and true, this cosmic matchup urges you to check your work and ensure all details are in order. Master the rules before you attempt to break them. You may discover that certain guidelines are there for a reason, and only a few need tweaking. See how much work you just saved yourself? Whew.

## SEP 18

### MERCURY IN LIBRA (SEP 18-OCT 6)

Stop clutching your pearls and start pricing out diamonds. Messenger Mercury swaps signs, ending a tour through critical, analytical Virgo. The messenger planet's next stop is in lighthearted Libra, the sign of peaceful cooperation, diplomacy and decadent romance. Petty squabbles could dissolve, paving the way for long-overdue compromises. But giving an inch doesn't mean letting people take a mile. Libra is governed by the symbol of the scales, reminding us to retain a healthy balance of give and take. In this partnership-oriented sign, communicative Mercury helps us negotiate healthy agreements in our relationships. Culture vultures, come out to play! Now's the time to appreciate art, get tickets for live music and mingle with the cognoscenti. Fete the fall with fashionable gatherings: signature cocktails, curated playlists AND guest lists.

### MERCURY-NEPTUNE OPPOSITION

Decision-making could get tricky as precise Mercury in harmony-seeking Libra faces off against elusive Neptune in assertive Aries. If you're giving instructions, go over them multiple times to ensure clarity—miscommunication is likely with this planetary tussle. Finding it hard to focus? Libra's need for balance and Aries' impulsivity can make concentrating a challenge, so it's essential to take regular mental breaks. To keep track of all the details in a complex project, lean on the structured beauty of a digital spreadsheet or embrace the simplicity of a traditional notebook. This will help you navigate the confusion with a bit more grace.

## SEP 19

### MERCURY-URANUS TRINE

Eureka! The two most clever planets sync in sweet harmony today. Mercury in diplomatic Libra trines Uranus in witty Gemini, sparking a meeting of the minds. As they merge their energies in genius air signs, entire industries can be disrupted—or maybe you'll just pull yourself out of a longstanding rut. Planning to make a pitch? Remember, you can only prep so much in advance. Stay present while avoiding the hard sell. You'll win people over with your relatable approach.

### MERCURY-PLUTO TRINE

Make your move! Today's cosmic alignment between Mercury in savvy Libra and Pluto in forward-thinking Aquarius supercharges your persuasive skills. This potent trine infuses you with a winning combination of charm and intelligence, making you nearly irresistible in negotiations. Trust in your ability to nail the perfect pitch or steer any conversation with grace. For an extra boost of confidence, keep a few key points handy in your Notes app or scribble them on a slip of paper. With this stellar support, you're set to sway any audience in your favor!

### VENUS IN VIRGO (SEP 19-OCT 13)

Romantic Venus tucks into virtuous Virgo, returning us all to modesty for a few weeks. Hang on to your corset strings! Love (and fashion) might get downright Regency Era for the next four weeks as fans go a-fluttering. Anything NSFW should be kept strictly private during this three-week cycle, which favors subtlety and stability. This downshift may feel sudden after Venus in Leo's hair-flipping excess. The highs and lows, the dramatic arcs—we could all use a break from Cupid's reality shows. Tone down the pyrotechnics and opt for earthy sensuality. There's so much to enjoy when you slow down and savor the simple things, from the warmth of someone's touch to the radiance of a fresh-faced glow. With beauty queen Venus in au natural Virgo, apply product with a lighter touch or skip it and slay with a no-makeup look. From decor to wardrobe, the classics win, especially if they are sustainably sourced and eco-chic.

## SEP 20 VENUS-URANUS SQUARE

Need some breathing room? Even the smoothest relationships may experience turbulence as Venus in fastidious Virgo squares rebellious Uranus in duplicitous Gemini. Minor discrepancies can feel like major chasms. Compromise might seem like a foreign concept today. It's easy to fault-find or feel like nothing that either of you do is right. However, remember that today's fussy energy will dissipate as quickly as it arrived. Opt for a time-out rather than make any knee-jerk decisions that can't be undone. There's a fine line between offering helpful advice and unfairly judging people. Under these reckless skies, a fleeting romantic adventure might seem enticing, but don't lose sight of your core values in the rush of excitement.

## SEP 21

### SUN-SATURN OPPOSITION

Reality check or total buzzkill? Today's opposition between the Virgo Sun and cautious Saturn in Pisces might feel like a harsh splash of cold water on your dreams. But don't let this dampen your spirit or water down your convictions. Use this moment to glean valuable insights from any criticism or obstacles that come your way. Perhaps it's time to pare down, wrap up lingering projects, or solidify your schedule and budget. Slow down, but don't come to a complete halt. This is just a bump in the road, not the end of your journey!

### NEW MOON IN VIRGO #2 (3:54PM; 29°05') (PARTIAL SOLAR ECLIPSE)

9

Eclipse season comes to a masterful finale with today's solar eclipse in vigilant Virgo. This one's doubly special, since it's also the second of a rare, back-to-back pair of Virgo new moons. Productivity has been in high gear since August 23, when the first Virgo new moon set the stage for disciplined developments. The pace could accelerate today, but that's not all. Since eclipses are known for bringing plot twists, your projects can move in unexpected directions. Brace yourself for potential changes with support staff and suppliers. While you may discover ways to improve your efforts, don't rush to tear up all the hard work you've put in. Watch out for perfectionism, Virgo's pitfall. New moons are starting blocks, so trust the process and embrace the lessons that come from acquiring new skills. If you want to add cachet to your resume, look for growth opportunities within your company. It may be time to sign up for specialized training that can bump you to a new paygrade. Want to make a difference in the world, or at least your corner of it? Virgo is the sign of selfless service. Seek volunteer opportunities where you can earn your earth angel halo. But whatever you do, make sure you have a solid plan in place for how to accomplish it. The eclipse will oppose structure-obsessed Saturn, underscoring the need to project-manage any pipe dreams if you want them to become tangible realities.

## SEP 22

### MARS IN SCORPIO (SEP 22–NOV 4)

Prepare for a season of deep dives and intense emotions as fiery Mars plunges into the enigmatic depths of Scorpio. This potent transit may stir up competitive urges or spark flares of jealousy. As power plays become more pronounced, you also have a golden opportunity to climb the ladder in any hierarchy. Just be careful not to come off as ruthless or too self-centered. As lusty Mars heats up sultry Scorpio over the coming six weeks, expect your romantic life to sizzle like never before. A smoldering connection could suddenly ignite, transforming into a passionate conflagration. However, this transit can also fan the flames of jealousy and possessiveness, so keep your cool. If you sense a genuine betrayal, Mars gives you the courage to address it head-on or even walk away. But a word of caution: Intense emotions might lead to paranoia. Before you point fingers, make sure your suspicions are based on facts, not fears. Remember, true investigation respects privacy—no snooping qllowed!

## SUN IN LIBRA (2:19PM) (SEP 22-OCT 22)

Collaborate, cooperate, co-create! Dynamic duos are all the rage for the next month as Libra season begins with the autumnal equinox. Pair up for the win, but not necessarily with someone who is basically your twin. Libra is the sign of the scales, encouraging you to achieve a happy equilibrium by finding a complementary force who can balance you out. Is it time to make a peace offering? Libra's harmonious vibes smooth over rough patches in our most important unions. It's rarely too late to at least TRY to make amends. The gracious diplomacy of Libra season will make others more amenable to accepting apologies. The spirit of justice is in the air! On a personal level, make sure you're playing fair in all your dealings. Legal matters come into focus under this sign's watch. Make agreements official, hire an attorney to review contracts or help you pursue an outstanding case.

## SEP 23

## SUN-NEPTUNE OPPOSITION

Lost in a vortex of indecision? As the vacillating Libra Sun opposes elusive Neptune in Aries, the mental fog thickens. With logic on hiatus, it's virtually impossible to figure out next steps. The second the "right" choice appears, someone discovers another option, which MIGHT be better, but then again... No matter how hard you try to find qualified people to advise you, this transit can obscure the clearest of intentions. Don't even bother poking the bear. Whatever is hidden behind Neptune's smoke screens won't be revealed today. Focus your energy on what you can directly influence and lean into Libra's diplomatic approach when dealing with difficult people.

## SUN-URANUS TRINE

If you've reached a plateau, you may get the urge to shake things up today, but don't throw all common sense out the window. As the balanced Libra Sun gets swayed by cagey Uranus in Gemini, you won't have the best gauge of what's "too much" versus what's "not quite enough." This dynamic cosmic connection brings a flash of "Eureka!" to your endeavors, inspiring bold leaps into uncharted territories. If your intuition nudges you toward a risky move, you may be tempted to act on impulse. However, temper your spontaneity with a bit of caution—make sure to do your homework before diving headfirst into unexplored waters. Experimenting could blow up in your face if you haven't considered the impact it will have on other areas of your life.

## SEP 24

## SUN-PLUTO TRINE

Your charisma is electrifying today as the Libra Sun sings a dynamic duet with magnetic Pluto in Aquarius. Harness this potent energy wisely! A witty quip can pack a powerful punch, but if there's too much truth or taunting, it could come across as a backhanded compliment. Keep an eye on your intensity level and give people a chance to respond to your questions before flooding them with more information. Looking to amplify your influence? Don't reveal your entire hand. Keeping an air of mystery about your intentions can work wonders to bring people back for more (and more!).

## MARS-PLUTO SQUARE

All is NOT fair in love, lust or war, as cutthroat Mars in Scorpio squares off with domineering Pluto in Aquarius. This intense astrological combat stirs up a cauldron of emotions like resentment, jealousy, and possessiveness. Everyone will be easily triggered, making this one of 2025's worst days for attempting to negotiate a compromise. Keep your cards close to your vest when around anyone who might be considered future competition. Feeling tension in a relationship?

Now is not the time to demand a deep, revealing conversation. You won't get a straight answer out of anyone under these tight-lipped skies. Erotic innuendos may be both titillating and insanely difficult to read. To avoid sending out mixed signals yourself, wait a couple days before pursuing anything (or anyone) that's questionable.

## SEP 29 WAXING QUARTER MOON IN CAPRICORN (7:54PM)

Struggling with the elusive "work-life" balance? It might be time for a rapid realignment, courtesy of today's waxing quarter moon in goal-oriented Capricorn. It's fulfilling to chase achievements, but how you get to the finish line matters. Are you overextending yourself instead of handing off tasks? Trying to juggle everything solo could stall crucial projects. If your professional ambitions are hiking up your stress, consider making strategic adjustments. Instead of cramming in "just one more task," what if you logged off and hit an exercise class to rejuvenate? And if your career progress has been more of a crawl lately, the illuminating energy of this moon phase might spotlight a valuable work opportunity that helps enhance your skills. Whether it's picking up an extra shift or enrolling in a webinar, small steps could soon restore your momentum and your finances!

# October

## MONTHLY HOROSCOPE

# 10

October is peak season for your professional life as the Libra Sun directs its rays straight into your tenth house of ambition and success. Push ahead on those goals, whether you're angling for a promotion, launching one of your impressive projects or stepping out as a leader in your field. Important people will take note, so find a way to get on their radar, even if that means joining an elite club or volunteering for a charity that they support. Love goals will also be in your crosshairs once Venus shifts into Libra on the 13th. Prior to that, you may be too distracted by all the eye candy to notice someone's enduring traits. With magnetic, intimate Pluto turning direct, also on the 13th, you may suddenly change your tune, remembering how sweet it can feel to "settle down." Pluto's about-face can help you gain command of your resources and make some strategic moves that have a lasting impact on your financial landscape. Lift your nose from the grindstone on the 22nd! The Sun streams into Scorpio, bringing a seductively fun energy to your communal, collaborative eleventh house. If you've been lonely at the top, that ends now. Join forces with innovative people who aren't afraid to disrupt the status quo in the name of progress. You may find it difficult to put all your thoughts into words, however. That same day, hazy Neptune retrogrades back into Pisces, finishing its retreat (until December 10) in your communication house. Listen, observe and let those ideas marinate. Those napkin sketches and 3AM doodles will come in handy by the end of the year!

**10**

*Read your extended monthly forecast for life, love, money and career! astrostyle.com*

# OCTOBER
## Moon Phase Calendar

| SUN | MON | TUE | WED | THU | FRI | SAT |
|---|---|---|---|---|---|---|
| | | | **1** ☾ ♑ ♒ 3:52PM | **2** ☽ ♒ | **3** ☽ ♒ ♓ 10:07PM | **4** ☽ ♓ |
| **5** ☽ ♓ | **6** ☽ ♓→♈ 12:48AM ♈ Full Moon 11:48PM | **7** ☽ ♈ | **8** ☽ ♈ ♉ 1:12AM | **9** ☽ ♉ | **10** ☽ ♉ ♊ 1:12AM | **11** ☽ ♊ |
| **12** ☽ ♊ ♋ 2:37AM | **13** ☽ ♋ 4th Quarter | **14** ☽ ♋ ♌ 6:47AM | **15** ☽ ♌ | **16** ☽ ♌ ♍ 2:06PM | **17** ☽ ♍ | **18** ☽ ♍ |
| **19** ☽ ♍ ♎ 12:01AM | **20** ● ♎ | **21** ● ♎ New Moon 8:25AM ♎→♏ 11:42AM | **22** ● ♏ | **23** ● ♏ | **24** ● ♏ ♐ 12:19AM | **25** ☾ ♐ |
| **26** ☾ ♐ 12:53PM | **27** ☾ ♐ | **28** ☾ ♐ ♑ 11:55PM | **29** ☽ ♒ 2nd Quarter | **30** ☽ ♒ | **31** ☽ ♒ ♓ 7:46AM | |

*Times listed are Eastern US Time Zone*

| | | | | | |
|---|---|---|---|---|---|
| ♈ ARIES | ♌ LEO | ♐ SAGITTARIUS | **FM** FULL MOON |
| ♉ TAURUS | ♍ VIRGO | ♑ CAPRICORN | **NM** NEW MOON |
| ♊ GEMINI | ♎ LIBRA | ♒ AQUARIUS | **LE** LUNAR ECLIPSE |
| ♋ CANCER | ♏ SCORPIO | ♓ PISCES | **SE** SOLAR ECLIPSE |

OCTOBER 6, 11:48PM

# full moon in
# Aries (14°08′)

## ARIES FULL MOON CRYSTAL

### BLOODSTONE

A dramatic dark-green with flecks of red, this stone is historically given to brave warriors. Use bloodstone to build resilience and pump up self-confidence as you step out as an individual. This circulation-boosting crystal enhances vitality and motivation.

---

*What's one thing you're celebrating under this full moon?*

---

## ARIES FULL MOON = CELEBRATE!

*Your inner (and outer) baddie*

*New experiences you're brave enough to try*

*Your competitive nature*

*Every unique feature that makes you a rare individual*

*Your fighting spirit that won't give up*

**10**

OCTOBER 21, 8:25AM

# new moon in
# Libra (28°22')

## LIBRA NEW MOON CRYSTAL

### MALACHITE
Green like the heart chakra, this stone supports the profound emotional transformations we can make during Libra season. Malachite also invites wealth and prosperity into your home, perfect for this time of beauty and abundance.

*What's one fresh intention you're ready to set under this new moon?*

## LIBRA NEW MOON = FOCUS

*Find synergies*

*Nurture romantic relationships*

*Enjoy art, music and fashion*

*Beautify everything*

*Network to build your contact list*

## October 2025

Longitude & Retrograde Ephemeris [00:00 UT]

| Day | Sid.time | ☉ | ☽ | +12h☽ | ☿ | ♀ | ♂ | ♃ | ♄ | ♅ | ♆ | ♇ | ☊ | ☊ | ⚸ | ⚷ | Day |
|---|---|---|---|---|---|---|---|---|---|---|---|---|---|---|---|---|---|
| 1 We | 00:39:56 | ♎08°04'45 | ♑19°31'24 | ♑25°49'29 | ♎21°11 | ♍14°04 | ♏05°51 | ♋22°27 | ℞ 27°45 | ℞ 01°12 | ℞ 00°33 | ℞ 01°24 | ℞ 17°02 | ♓18°10 | ♏20°57 | ℞ 25°37 | 1 We |
| 2 Th | 00:43:52 | ♎09°03'45 | ♒02°13'02 | ♒08°42'05 | ♎22°46 | ♍15°18 | ♏06°32 | ♋22°35 | ♓27°40 | ♊01°11 | ♈00°31 | ♒01°24 | ♓16°59 | ♓18°11 | ♏21°04 | ♈25°34 | 2 Th |
| 3 Fr | 00:47:49 | ♎10°02'46 | ♒15°17'27 | ♒21°59'01 | ♎24°19 | ♍16°32 | ♏07°13 | ♋22°42 | ♓27°36 | ♊01°10 | ♈00°29 | ♒01°23 | ♓16°56 | ♓18°12 | ♏21°10 | ♈25°32 | 3 Fr |
| 4 Sa | 00:51:45 | ♎11°01'49 | ♒28°47'23 | ♓05°42'10 | ♎25°53 | ♍17°46 | ♏07°54 | ♋22°49 | ♓27°31 | ♊01°08 | ♈00°28 | ♒01°23 | ♓16°52 | ♓18°14 | ♏21°17 | ♈25°29 | 4 Sa |
| 5 Su | 00:55:42 | ♎12°00'53 | ♓12°43'44 | ♓19°51'24 | ♎27°25 | ♍19°00 | ♏08°35 | ♋22°55 | ♓27°27 | ♊01°07 | ♈00°26 | ♒01°23 | ♓16°49 | ♓18°15 | ♏21°24 | ♈25°26 | 5 Su |
| 6 Mo | 00:59:38 | ♎13°00'00 | ♓27°05'10 | ♈04°24'00 | ♎28°56 | ♍20°14 | ♏09°16 | ♋23°02 | ♓27°23 | ♊01°05 | ♈00°24 | ♒01°22 | ♓16°46 | ℞ 18°15 | ♏21°30 | ♈25°24 | 6 Mo |
| 7 Tu | 01:03:35 | ♎13°59'08 | ♈11°47'37 | ♈19°14'36 | ♏00°27 | ♍21°28 | ♏09°58 | ♋23°09 | ♓27°18 | ♊01°04 | ♈00°23 | ♒01°22 | ♓16°43 | ♓18°13 | ♏21°37 | ♈25°21 | 7 Tu |
| 8 We | 01:07:32 | ♎14°58'18 | ♈26°44'26 | ♉04°15'30 | ♏01°57 | ♍22°42 | ♏10°39 | ♋23°15 | ♓27°14 | ♊01°03 | ♈00°21 | ♒01°22 | ♓16°40 | ♓18°11 | ♏21°44 | ♈25°18 | 8 We |
| 9 Th | 01:11:28 | ♎15°57'31 | ♉11°47'08 | ♉19°17'42 | ♏03°26 | ♍23°56 | ♏11°20 | ♋23°21 | ♓27°10 | ♊01°01 | ♈00°20 | ♒01°22 | ♓16°37 | ♓18°07 | ♏21°51 | ♈25°16 | 9 Th |
| 10 Fr | 01:15:25 | ♎16°56'46 | ♉26°46'33 | ♊04°12'13 | ♏04°54 | ♍25°10 | ♏12°01 | ♋23°27 | ♓27°05 | ♊00°59 | ♈00°18 | ♒01°22 | ♓16°33 | ♓18°03 | ♏21°57 | ♈25°13 | 10 Fr |
| 11 Sa | 01:19:21 | ♎17°56'03 | ♊11°34'18 | ♊18°51'36 | ♏06°22 | ♍26°25 | ♏12°43 | ♋23°33 | ♓27°01 | ♊00°58 | ♈00°16 | ♒01°22 | ♓16°30 | ♓17°59 | ♏22°04 | ♈25°10 | 11 Sa |
| 12 Su | 01:23:18 | ♎18°55'23 | ♊26°04'01 | ♋03°10'44 | ♏07°48 | ♍27°39 | ♏13°24 | ♋23°39 | ♓26°57 | ♊00°56 | ♈00°15 | ♒01°22 | ♓16°27 | ♓17°56 | ♏22°11 | ♈25°07 | 12 Su |
| 13 Mo | 01:27:14 | ♎19°54'45 | ♋10°11'56 | ♋17°07'07 | ♏09°14 | ♍28°53 | ♏14°06 | ♋23°44 | ♓26°53 | ♊00°55 | ♈00°13 | ♒01°22 | ♓16°24 | ♓17°54 | ♏22°17 | ♈25°05 | 13 Mo |
| 14 Tu | 01:31:11 | ♎20°54'09 | ♋23°56'47 | ♌00°40'38 | ♏10°39 | ♎00°08 | ♏14°48 | ♋23°50 | ♓26°49 | ♊00°53 | ♈00°12 | ♒01°22 | ♓16°21 | D 17°54 | ♏22°24 | ♈25°02 | 14 Tu |
| 15 We | 01:35:07 | ♎21°53'35 | ♌07°19'21 | ♌13°52'49 | ♏12°03 | ♎01°22 | ♏15°29 | ♋23°55 | ♓26°45 | ♊00°51 | ♈00°10 | D 01°22 | ♓16°18 | ♓17°55 | ♏22°31 | ♈24°59 | 15 We |
| 16 Th | 01:39:04 | ♎22°53'04 | ♌20°21'48 | ♌26°46'15 | ♏13°26 | ♎02°37 | ♏16°11 | ♋24°00 | ♓26°41 | ♊00°49 | ♈00°09 | ♒01°22 | ♓16°14 | ♓17°56 | ♏22°38 | ♈24°56 | 16 Th |
| 17 Fr | 01:43:01 | ♎23°52'35 | ♍03°06'58 | ♍09°23'53 | ♏14°48 | ♎03°51 | ♏16°53 | ♋24°05 | ♓26°37 | ♊00°47 | ♈00°07 | ♒01°22 | ♓16°11 | ♓17°58 | ♏22°44 | ♈24°54 | 17 Fr |
| 18 Sa | 01:46:57 | ♎24°52'08 | ♍15°37'48 | ♍21°48'37 | ♏16°09 | ♎05°06 | ♏17°35 | ♋24°10 | ♓26°33 | ♊00°46 | ♈00°06 | ♒01°22 | ♓16°08 | ♓17°59 | ♏22°51 | ♈24°51 | 18 Sa |
| 19 Su | 01:50:54 | ♎25°51'43 | ♍27°57'04 | ♎04°03'02 | ♏17°29 | ♎06°21 | ♏18°17 | ♋24°14 | ♓26°30 | ♊00°44 | ♈00°04 | ♒01°22 | ♓16°05 | ℞ 17°58 | ♏22°58 | ♈24°48 | 19 Su |
| 20 Mo | 01:54:50 | ♎26°51'20 | ♎10°07'11 | ♎16°09'20 | ♏18°48 | ♎07°35 | ♏18°59 | ♋24°19 | ♓26°26 | ♊00°42 | ♈00°03 | ♒01°22 | ♓16°02 | ♓17°56 | ♏23°04 | ♈24°45 | 20 Mo |
| 21 Tu | 01:58:47 | ♎27°51'00 | ♎22°10'08 | ♎28°09'21 | ♏20°06 | ♎08°50 | ♏19°41 | ♋24°23 | ♓26°22 | ♊00°40 | ♈00°01 | ♒01°22 | ♓15°58 | ♓17°52 | ♏23°11 | ♈24°42 | 21 Tu |
| 22 We | 02:02:43 | ♎28°50'42 | ♏04°07'36 | ♏10°04'40 | Rs 21°23 | ♎10°05 | ♏20°23 | ♋24°27 | ♓26°19 | ♊00°38 | ♈00°00 | ♒01°22 | ♓15°55 | ♓17°45 | ♏23°18 | ♈24°40 | 22 We |
| 23 Th | 02:06:40 | ♎29°50'25 | ♏16°01'08 | ♏21°56'49 | ♏22°38 | ♎11°19 | ♏21°05 | ♋24°31 | ♓26°15 | ♊00°36 | ♓29°59 | ♒01°23 | ♓15°52 | ♓17°38 | ♏23°25 | ♈24°37 | 23 Th |
| 24 Fr | 02:10:36 | ♏00°50'11 | ♏27°52'21 | ♐03°47'34 | ♏23°51 | ♎12°34 | ♏21°47 | ♋24°35 | ♓26°12 | ♊00°34 | ♓29°57 | ♒01°23 | ♓15°49 | ♓17°29 | ♏23°31 | ♈24°34 | 24 Fr |
| 25 Sa | 02:14:33 | ♏01°49'58 | ♐09°43'09 | ♐15°39'01 | ♏25°03 | ♎13°49 | ♏22°30 | ♋24°38 | ♓26°08 | ♊00°32 | ♓29°56 | ♒01°23 | ♓15°46 | ♓17°21 | ♏23°38 | ♈24°31 | 25 Sa |
| 26 Su | 02:18:30 | ♏02°49'48 | ♐21°35'53 | ♐27°33'46 | ♏26°13 | ♎15°04 | ♏23°12 | ♋24°41 | ♓26°05 | ♊00°29 | ♓29°55 | ♒01°24 | ♓15°43 | ♓17°13 | ♏23°45 | ♈24°29 | 26 Su |
| 27 Mo | 02:22:26 | ♏03°49'39 | ♑03°33'29 | ♑09°35'05 | ♏27°22 | ♎16°19 | ♏23°55 | ♋24°45 | ♓26°02 | ♊00°27 | ♓29°53 | ♒01°24 | ♓15°39 | ♓17°07 | ♏23°51 | ♈24°26 | 27 Mo |
| 28 Tu | 02:26:23 | ♏04°49'31 | ♑15°39'28 | ♑21°46'46 | ♏28°28 | ♎17°34 | ♏24°37 | ♋24°47 | ♓25°59 | ♊00°25 | ♓29°52 | ♒01°24 | ♓15°36 | ♓17°02 | ♏23°58 | ♈24°23 | 28 Tu |
| 29 We | 02:30:19 | ♏05°49'26 | ♑27°57'57 | ♒04°13'09 | ♏29°31 | ♎18°48 | ♏25°20 | ♋24°50 | ♓25°56 | ♊00°23 | ♓29°51 | ♒01°25 | ♓15°33 | ♓17°00 | ♏24°05 | ♈24°21 | 29 We |
| 30 Th | 02:34:16 | ♏06°49'22 | ♒10°33'21 | ♒16°58'43 | ♐00°32 | ♎20°03 | ♏26°02 | ♋24°53 | ♓25°53 | ♊00°21 | ♓29°49 | ♒01°25 | ♓15°30 | D 17°00 | ♏24°12 | ♈24°18 | 30 Th |
| 31 Fr | 02:38:12 | ♏07°49'19 | ♒23°30'10 | ♓00°07'48 | ♐01°30 | ♎21°18 | ♏26°45 | ♋24°55 | ♓25°50 | ♊00°18 | ♓29°48 | ♒01°26 | ♓15°27 | ♓17°01 | ♏24°18 | ♈24°15 | 31 Fr |
| Δ Delta | 01:58:15 | 29°44'33" | 393°58'45" | 394°18'18" | 40°19' | 37°14' | 20°53' | 2°27' | -1°54' | -0°53' | 0°44' | 0°01' | -1°35' | -1°08' | 3°21' | -1°21' | Delta |

Ephemeris tables and data provided by **Astro-Seek.com.** All times in UTC.

10

| S | M | T | W | T | F | S |
|---|---|---|---|---|---|---|
| | | | 1 | 2 | 3 | 4 |
| 5 | 6 | 7 | 8 | 9 | 10 | 11 |
| 12 | 13 | 14 | 15 | 16 | 17 | 18 |
| 19 | 20 | 21 | 22 | 23 | 24 | 25 |
| 26 | 27 | 28 | 29 | 30 | 31 | |

## MONTHLY INTENTION

**1** WED

○ ♐
♒ 3:52PM
Mercury-Jupiter square

**2** THU

○ ♒

**3** FRI

○ ♒
♄ 10:07PM

**4** SAT

○ ♓

**OCTOBER 2025**

| S | M | T | W | T | F | S |
|---|---|---|---|---|---|---|
|  |  |  | 1 | 2 | 3 | 4 |
| 5 | 6 | 7 | 8 | 9 | 10 | 11 |
| 12 | 13 | 14 | 15 | 16 | 17 | 18 |
| 19 | 20 | 21 | 22 | 23 | 24 | 25 |
| 26 | 27 | 28 | 29 | 30 | 31 |  |

## WEEKLY INTENTION

## TOP 3 TO-DOS

◯

◯

◯

**5** SUN ◯♓

**10**

**6** MON ◯♓
**♈ 12:48AM**
**FULL MOON IN ARIES**
(11:48PM; 14°08')
Mercury in Scorpio until Oct 29 (12:41PM)

**7** TUE

○♈

Mercury-Pluto square

---

**8** WED

○♈

♉ 1:12AM

---

**9** THU

○♉

---

**10** FRI

◐♉

♊ 1:12AM

---

**11** SAT

◑♊

Venus-Saturn opposition

| S | M | T | W | T | F | S |
|---|---|---|---|---|---|---|
|  |  |  | 1 | 2 | 3 | 4 |
| 5 | 6 | 7 | 8 | 9 | 10 | 11 |
| 12 | 13 | 14 | 15 | 16 | 17 | 18 |
| 19 | 20 | 21 | 22 | 23 | 24 | 25 |
| 26 | 27 | 28 | 29 | 30 | 31 |  |

## WEEKLY INTENTION

## TOP 3 TO-DOS

◯

◯

◯

**12** SUN ◐ ♊
♋ 2:37AM

**10**

**13** MON ◑ ♋
Waning Quarter moon in Cancer (2:13PM)
Venus in Libra until Nov 6 (5:19PM)
Venus-Neptune opposition
Pluto direct in Aquarius (10:54PM)

**14** TUE

◑ ♋
♌ 6:47AM
Venus-Uranus trine
Venus-Pluto trine

---

**15** WED

◑ ♌

---

**16** THU

◑ ♌
♍ 2:06PM

---

**17** FRI

● ♍
Sun-Jupiter square

---

**18** SAT

● ♍

### OCTOBER 2025

| S | M | T | W | T | F | S |
|---|---|---|---|---|---|---|
|   |   |   | 1 | 2 | 3 | 4 |
| 5 | 6 | 7 | 8 | 9 | 10 | 11 |
| 12 | 13 | 14 | 15 | 16 | 17 | 18 |
| **19** | **20** | **21** | **22** | **23** | **24** | **25** |
| 26 | 27 | 28 | 29 | 30 | 31 |   |

## WEEKLY INTENTION

## TOP 3 TO-DOS

○

○

○

**19** SUN

●♍︎
♎︎ 12:01AM

**10**

**20** MON

●♎︎
Mercury-Mars meetup

**21** TUE                                          ●︎ ♎︎

NEW MOON IN LIBRA
(8:25AM; 28°22')
♏︎ 11:42AM

---

**22** WED                                          ●︎ ♏︎

Neptune retrograde in Pisces until Dec 10 (5:48AM)
Sun in Scorpio (11:51PM)

**SCORPIO SEASON UNTIL NOV 21**

---

**23** THU                                          ●︎ ♏︎

---

**24** FRI                                          ●︎ ♏︎

♐︎ 12:19AM
Sun-Pluto square
Mercury-Jupiter trine #1 of 3

---

**25** SAT                                          ●︎ ♐︎

Mercury-Saturn trine #1 of 3

| S | M | T | W | T | F | S |
|---|---|---|---|---|---|---|
|   |   |   | 1 | 2 | 3 | 4 |
| 5 | 6 | 7 | 8 | 9 | 10 | 11 |
| 12 | 13 | 14 | 15 | 16 | 17 | 18 |
| 19 | 20 | 21 | 22 | 23 | 24 | 25 |
| 26 | 27 | 28 | 29 | 30 | 31 |   |

## WEEKLY INTENTION

## TOP 3 TO-DOS

○

○

○

**26** SUN

◐ ♐
♑ 12:53PM

**10**

**27** MON

◐ ♑

**28** TUE

●♐
♒ 11:55PM
Mars-Jupiter trine

---

**29** WED

◐♒
Mercury-Neptune trine #1 of 3
Mercury in Sagittarius until Nov 18 (7:02AM)
Waxing Quarter moon in Aquarius (12:21PM)
Mars-Saturn trine
Mercury-Uranus opposition

---

**30** THU

◑♒

---

**31** FRI

◑♒
♓ 7:46AM

---

## NOTES & THOUGHTS

# OCTOBER
## MONTHLY HOTSPOTS

# 10

### OCT 1 MERCURY-JUPITER SQUARE

As Mercury in diplomatic Libra squares off against expansive Jupiter in nurturing Cancer, your words carry weight—perhaps more than you intend. This expressive cosmic duo amplifies communication, but watch out! It's easy to promise more than you can humanly deliver. You're likely coming from a good place. You want to be helpful or shore up someone's mood. Remember: You can't solve the world's problems in a single conversation. Be mindful of overstepping emotional boundaries or getting overly involved in problems that aren't yours to solve. Think big, but speak judiciously to ensure that your intentions align with your impact.

### OCT 6

#### MERCURY IN SCORPIO (OCT 6-29)

Messenger Mercury slides into secretive Scorpio, urging you to strengthen your filters and adopt an air of mystery. Maintain a measure of control to build intrigue by keeping them guessing. If you're not ready for a big announcement, it's wise to hold off on the grand reveals and press statements for now. The upcoming weeks are perfect for behind-the-scenes work—researching, editing, and crafting your magnum opus. Secure any confidential information and bolster your passwords. During this transit, expect a loyalty test or two, as suspicion tends to increase. If you find your trust alarms sounding, be mindful not to question others too intensely. Avoid the temptation to conduct an FBI-level interrogation— instead, allow trust to develop or repair slowly and naturally.

## FULL MOON IN ARIES (11:48PM; 14°08')

Work the room! Steal the spotlight! And don't you dare apologize for being over the top. The annual full moon in Aries unleashes a tsunami of boldness, cueing you to let your most flamboyant self shine. Who cares if tongues wag? Take the focus off of audience approval and make the day about unleashing a daring round of raw self-expression. The Aries drive to be #1 may spike the competitive energy. Nothing wrong with a healthy desire to be the best. But if the vibe begins to verge on cutthroat, diffuse the tension before a fight breaks out. One savvy way to do that? Share the glory and signal boost some of the other deserving talents in your midst. The full moon touches base with deep-feeling Neptune, which could unlock a floodgate of bottled-up emotions, especially anger. Channel any rage constructively. A vigorous workout or karaoke power ballads— whatever it takes to deescalate drama and metabolize those feels!

## OCT 7 MERCURY-PLUTO SQUARE

Dialogues may turn into diatribes as Mercury in secretive Scorpio battles Pluto in renegade Aquarius. Speaking truth to power is one thing. But if someone attempts to draw you into an ideological wrestling match, get out of the ring before egos get bruised. This investigative energy can help you uncover hidden truths and renew your mindset once you do. Guard against the darker undertones that might lead to paranoid thinking or manipulative tactics. You may have no choice but to face tough issues head-on, but maintain integrity and strive for clarity and fairness in all exchanges.

## OCT 11 VENUS-SATURN OPPOSITION

Have your relationship boundaries been too porous? If you've been setting aside your own instincts for the sake of harmony, today's Venus-Saturn opposition blows the whistle. You know you need clearly defined limits; yet in the heat of a certain connection, you could have lost your steely determination. Today's cosmic climate offers a chance to step back and reassess. Feeling uncertain about someone in particular? Hold off on making any hasty decisions while the stars cast a somewhat gloomy shadow over your judgment. While it's crucial to heed any warning signs, recognize that your current ability to differentiate a minor issue from a crisis might be a bit clouded. Take this time to reflect and ensure you're not overreacting or underreacting—balance is key.

## OCT 13

### WANING QUARTER MOON IN CANCER (2:13PM)

Cozy season vibes are calling today as the waning Cancer moon brings visions of chunky knit sweaters and pumpkin spice everything into your field. Where could you bring more homey touches to your daily life? Tuck slippers under your desk, frame a few family photos, splurge on that espresso maker for your kitchen. (If you're a regular coffeeshop-goer, it will pay for itself in a few months!) Pause between professional duties to connect with coworkers. Call a relative you've lost touch with. When you're back at base camp, set up your living room for movie, craft and game nights. On the lookout for a new space? Set up alerts from Zillow and Redfin. A lucky listing could pop up while you're organizing your office supplies or folding laundry.

### VENUS IN LIBRA (OCT 13–NOV 6)

Elevate, luxuriate, decorate! Beauty queen Venus dons a tiara and floats into Libra for her annual homecoming parade. Willpower is fairly nonexistent while Venus is in Libra, which can make us go weak in the face of bespoke, luxury treasures: cashmere sweaters from a capsule collection, reserve Pinots aged in oak barrels. Lovers, rejoice! The next few weeks are peak cuffing season as Venus unites kindred souls. Situationships may evolve into exclusive relationships or simply fade away, clearing space for the real deal. In a relationship? Spoil your S.O. mercilessly and speak up about your own desires. If you don't ask, you don't get! With Venus in gentle Libra, slow and steady devotion wins the race in all realms. Dial down the pressure, dial up the sweet gestures and charm. Pay attention to visuals, too. Taking care of your body and looking your personal best doesn't make you vain. It's called valuing yourself and it can help you attract people who will do the same!

**10**

## VENUS-NEPTUNE OPPOSITION

The line between fantasy and reality may become imperceptible today. Shortly after Venus takes its first step in Libra, it gets into standoff with quixotic Neptune in Aries. You may be swept up in a whirlwind attraction or put someone on a pedestal, only to realize later that you completely misread their character. While it's tempting to lose yourself in the allure of idealized love, remember that true connection is built on authenticity, not illusions. Stay grounded and keep your heart open, but don't ignore red flags. This cosmic combo can inspire creative passion, but be mindful of seeing what you want to see rather than what's really there.

## PLUTO DIRECT IN AQUARIUS

Viva la revolución! After five months spent simmering in a low-power retrograde, alchemical Pluto wakes up and turns direct in humanitarian Aquarius. Pluto's backspin, which began on May 4, inspired deep reflection—especially around the systems, structures, and social circles that needed a serious transformation. Now that the metamorphic planet is back in forward motion, you have the green light to start acting on those game-changing visions. But no need to rush! Pluto is in the early stages of its long transit through the Water Bearer's realm, which lasts until January 19, 2044! Over the next two decades, it will bring radical shifts in technology, social justice, and how we connect with our communities. Look for ways to improve your corner of the not-so-lonely planet. Whether you're syncing up with family, starting an organization or joining an existing one, you'll find strength in numbers.

## OCT 14

## VENUS-URANUS TRINE

Relationships could take an unexpected but exhilarating turn today as Venus in Libra flows into a harmonious trine with change-agent Uranus in Gemini. Couples who've been at odds for the past few days could suddenly tap into a creative (and potentially hilarious) solution. Don't walk around in a tech trance when you're waiting for your coffee or picking up dry cleaning. You could miss the chance to exchange witty banter—and contact 'deets—with a charming person the universe places in your path. This cosmic connection favors unconventional attractions and out-of-the-box thinking. The person who stimulates your intellect wins!

## VENUS-PLUTO TRINE

Deep, transformative vibes will also permeate today's interactions as Venus in Libra forms her second trine of the day, this time with intense Pluto, who's just wrapped up its retrograde in Aquarius. This cosmic combo invites you to connect on a soul level. Cut through surface-level interactions and reveal something that you don't share often—with the caveat that this won't give you a vulnerability hangover tomorrow. (Rule of thumb: Share your partially healed scars instead of the trauma of fresh wounds.) Pluto's influence can bring powerful breakthroughs and healing. Under these sultry skies, a magnetic attraction could take your breath away. Relationships formed today may feel fated, as if destiny is pulling the strings!

## OCT 17 SUN-JUPITER SQUARE

Emotional attachments make it hard to play fair under today's cosmic clash. You can see the path to compromise, thanks to the diplomatic Libra Sun. But Jupiter in sensitive Cancer cranks up your personal bias, making it hard to be impartial, even when you're playing peacemaker. Think twice about getting in the middle of complex family dynamics. In your efforts to assuage someone who is moody and difficult, you might wind up taking on more than you can honestly handle. Is this actually your cross to bear? Be helpful from a distance rather than jumping into the line of other people's fire. Be supportive without sacrificing yourself. The deeper emotional needs that surface today may require multiple conversations—and the support of a professional like a therapist or mediator—to be resolved.

## OCT 20 MERCURY-MARS MEETUP

Retract those claws...or maybe just sharpen them first. With Mercury and Mars entwined in fierce, calculating Scorpio, conversations could

10

cut deep today. Power struggles, hidden agendas, and under-the-table tactics might surface, so keep your guard up. Don't fan the flames with biting, venomous remarks. Scorpio's sting can leave lasting wounds, and once those words are out, there's no taking them back. Instead, embrace Scorpio's strategic side. Know your limits and what you're willing to settle for before you even enter the ring. This is a day to negotiate with precision, staying laser-focused on your ultimate goal. If things start to get too intense, don't be afraid to step back, cool down, and strike when the moment is right. Scorpio's energy favors those who play the long game, so use this passionate surge to speak your truth...but with the right amount of stealth and control.

## OCT 21 NEW MOON IN LIBRA (8:25AM; 28°22')

The year's only new moon in Libra revs up romance today, serving important lessons in chemistry. Under this pink-hued glow, it's easy to fall in love with people's potential but we won't be so gifted at spotting red flags. Even the greatest person on the planet is still prone to human flaws. This new moon encourages a balanced perspective in all realms. With Jupiter in Cancer squaring la luna, your inner circle may have some pretty strong opinions about your partnership choices. Similarly, you could find yourself getting overly involved in other people's love lives. Keep the focus on your own desires and close the opinion polls. Your heart wants what it wants and unless they are personally affected by your choices, you don't owe the bystanders an explanation. Couples may have those important talks about supporting each other's independence without feeling threatened. Autonomy and togetherness can coexist beautifully, but it takes some finesse!

## OCT 22

### NEPTUNE RETROGRADE IN PISCES (OCT 22–DEC 10)

Numinous Neptune, who's been retrograde in Aries since July 4, backstrokes into its home sign of Pisces. Deeper waters beckon as the celestial mystic amplifies the introspective, dreamlike energy of this transit. Since Neptune first entered Aries on March 30, you may have felt called to redefine your entire identity. A burst of pioneering energy sparked trailblazing visions and idealistic pursuits. Once the retrograde began on July 4, Neptune's fog may have clouded the path forward, creating tension between your desire for action and the haziness of what comes next. Now, as Neptune slips back into Pisces, the focus shifts to surrender and spiritual reflection, allowing you to gracefully integrate the lessons of these past months. If you've been on the fence about travel plans, think "escape"—but with intention. This is prime time for a soulful retreat, whether that's a weekend of yoga and sound baths or a painting workshop in Positano. Just watch out for Neptune's tendency to blur reality and fantasy. While you may feel drawn to mystical or healing experiences, choose your guides carefully. Boundless Neptune in reverse drops our defenses, making us more impressionable and open to suggestion. Shield your psychic space with salt baths, crystal jewelry and protective rituals. Hydrate well—Neptune rules the seas, so a refillable water bottle might just be your best travel companion.

## SUN IN SCORPIO (11:51PM) (OCT 22–NOV 21)

Money, power, success! With the Sun blazing into magnetic Scorpio, you've got a month to tap into hidden financial opportunities and rev up your earning potential. Instead of dwelling on what's missing from your bank account, get strategic. A deep dive into your closet could unearth treasures to flip on Depop or Poshmark. Maybe a local business could use your freelance Canva skills for social media graphics. During this magnetic Scorpio solar cycle, energy flows where your attention goes, so make sure you're radaring in on people, places and things that stoke your inner fire. Scorpio also rules long-term investments and joint ventures. Curious about cryptocurrency or real estate? Now's the time to learn! Thinking about partnering up for a big venture? Schedule that chemistry meeting with a potential business partner. If you need startup capital, this zodiac season's magic could connect you with the perfect investor. And don't limit yourself to the 9-5 grind—Scorpio turns us into night owls. A passive revenue stream, like a downloadable product or rental equipment, could earn you money while you sleep.

10

## OCT 24

### SUN-PLUTO SQUARE
Buried tensions are bubbling below the surface, but with the secretive Scorpio sun squaring surreptitious Pluto, no one is in a rush to bring them out into the open. While you don't want an active emotional volcano to erupt, consider the cost of avoidance. The anticipation of conflict may be more stressful than the conflict itself. Nevertheless, this will not be an easy situation to navigate. Scorpio's probing energy wants to uncover the truth, while rebellious Pluto in Aquarius demands radical change and independence. You may feel caught between holding on to what feels safe and diving into the unknown. Use this cosmic friction to break through old patterns but be mindful of not forcing things. Power struggles could arise, but with awareness, this aspect can help you transform and evolve—on your own terms!

### MERCURY-JUPITER TRINE #1 OF 3
Your inner world may be far more alluring than anything that's happening "out there" today. As Mercury in sultry Scorpio forms a provocative trine with limitless Jupiter in Cancer, there's no telling what fantasies you'll spin up. This cosmic combo could spark spicy pillow talk and inspire seductive moves to match. The only imperative is that you and your partner are both into it. Whether with a love interest or trusted bestie, you may be motivated to initiate a conversation about your private thoughts and emotions. Since Jupiter can create big energy, stay aware. You don't want to flood people with your revelations. Gauge their moods before you start pulling skeletons out of the closet.

### OCT 25 MERCURY-SATURN TRINE #1 OF 3
Every detail counts today as analytical Mercury gets swept into Saturn's grind. Whether you're putting the final touches on a project for work or making a weighty decision about your personal life, stay hypervigilant through every aspect of the process. With both planets in sensitive water signs (Scorpio and Cancer), intuitive hits will be strong. If your

Spidey senses start to tingle, investigate! Your curiosity could lead you to a growth opportunity that helps you create lasting security for yourself. A well-connected or experienced person could help you get to the next level. Be prepared to follow through if you ask them to make an introduction. Remember: Your work will reflect on the person who vouched for you.

## OCT 28 MARS-JUPITER TRINE

Today's energy is outright alchemical thanks to a free-flowing trine between Mars in Scorpio and Jupiter in Cancer. This dynamic duet brings penetrating insights, extreme willpower and the energy to act upon your deepest convictions. Supersized ideas spring to life, and you'll be inspired to give them your all. The wholehearted devotion of these two planets can help you move mountains in a remarkably short period of time. The pitfall would be playing too small or underestimating your impact. While empathy is favored, this is not the time for modesty or extreme caution. Jupiter the gambler and Mars the warrior call for epic leaps—or plunges! With both planets in deep-feeling water signs, mine the magic that's hidden below the surface. Don't overlook the obvious!

## OCT 29

### MERCURY-NEPTUNE TRINE #1 OF 3

Ask, believe, receive! Today, as mental Mercury in Scorpio tunes in to mystical Neptune's Piscean frequency, use the Law of Attraction to your advantage and visualize what you desire. Manifestation doesn't require a laborious effort to pull off. With these planets in intuitive, magnetic water signs, try holding a vision of what it would feel like to already have what you want. That alone will send a powerful message to the universe. Instead of swimming upstream, float WITH the current. Under this flowing mashup, your intuition may be borderline psychic. Read the reports and check the data, but also follow your gut.

### MERCURY IN SAGITTARIUS (OCT 29–NOV 18)

After weeks of mind games and hidden agendas, clarity is finally on the horizon. Mercury shifts out of secretive Scorpio and into straightforward Sagittarius for its annual tour through this philosophical, outspoken fire sign. With the messenger planet firing arrows into Sagittarius' domain, authenticity is back in vogue. But with so many truth arrows flying around, no one is keen to listen. Go easy on the opinionated rants and zealous preaching over the next few weeks. Sagittarius is the sign of global expansion and cross-cultural connections. You may discover surprising common ground by reaching across the proverbial aisle. Mediamakers and entrepreneurs will have no shortage of big ideas. Capture them all for consideration! Just don't rush to pull the trigger on any venture until you've thoroughly mapped it out, especially if doing so means taking a gamble on your essential resources.

## WAXING QUARTER MOON IN AQUARIUS (12:21PM)

Today's quarter moon in forward-thinking Aquarius urges you to scrutinize your digital footprint. Whether it's turning off location services, beefing up your privacy settings, or blocking cookies, reclaim control over the relentless data-tracking from the apps and websites you frequent. In the analog world, assess the dynamics of your social circle. Are trust and discretion upheld among your colleagues? Distance yourself from the gossips or people whose questionable activities could sully your good name. Need to get your squad back on the same page? Propose a team-building session or an offsite retreat to reenergize and refocus. If it's been too long since you've connected with your core crew, this is also an ideal time to organize a seasonal get-together. Keep it lighthearted and casual, like pub trivia or costumed karaoke to fete Halloween!

## MARS-SATURN TRINE

Hit your cruising altitude and let the tailwind guide you! Speedy Mars in Scorpio plays nice with cautious Saturn in Pisces today, helping you advance at a pace that won't throw you into an anxiety spiral. Be excited but not desperate, direct but diplomatic. You can even make a strongly worded statement about your competitive advantage and why you're the best person for a job. Just be prepared to back up your claims with action and evidence.

Radar in on people's emotions, pain points and deepest desires. With Mars and Pluto both in sensitive water signs, you'll need to make people FEEL something if you want to spur them to action.

## MERCURY-URANUS OPPOSITION

Brace yourself for a whirlwind of ideas and sudden insights! No subject is too out there today as Mercury in philosophical Sagittarius opposes Uranus in whimsical Gemini. Together, they'll whip up your curiosity, which could lead you down a research rabbit hole or pull you into hours of scrolling for quick, catchy information. Conversations may shift directions unexpectedly, sparking brilliant, if fleeting, revelations. Fast friendships may form under these skies, but don't bank on most of them being permanent. Enjoy the day's exchanges for what they are—dynamic bursts of inspiration that can help you break through any creative blocks.

# NOTES & THOUGHTS

# November

## MONTHLY HOROSCOPE

Summon your supergroup! The Sun swirls through Scorpio and your community-oriented eleventh house until the 21st, inviting you to deepen connections within your network. With Venus gliding through Scorpio from November 6 to 30, creative brainstorms could turn into mental monsoons. Capture all those "wouldn't it be crazy if" ideas, even if you don't take action on them until early next year. Your subconscious mind is working overtime as busy, buzzy Mars catapults into Sagittarius on November 4 and activates your imagination until December 15. While your visionary plans could be epic, also use this time to clean house—physically and energetically—and to let go of what no longer serves you. With Mercury turning retrograde in Sagittarius from the 9th, and slipping back into Scorpio from the 18th to the 29th, some old collaborations or group dynamics may need review. This is your cue to reassess which relationships are pulling their weight—and which ones are draining you. Meanwhile, Uranus retrogrades back into Taurus and your fifth house of creative self-expression on November 7, encouraging you to push the envelope until February 3. Romantic experimentation could also lead to new levels of pleasure and fulfillment. Just make sure you choose a safe word and safe playmates. The month's end offers relief when stabilizing Saturn turns direct in Pisces and your third house of communication on the 27th. You'll finally feel like you're speaking a language that others understand, and that your words are carrying weight.

*Read your extended monthly forecast for*
*life, love, money and career! astrostyle.com*

# NOVEMBER
## Moon Phase Calendar

| SUN | MON | TUE | WED | THU | FRI | SAT |
|---|---|---|---|---|---|---|
| | | | | | | **1** ♓ |
| **2** ♓ ♈ 10:39AM | **3** ♈ | **4** ♈ ♉ 11:16AM | **5** Full Moon 8:19AM | **6** ♉ ♊ 10:20AM | **7** ♊ | **8** ♊ ♋ 10:06AM |
| **9** ♋ | **10** ♋ ♌ 12:34PM | **11** ♌ | **12** ♌ 4th Quarter ♌→♍ 6:52PM | **13** ♍ | **14** ♍ | **15** ♍ ♎ 4:44AM |
| **16** ♎ | **17** ♎ ♏ 4:44PM | **18** ♏ | **19** ♏ | **20** ♏ New Moon 1:47AM ♏→♐ 5:26AM | **21** ♐ | **22** ♐ ♑ 5:53PM |
| **23** ♑ | **24** ♑ | **25** ♑ ♒ 5:16AM | **26** ♒ | **27** ♒ ♓ 2:24PM | **28** ♓ 2nd Quarter | **29** ♓ ♈ 8:07PM |
| **30** ♈ | | | | | | |

*Times listed are Eastern US Time Zone*

**KEY**

| | | | |
|---|---|---|---|
| ♈ ARIES | ♌ LEO | ♐ SAGITTARIUS | **FM** FULL MOON |
| ♉ TAURUS | ♍ VIRGO | ♑ CAPRICORN | **NM** NEW MOON |
| ♊ GEMINI | ♎ LIBRA | ♒ AQUARIUS | **LE** LUNAR ECLIPSE |
| ♋ CANCER | ♏ SCORPIO | ♓ PISCES | **SE** SOLAR ECLIPSE |

NOVEMBER 5, 8:19AM
# full moon in
# Taurus (13°23')

## TAURUS FULL MOON CRYSTAL

### COPPER
One of the Earth's most healing materials, copper brings the signature stability of earth-sign Taurus. This gem balances the chakras and shifts stagnant energy, charging you up to connect with loved ones during holiday celebrations. The weight of copper grounds you as you tap into the quantum field—the place of limitless ideas and possibilities.

---

*What's one thing you're celebrating under this full moon?*

---

## TAURUS FULL MOON = CELEBRATE!
*The simple things that bring you joy*
*The beauty of nature*
*Your favorite music and artists*
*Finding holiday gifts that are sustainable and earth-friendly*
*Creating a comfortable home environment*
*Food that you love*

**11**

NOVEMBER 20, 1:47AM

# new moon in
# Scorpio (28° 12′)

## SCORPIO NEW MOON CRYSTAL

### SERPENTINE

With its dramatic swirls of pale yellow and ash grey, this crystal activates the Scorpio kundalini energy, helping you transcend your ego and detoxify your body. Serpentine creates a bridge between the physical and spiritual realms so you can access ancient wisdom and messages from your guides.

---

**What's one fresh intention you're ready to set under this new moon?**

---

## SCORPIO NEW MOON = FOCUS

*Build trusted bonds*

*Share secrets*

*Form strategic partnerships*

*Explore your erotic nature*

*Join forces (and finances)*

*Give everything you do more sizzle and spice*

## November 2025

Longitude & Retrograde Ephemeris [00:00 UT]

| Day | Sid.time | ☉ | ☽ | +12h☽ | ☿ | ♀ | ♂ | ♃ | ♄ | ♅ | ♆ | ♇ | ☊ | ☊ | ⚸ | ⚷ | Day |
|---|---|---|---|---|---|---|---|---|---|---|---|---|---|---|---|---|---|
| 1 Sa | 02:42:09 | ♏08°49'18 | ♓06°52'24 | ♓13°43'51 | ℞s 02°25 | ♎22°33 | ♏27°28 | ♋24°57 | ℞ 25°47 | ℞ 00°16 | ℞ 29°47 | ♒01°26 | ℞ 15°24 | ♓17°02 | ♏24°25 | ℞ 24°12 | 1 Sa |
| 2 Su | 02:46:05 | ♏09°49'19 | ♓20°42'47 | ♓27°48'44 | ♐03°16 | ♎23°48 | ♏28°10 | ♋24°59 | ♓25°45 | ♊00°14 | ♓29°46 | ♒01°27 | ♓15°20 | ℞ 17°02 | ♏24°32 | ♈24°10 | 2 Su |
| 3 Mo | 02:50:02 | ♏10°49'21 | ♈05°01'59 | ♈12°21'42 | ♐04°03 | ♎25°03 | ♏28°53 | ♋25°01 | ♓25°42 | ♊00°12 | ♓29°45 | ♒01°27 | ♓15°17 | ♓17°01 | ♏24°38 | ♈24°07 | 3 Mo |
| 4 Tu | 02:53:59 | ♏11°49'25 | ♈19°47'43 | ♈27°18'43 | ♐04°45 | ♎26°18 | ♏29°36 | ♋25°03 | ♓25°39 | ♊00°09 | ♓29°44 | ♒01°28 | ♓15°14 | ♓16°57 | ♏24°45 | ♈24°05 | 4 Tu |
| 5 We | 02:57:55 | ♏12°49'31 | ♉04°54'10 | ♉12°32'18 | ♐05°22 | ♎27°34 | ♐00°19 | ♋25°04 | ♓25°37 | ♊00°07 | ♓29°42 | ♒01°28 | ♓15°11 | ♓16°51 | ♏24°52 | ♈24°02 | 5 We |
| 6 Th | 03:01:52 | ♏13°49'39 | ♉20°12'16 | ♉27°52'07 | ♐05°54 | ♎28°49 | ♐01°02 | ♋25°05 | ♓25°35 | ♊00°05 | ♓29°41 | ♒01°29 | ♓15°08 | ♓16°43 | ♏24°59 | ♈23°59 | 6 Th |
| 7 Fr | 03:05:48 | ♏14°49'48 | ♊05°30'54 | ♊13°06'42 | ♐06°19 | ♏00°04 | ♐01°45 | ♋25°06 | ♓25°33 | ♊00°02 | ♓29°40 | ♒01°30 | ♓15°04 | ♓16°34 | ♏25°05 | ♈23°57 | 7 Fr |
| 8 Sa | 03:09:45 | ♏15°50'00 | ♊20°38'46 | ♊28°05'31 | ♐06°38 | ♏01°19 | ♐02°28 | ♋25°07 | ♓25°30 | ♊00°00 | ♓29°39 | ♒01°30 | ♓15°01 | ♓16°25 | ♏25°12 | ♈23°54 | 8 Sa |
| 9 Su | 03:13:41 | ♏16°50'13 | ♋05°26'31 | ♋12°40'41 | ♐06°48 | ♏02°34 | ♐03°12 | ♋25°08 | ♓25°28 | ♉29°57 | ♓29°38 | ♒01°31 | ♓14°58 | ♓16°18 | ♏25°19 | ♈23°52 | 9 Su |
| 10 Mo | 03:17:38 | ♏17°50'29 | ♋19°48'02 | ♋26°47'54 | ℞ 06°51 | ♏03°49 | ♐03°55 | ♋25°08 | ♓25°26 | ♉29°55 | ♓29°37 | ♒01°32 | ♓14°55 | ♓16°12 | ♏25°25 | ♈23°49 | 10 Mo |
| 11 Tu | 03:21:34 | ♏18°50'46 | ♌03°40'45 | ♌10°26'18 | ♐06°45 | ♏05°04 | ♐04°38 | ♋25°09 | ♓25°25 | ♉29°52 | ♓29°36 | ♒01°33 | ♓14°52 | ♓16°09 | ♏25°32 | ♈23°47 | 11 Tu |
| 12 We | 03:25:31 | ♏19°51'05 | ♌17°05'18 | ♌23°37'43 | ♐06°29 | ♏06°20 | ♐05°22 | ℞ 25°09 | ♓25°23 | ♉29°50 | ♓29°35 | ♒01°33 | ♓14°49 | ♓16°08 | ♏25°39 | ♈23°44 | 12 We |
| 13 Th | 03:29:28 | ♏20°51'27 | ♍00°04'28 | ♍06°25'42 | ♐06°03 | ♏07°35 | ♐06°05 | ♋25°08 | ♓25°21 | ♉29°48 | ♓29°34 | ♒01°34 | ♓14°45 | D 16°08 | ♏25°46 | ♈23°42 | 13 Th |
| 14 Fr | 03:33:24 | ♏21°51'50 | ♍12°42'22 | ♍18°54'38 | ♐05°27 | ♏08°50 | ♐06°49 | ♋25°08 | ♓25°20 | ♉29°45 | ♓29°34 | ♒01°35 | ♓14°42 | ♓16°08 | ♏25°52 | ♈23°40 | 14 Fr |
| 15 Sa | 03:37:21 | ♏22°52'14 | ♍25°03'28 | ♎01°09'01 | ♐04°41 | ♏10°05 | ♐07°32 | ♋25°08 | ♓25°18 | ♉29°43 | ♓29°33 | ♒01°36 | ♓14°39 | ℞ 16°08 | ♏25°59 | ♈23°37 | 15 Sa |
| 16 Su | 03:41:17 | ♏23°52'41 | ♎07°12'10 | ♎13°13'01 | ♐03°45 | ♏11°21 | ♐08°16 | ♋25°07 | ♓25°17 | ♉29°40 | ♓29°32 | ♒01°37 | ♓14°36 | ♓16°06 | ♏26°06 | ♈23°35 | 16 Su |
| 17 Mo | 03:45:14 | ♏24°53'10 | ♎19°12'22 | ♎25°10'13 | ♐02°40 | ♏12°36 | ♐09°00 | ♋25°06 | ♓25°16 | ♉29°38 | ♓29°31 | ♒01°38 | ♓14°33 | ♓16°01 | ♏26°12 | ♈23°33 | 17 Mo |
| 18 Tu | 03:49:10 | ♏25°53'40 | ♏01°07'17 | ♏07°03'29 | ♐01°28 | ♏13°51 | ♐09°43 | ♋25°05 | ♓25°14 | ♉29°35 | ♓29°30 | ♒01°39 | ♓14°30 | ♓15°53 | ♏26°19 | ♈23°30 | 18 Tu |
| 19 We | 03:53:07 | ♏26°54'13 | ♏12°59'27 | ♏18°55'01 | ♐00°11 | ♏15°07 | ♐10°27 | ♋25°03 | ♓25°13 | ♉29°33 | ♓29°30 | ♒01°40 | ♓14°26 | ♓15°43 | ♏26°26 | ♈23°28 | 19 We |
| 20 Th | 03:57:03 | ♏27°54'46 | ♏24°50'47 | ♐00°46'30 | ♏28°50 | ♏16°22 | ♐11°11 | ♋25°02 | ♓25°13 | ♉29°30 | ♓29°29 | ♒01°41 | ♓14°23 | ♓15°30 | ♏26°33 | ♈23°26 | 20 Th |
| 21 Fr | 04:01:00 | ♏28°55'22 | ♐06°42'43 | ♐12°39'15 | ♏27°29 | ♏17°37 | ♐11°55 | ♋25°00 | ♓25°12 | ♉29°28 | ♓29°28 | ♒01°42 | ♓14°20 | ♓15°16 | ♏26°39 | ♈23°24 | 21 Fr |
| 22 Sa | 04:04:57 | ♏29°55'59 | ♐18°36'36 | ♐24°34'34 | ♏26°09 | ♏18°53 | ♐12°39 | ♋24°58 | ♓25°11 | ♉29°25 | ♓29°28 | ♒01°43 | ♓14°17 | ♓15°01 | ♏26°46 | ♈23°22 | 22 Sa |
| 23 Su | 04:08:53 | ♐00°56'37 | ♑00°33'45 | ♑06°33'59 | ♏24°55 | ♏20°08 | ♐13°23 | ♋24°56 | ♓25°10 | ♉29°23 | ♓29°27 | ♒01°44 | ♓14°14 | ♓14°48 | ♏26°53 | ♈23°20 | 23 Su |
| 24 Mo | 04:12:50 | ♐01°57'16 | ♑12°35'55 | ♑18°39'28 | ♏23°47 | ♏21°23 | ♐14°07 | ♋24°53 | ♓25°10 | ♉29°20 | ♓29°26 | ♒01°45 | ♓14°10 | ♓14°37 | ♏26°59 | ♈23°18 | 24 Mo |
| 25 Tu | 04:16:46 | ♐02°57'57 | ♑24°45'22 | ♒00°53'36 | ♏22°49 | ♏22°39 | ♐14°51 | ♋24°51 | ♓25°09 | ♉29°18 | ♓29°26 | ♒01°46 | ♓14°07 | ♓14°29 | ♏27°06 | ♈23°16 | 25 Tu |
| 26 We | 04:20:43 | ♐03°58'39 | ♒07°05'00 | ♒13°19'39 | ♏22°01 | ♏23°54 | ♐15°35 | ♋24°48 | ♓25°09 | ♉29°15 | ♓29°25 | ♒01°47 | ♓14°04 | ♓14°23 | ♏27°13 | ♈23°14 | 26 We |
| 27 Th | 04:24:39 | ♐04°59'22 | ♒19°38'26 | ♒26°01'27 | ♏21°24 | ♏25°10 | ♐16°20 | ♋24°45 | ♓25°09 | ♉29°12 | ♓29°25 | ♒01°49 | ♓14°01 | ♓14°21 | ♏27°20 | ♈23°12 | 27 Th |
| 28 Fr | 04:28:36 | ♐06°00'06 | ♓02°29'39 | ♓09°03'07 | ♏20°59 | ♏26°25 | ♐17°04 | ♋24°42 | ♓25°09 | ♉29°10 | ♓29°25 | ♒01°50 | ♓13°58 | ♓14°20 | ♏27°26 | ♈23°10 | 28 Fr |
| 29 Sa | 04:32:33 | ♐07°00'51 | ♓15°42'46 | ♓22°28'36 | ♏20°45 | ♏27°41 | ♐17°48 | ♋24°39 | D 25°09 | ♉29°08 | ♓29°24 | ♒01°51 | ♓13°55 | ♓14°20 | ♏27°33 | ♈23°08 | 29 Sa |
| 30 Su | 04:36:29 | ♐08°01'36 | ♓29°21'22 | ♈06°20'51 | Ds 20°42 | ♏28°56 | ♐18°33 | ♋24°35 | ♓25°09 | ♉29°05 | ♓29°24 | ♒01°52 | ♓13°51 | ♓14°19 | ♏27°40 | ♈23°06 | 30 Su |
| Δ Delta | 01:54:19 | 29°12'18" | 382°28'58" | -382°37'00" | -11°42' | 36°22' | 21°05' | -0°22' | -0°38' | -1°11' | -0°23' | 0°26' | -1°32' | -2°42' | 3°14' | -1°06' | Delta |

Ephemeris tables and data provided by **Astro-Seek.com.** All times in UTC.

## NOVEMBER 2025

| S | M | T | W | T | F | S |
|---|---|---|---|---|---|---|
|   |   |   |   |   |   | 1 |
| 2 | 3 | 4 | 5 | 6 | 7 | 8 |
| 9 | 10 | 11 | 12 | 13 | 14 | 15 |
| 16 | 17 | 18 | 19 | 20 | 21 | 22 |
| 23 | 24 | 25 | 26 | 27 | 28 | 29 |
| 30 |   |   |   |   |   |   |

## MONTHLY INTENTION

1 SAT

O♓

**NOVEMBER 2025**

| S | M | T | W | T | F | S |
|---|---|---|---|---|---|---|
|  |  |  |  |  |  | 1 |
| 2 | 3 | 4 | 5 | 6 | 7 | 8 |
| 9 | 10 | 11 | 12 | 13 | 14 | 15 |
| 16 | 17 | 18 | 19 | 20 | 21 | 22 |
| 23 | 24 | 25 | 26 | 27 | 28 | 29 |
| 30 |  |  |  |  |  |  |

## WEEKLY INTENTION

## TOP 3 TO-DOS

○

○

○

**2** SUN

☉ ♓
♈ 10:39AM
Venus-Jupiter square

**3** MON

☉ ♈
Mars-Neptune trine

**4** TUE

○♈

♂ 11:16AM

Mars in Sagittarius until Dec 15 (8:01AM)
Mars-Uranus opposition

---

**5** WED

○♉

**FULL SUPERMOON IN TAURUS**
**(8:19AM EDT; 13°23′;)**

---

**6** THU

○♉

♊ 10:20AM

Venus in Scorpio until Nov 30 (5:39PM)

---

**7** FRI

○♊

Uranus retrograde in Taurus until
Feb 3, 2026 (9:22PM)
Venus-Pluto square

---

**8** SAT

○♊

♋ 10:06AM

## NOVEMBER 2025

| S | M | T | W | T | F | S |
|---|---|---|---|---|---|---|
|   |   |   |   |   |   | 1 |
| 2 | 3 | 4 | 5 | 6 | 7 | 8 |
| 9 | 10 | 11 | 12 | 13 | 14 | 15 |
| 16 | 17 | 18 | 19 | 20 | 21 | 22 |
| 23 | 24 | 25 | 26 | 27 | 28 | 29 |
| 30 |   |   |   |   |   |   |

## WEEKLY INTENTION

## TOP 3 TO-DOS

○

○

○

---

**9** SUN ☽♋

Mercury retrograde in Sagittarius
until Nov 18 (2:02PM)

---

**10** MON ☽♋

♌ 12:34PM

II

**11** TUE

◐♌

Jupiter retrograde in Cancer
until Mar 10, 2026 (11:41AM)

---

**12** WED

◐♌

Waning Quarter moon in Leo (12:28AM)
Mercury-Mars meetup

♍ **6:52PM**

---

**13** THU

◑♍

---

**14** FRI

◑♍

---

**15** SAT

◑♍

♎ **4:44AM**

| S | M | T | W | T | F | S |
|---|---|---|---|---|---|---|
|   |   |   |   |   |   | 1 |
| 2 | 3 | 4 | 5 | 6 | 7 | 8 |
| 9 | 10 | 11 | 12 | 13 | 14 | 15 |
| **16** | **17** | **18** | **19** | **20** | **21** | **22** |
| 23 | 24 | 25 | 26 | 27 | 28 | 29 |
| 30 |   |   |   |   |   |   |

## WEEKLY INTENTION

## TOP 3 TO-DOS

○

○

○

**16** SUN ● ♎

**17** MON ● ♎

♏ **4:44PM**
Sun-Jupiter trine
Sun-Saturn trine

**18** TUE

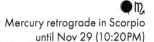

Mercury retrograde in Scorpio
until Nov 29 (10:20PM)

---

**19** WED

● ♏

Mercury-Uranus opposition
Mercury-Neptune trine #2 of 3

---

**20** THU

● ♏

## NEW MOON IN SCORPIO
(1:47AM; 28°12')
♐ 5:26AM

Sun-Mercury retrograde meetup

---

**21** FRI

● ♐

Sun-Uranus opposition
Sun-Neptune trine
Sun in Sagittarius (8:36PM)

## SAGITTARIUS SEASON UNTIL DEC 21

**22** SAT

● ♐

♑ 5:53PM

Mercury-Saturn trine #2 of 3
Mercury-Jupiter trine #2 of 3

## NOVEMBER 2025

| S | M | T | W | T | F | S |
|---|---|---|---|---|---|---|
|   |   |   |   |   |   | 1 |
| 2 | 3 | 4 | 5 | 6 | 7 | 8 |
| 9 | 10 | 11 | 12 | 13 | 14 | 15 |
| 16 | 17 | 18 | 19 | 20 | 21 | 22 |
| 23 | 24 | 25 | 26 | 27 | 28 | 29 |
| 30 |   |   |   |   |   |   |

## WEEKLY INTENTION

## TOP 3 TO-DOS

○

○

○

**23** SUN ●☽♑

**24** MON ●☽♑
Mercury-Venus meetup

II

**25** TUE

●♑
♒ 5:16AM

---

**26** WED

●♒
Venus-Jupiter trine
Venus-Saturn trine

---

**27** THU

◗♒
♓ 2:24PM
Saturn retrograde ends (10:52PM)

---

**28** FRI

◗♓
Waxing Quarter moon in Pisces (1:59AM)

---

**29** SAT

◗♓
♈ 8:07PM
Mercury retrograde ends (12:38PM)
Venus-Uranus opposition

## NOVEMBER 2025

| S | M | T | W | T | F | S |
|---|---|---|---|---|---|---|
|   |   |   |   |   |   | 1 |
| 2 | 3 | 4 | 5 | 6 | 7 | 8 |
| 9 | 10 | 11 | 12 | 13 | 14 | 15 |
| 16 | 17 | 18 | 19 | 20 | 21 | 22 |
| 23 | 24 | 25 | 26 | 27 | 28 | 29 |
| 30 |   |   |   |   |   |   |

## WEEKLY INTENTION

## TOP 3 TO-DOS

○

○

○

**30** SUN

☽♈

Venus-Neptune trine
Venus in Sagittarius until Dec 24 (3:14PM)

## NOTES & THOUGHTS

# NOVEMBER

**11**

## MONTHLY HOTSPOTS

### NOV 2 VENUS-JUPITER SQUARE

Feeling torn between head and heart? With Jupiter in Cancer squaring off against Venus in Libra, you're craving deep emotional connections, but also trying to keep things smooth and balanced. Jupiter's all about big feelings and nurturing vibes, while Venus wants harmony and beauty in your relationships. It's a cosmic tug-of-war between going all-in on love and making sure everything stays just right. The sweet spot? Let your heart lead, but don't overdo it—keep those emotions in check while still honoring your deeper desires. Balance is key, so find your flow without tipping the scales too far!

### NOV 3 MARS-NEPTUNE TRINE

Trust your gut, because today the universe is practically trolling you with hints. With insistent Mars in psychic Scorpio vibing with Neptune in intuitive Pisces, the signs and serendipities are impossible to miss. Don't brush them off—these cosmic nudges are guiding you to exactly where you need to be. Couples will feel a perfect balance between passion and deep trust, as Neptune's compassion cools Mars' fiery intensity. Single? You'll be drawn to someone with spiritual depth, not just raw chemistry. Forget the sparkly unicorns. Soulful connection will captivate your heart today.

### NOV 4

#### MARS IN SAGITTARIUS (NOV 4–DEC 15)

Your visionary dreams are set to soar as Mars charges into entrepreneurial Sagittarius, lighting a fire under your feet. Got a bucket-list adventure in mind? Thinking about launching a world-changing project or business? This transit fills your tank with unstoppable go-for-it energy. Skip the holiday comfort comas and endless social media scrolling. Instead, fuel up with an inspiring workshop or dive into a metaphysical book to keep the momentum going. In love, Mars dares you to venture into uncharted territory. Single? Give someone totally out of your usual orbit a shot. Coupled up? Plan an adventurous trip or sneak away from family gatherings for a romantic escape. Whether it's a sun-soaked beach or city lights, a change of scenery could seriously reignite the spark. With Mars in Sagittarius, your end-of-year vibe is all about bold moves and passionate amour.

## MARS-URANUS OPPOSITION

Hold on tight! Mars in Sagittarius is firing up your ambitions, but with Uranus in Gemini hurling curveballs into the mix, it's going to be a wild ride! This cosmic clash brings spontaneous plot twists, pushing you to think fast and adapt on the fly. Got big plans? Be flexible because Uranus loves to shake things up when you least expect it. But here's the thing—chaos can be your secret weapon. Lean into the unpredictability, and you might stumble upon a breakthrough idea or an unexpected opportunity that blows your mind. Relationships could get a jolt, too! You or your partner may crave more freedom, leading to some intense "let's change things up" moments. Single? You might meet someone totally out of the blue, who challenges everything you thought you wanted. This isn't the time to play it safe—Mars and Uranus are daring you to take bold risks and embrace the unexpected. Buckle up, because this opposition will take you places you never saw coming!

## NOV 5 FULL MOON IN TAURUS (8:19AM; 13°23'; SUPERMOON)

The earth moves under your feet as the full supermoon rises in grounded Taurus! This lunation shines a light on your values, security, and everything you've been building since the spring. Anchor your visionary ideas into reality. With some thoughtful planning you can make them tangible, even profitable, over the coming weeks. Taurus loves luxury, and this supermoon invites you to indulge in sensual pleasures, like a decadent dinner reservation, booking spa treatments for the upcoming weekend (seaweed mud wraps and collagen-stimulating facials, please!) or an evening of visual stimulation at an art exhibit. This moon also brings emotional clarity around your values, helping you sort through what really matters. If you've been feeling off balance, this is your moment to slow down, regroup, and focus on creating more stability.

## NOV 6–30 VENUS IN SCORPIO

Venus shimmies into smoldering Scorpio, cranking up the sex appeal. Just talking about what turns you on could get pulses racing, and chemistry heats up fast behind closed doors. Channel your erotic energy through dance, sensual movement, or spicy adventures between the sheets. With Venus here, secrecy and mystery are irresistibly hot, but be careful—temptations could take you into taboo territory. Trust and lust are equally important under Scorpio's watch. The green-eyed monster could rear its head during this cycle. Karma might be your kink, but vengeance? Don't get caught up in that. Let this Venus cycle take you to new levels of passion, without losing sight of honor and respect.

## NOV 7

### URANUS RETROGRADE IN TAURUS (NOV 7–FEB 3, 2026)

Uranus, who's been retrograde in duplicitous Gemini since September 6, slips back into Taurus for the final retrograde, of our lifetime, in this sign. Until February 3, it channels its rebellious energy toward our money, routines and personal values. This chaotic cycle may bring a few shakeups in your financial life or even your self-worth. Old money issues or unexpected expenses could pop up, pushing you to rethink how you handle your resources. But don't panic! This is your cosmic cue to get creative and find new ways to build lasting security. Uranus loves change, and though it can feel destabilizing, this transit is about finding freedom in places you've been stuck. Stay open to breaking out of old patterns—you might discover an unconventional path to financial freedom!

## VENUS-PLUTO SQUARE

Feel the heat, but watch out for power struggles! As Venus in seductive Scorpio squares off with intense Pluto in Aquarius, love and relationships take on a biting edge. This transit brings deep emotional currents to the surface. Expect a surge of passion, attraction, and even obsession. But with Pluto in the mix, things can get a little intense, and control issues may creep in. Be mindful of any hidden agendas or jealousy. While the chemistry is off the charts, this square can push you to confront deep fears around trust and vulnerability. Secrets could emerge, revealing the truth beneath the surface. In love, you'll be craving more depth, intimacy, and raw connection—but be careful not to let power dynamics take over. This is a time for emotional honesty while avoiding manipulative moves.

## NOV 9–18 MERCURY RETROGRADE IN SAGITTARIUS

Please DON'T say the quiet part out loud. Today, big-mouthed Mercury spins retrograde in tactless Sagittarius, flashing a code red blurt alert. This three-week cycle lasts until November 29, but before Mercury moves back into Scorpio on the 18th, honesty can be particularly brutal, smashing relationships to smithereens. If you don't want to spend the holidays estranged from your nearest and dearest, think twice about going on any attacks, even if you're "just trying to be helpful." Equally disruptive are off-color remarks and X-rated humor which could fall flat with a general audience. Visiting loved ones might require extra precautions during this argumentative time. If you need to cut a trip short or stay at a hotel to preserve the peace, err on the side of "personal space." Leave early for the airport and triple check all reservations since this retrograde can be particularly disruptive of travel.

## NOV 11–MAR 10, 2026 JUPITER RETROGRADE IN CANCER

How sturdy is your emotional foundation? As Jupiter pulls the brakes in nurturing Cancer, inward reflection is called for. Have you been chasing success at the expense of personal fulfillment? This four-month cycle can help you true up your outer ambitions with your longing for inner peace. Opportunities for growth may not come as fast during this period, but that's okay! Jupiter retrograde encourages you to redefine what abundance means on a more holistic level. Revisit your long-term goals with a nurturing touch, focusing on what brings you comfort and joy. Check in with your loved ones to make sure everyone is feeling safe and supported. With knowledge-seeking Jupiter in this family-friendly sign, dig in and discover more about your roots. Get a genetic test from 23andMe or reach out to relatives overseas. A pilgrimage might be in order!

## NOV 12

### WANING QUARTER MOON IN LEO (12:28AM)

When does "just a little more" cross the line into "hella extra"? The answer could reveal itself during today's moderating quarter moon in Leo. Have you fallen into a rut of basic-ness? Add a few glamorous, theatrical bells and whistles to your presentations. Already creeping into "Liberace Museum" terrain? This lunar leveling wags a bejeweled finger at anything too ostentatious. Leo style maven Coco Chanel advised people to remove one accessory before walking out the door. Apply this principle broadly today. If stress has been rising, book a massage (Leo rules the back) or stream an upbeat dance class. Pampering yourself pays off in productivity and pleasure!

### MERCURY-MARS MEETUP

Contentious much? With fiery Mars merging with retrograde Mercury in outspoken Sagittarius, you might fire off a zinger before your brain has a chance to catch up. Quick comebacks feel almost irresistible under this transit, but watch out—you may not have all the facts straight. With Mercury retrograde in the mix, misunderstandings are bound to pop up, and the truth could look very different from the drama unfolding in your head. Before you let those fiery words fly, take a moment to cool off, think it through, and separate fact from fiction. Sometimes silence really is golden!

## SUN-JUPITER TRINE

The divine feminine is rising and alchemizing! Jupiter in woman-powered Cancer dances into an ultra-rare trine with the Scorpio Sun, bringing a welcome reminder of the powerful role women play in shaping our world. With both heavenly bodies in water signs, emotions will be passionate and palpable. Don't hold back if you have feelings to express. Candid Jupiter can pull our deepest confessions out of Scorpio's vault. There's freedom in owning your truth and being witnessed. Start the sharing with people you know and trust before you unleash on TikTok and wind up on a million strangers' FYPs.

## SUN-SATURN TRINE

As the Scorpio Sun and disciplined Saturn in Pisces unite in a compassionate water trine, a calm but comforting approach will win the day. Know the difference between reacting and responding. Instead of flying into action at every provocation, step back and assess the best course of action. Smart solutions are best when backed by wisdom. If someone is pushing you to do something that feels out of alignment, opt for passive resistance rather than confronting them head on.

## NOV 18-29 MERCURY RETROGRADE IN SCORPIO

Cat and mouse games could go awry as Mercury slips back into manipulative Scorpio to complete its retrograde, which ends on November 29. On the one hand, this brings relief from fiery feuds that have been going on since the messenger planet pulled a U-turn in Sagittarius on November 9. But for the next eleven days, life could feel like an extended game of Clue. Prepared to pass those loyalty tests? Trust is a must with Mercury reversing through this suspicious sign, and don't expect anyone to extend the benefit of the doubt. Show and prove, AND pledge your allegiance, if you want the keys to anyone's kingdom.

11

## MERCURY-URANUS OPPOSITION

Your mind and mouth are moving at two totally different speeds under today's cosmic collision between irreverent Mercury, who's retrograde in Scorpio, and erratic Uranus in Taurus. With Mercury in sharp-tongued Scorpio, your zingers come with stingers. Just because you've thought of the prizewinning comeback, doesn't mean you should say it out loud. But hold your tongue before rebellious Uranus seizes the mic. Polarizing discussions can flame up fast today, and rabble-rouser Uranus won't want to back down from a debate. Consider whether you're sowing chaos and contention rather than actually promoting progress. You don't have to force everyone to agree (that's not happening today) but at least reach a place of common decency and respect.

## MERCURY-NEPTUNE TRINE #2 OF 3

Pay attention to what's bubbling beneath the surface today. With Mercury retrograde in investigative Scorpio dreamweaving with mystical Neptune in Pisces, you're being nudged to tap into your subconscious. This cosmic alignment may uncover hidden truths or forgotten visions buried deep in your imagination. Instead of getting caught up in overanalyzing, embrace a flow state through meditation, music, or creativity. Even with Mercury in reverse, your intuition is extra sharp now. Double-check your facts, but don't ignore that inner voice.

## NEW MOON IN SCORPIO (1:47AM; 28º12')

Want to turn a leaden aspect of your life into pure, shimmering gold? Get the ball rolling on those transformational efforts. Real change takes work—it never just happens overnight. But this is a NEW moon, so it's all about jumping off the starting block. Scorpio works in the shadows, so don't try to force the positive vibes—not without paying attention to the full range of feelings involved with making change. It can be scary to let go! The fear of the unknown is what keeps most people stuck in a cycle. With both curious Mercury and esoteric Neptune trine the new moon, you could just as easily channel the information you need as you could discover it on a deep Google search. Acknowledge where you're blocked, then search for savvy mentors and guides who can help you untangle the mysterious machinations of your mind. With Uranus opposite the new moon, you might even find some of them in the virtual realm.

## SUN-MERCURY MEETUP

Get ready for some deep introspection as the Sun merges with Mercury retrograde in the intense sign of Scorpio. This cosmic meetup shines a spotlight on buried truths and unfinished business, especially in relationships or personal goals. Mercury retrograde's influence slows things down, inviting you to revisit past decisions and rethink your next steps. Old secrets may resurface, or a former flame could reappear, demanding closure. Don't rush the process! This is a powerful time for reflection and recalibration. Tune in to your gut instincts and dig deep—you're on the verge of a major breakthrough.

NOV 21

## SUN-URANUS OPPOSITION

Everyone's skin is especially thin today as the sensitive Scorpio Sun faces down button-pushing Uranus in Taurus. Steer clear of trolls who are always spoiling for a fight. And don't go playing devil's advocate yourself. You can try to smooth things over by focusing on common ground, but easy does it. Attempts to break the tension with humor may go over like a lead balloon. Although you might feel anxious about a pending event, this isn't the day to demand a firm answer or make a binding decision. Plans could change at a moment's notice. If you must pivot quickly, adopt a flexible attitude instead of digging in your heels. (Tough, given that the Sun and Uranus are at loggerheads in tenacious fixed signs.) Stay nimble! A completely unexpected approach could actually lead to a breakthrough.

## SUN-NEPTUNE TRINE

Let your intuition take the wheel today as the soulful Scorpio Sun forms a harmonious trine with dreamy Neptune in Pisces. This cosmic connection heightens your empathy and creativity, making it easier to tap into the subtle energies around you. Loosen up a little control. Instead of forcing outcomes, trust your inner wisdom and let things unfold organically. In the end, you'll be grateful for the extra integration time that comes from a slower pace. Conversations could take on a spiritual or emotional tone. You could lose track of time creating art, playing music or daydreaming. The more you surrender to the flow, the more magic you'll manifest. Just stay grounded so you don't drift too far into fantasy.

## SUN IN SAGITTARIUS (8:36PM) (NOV 21–DEC 21)

Inclusivity is the name of the game as the Sun bursts into diversifying Sagittarius for a month. After huddling with your inner circle during Scorpio season, break out! Celebrate the differences that make us all dynamic. Play ambassador for people who haven't learned how to access the "one love" vibes. The spirit of transparency is in the air, so if you need to have an honest chat with someone before the holidays kick in, hash it out after Mercury turns direct on November 29. "Anywhere but home" always seems like the ideal destination for Sagittarius season; yes, even while Mercury is retrograde. With careful planning your holiday travel can go off without a hitch. This sporty solar cycle could get you bundled up and onto the slopes— or onto your yoga mat to warm your body from the inside out.

## NOV 22

## MERCURY-SATURN TRINE #2 OF 3

Slow your roll and think things through today as detail-oriented Mercury teams up with taskmaster Saturn. Whether you're sealing the deal or putting the finishing touches on a project, Saturn rewards thorough, no-nonsense work. With both planets in emotional water

signs, don't be shy about leaning on your inner circle for support.
A savvy mentor or well-connected friend might hold the key to
leveling up, but if you ask for an intro, be ready to follow through.
Remember, your actions reflect on the person who's vouching
for you, so bring your A-game once that door swings open!

## MERCURY-JUPITER TRINE #2 OF 3

Big ideas are bubbling to the surface today as investigative Mercury,
currently retrograde in Scorpio, forms a flowing trine to optimistic
Jupiter in nurturing Cancer. With these security-loving signs at the
helm, you'll be in the mood to research and brainstorm the particulars
around your long-term plans. Conversations today could lead to
major breakthroughs if you're willing to look underneath certain
rocks. This watery cosmic combo amps up your intuition, making it
easy to pick up on what's unsaid. But with Mercury retrograde, don't
ride on assumptions. Someone's silence does not necessarily mean
they are ghosting you. A close friend or relative might offer a golden
opportunity or priceless advice—listen closely! Just be mindful not to
bite off more than you can chew. Dream big but keep it manageable.

## NOV 24 MERCURY-VENUS MEETUP

Some secrets aren't meant to be kept in the vault forever. If you've been
agonizing over the right time to reveal your feelings, this day might
greenlight the dialogue, as messenger Mercury (retrograde) meets up
with heart-centered Venus at the same degree of Scorpio. A "coeur-a-
coeur" could spontaneously erupt! Should you bump into a person-of-
interest on the street—and dive right into a deep conversation—you may
decide to move your sidewalk talk to a coffee shop...or a more private
location. One caveat: While Venus loves to be swept away, this CAN be
a slippery slope, given Mercury's backspin. With both planets tangoing
through erotically charged (and vengeful) Scorpio, it might be better to
cut things short if you encounter someone surreptitious, like a shady client
who owes you money or someone you slept with who suddenly stopped
texting you back. Power struggles may arise, or you might get swept right
back into an old dynamic that leaves you feeling frustrated and out of

control. But if you're dealing with a beautiful soul, this could be the day to lay it all on the line and see what emerges!

NOV 26

## VENUS-JUPITER TRINE

"Warm and fuzzy" could be surprisingly seductive today, so give the nice ones a chance. Venus, gliding through passionate Scorpio, forms a harmonious trine to generous Jupiter in nurturing Cancer, which turns up the heat on all things heartfelt. Whether you're strengthening the bond with your significant other or forging meaningful connections with close friends, today serves a buffet of soul-stirring moments. Jupiter's expansive energy could bring game-changing surprises, like a friend date blossoming into something romantic or a creative collaboration taking off with an artist you've been fangirling over for years. Open your channels wide and let the magic unfold!

## VENUS-SATURN TRINE

Fantasy mingles with reality for a highly seductive cocktail. As romantic Venus in Scorpio connects with mature Saturn in Pisces, love could take a turn for the serious. Single? Don't rule out a slightly older prospect or a stable person you might have written off as "boring." (Those secure attachments have their benefits!) For couples, it's a great day to talk about the future and to make concrete plans for some holiday activities you can enjoy as a duo. Nostalgic activities may be on the menu, especially if you want to rev up romance.

## NOV 27 SATURN RETROGRADE ENDS

Taskmaster Saturn straightens out after a five-month retrograde period that began in fiery Aries on July 13, and moved into healing, watery Pisces on September 1. Saturn's backspin brought plenty of soul-searching and personal growth—along with a few harsh but necessary lessons. You may have learned a lot about the pitfalls of being both aggressive and passive. No one would call a transit like this fun, but the growth and maturity that it can bring is priceless. Got an artistic or spiritual gift to contribute to the world? While Saturn takes one more lap through Pisces, until February 13, 2026, practice the skills that lead to mastery. If you're already an expert, contribute to someone else's inner growth by sharing the wisdom of your own experience.

## NOV 28 WAXING QUARTER MOON IN PISCES (1:59AM)

Subtle energies speak volumes today as the quarter moon in intuitive Pisces amplifies your sixth sense. What aren't people saying out loud? Pay attention to prolonged silences, facial expressions and body language that don't match the mood. While it's still important to get the facts, these are reliable guides for assessing the temperature of your environment. If you've been an open book (and who hasn't during Sagittarius season?), keep a little more mystery to yourself. It's an alluring trait today, one that leaves people hungry to know more. And since Pisces is the master of illusion, it's a wise security measure. Establishing trust takes time. Pace yourself and let things flow organically. Don't be surprised if this "tuned in" approach leads you to a miraculous discovery! Serendipities are probably not mere coincidences today. If something seems like a sign, follow that thread.

## NOV 29

### MERCURY RETROGRADE ENDS

All those dodgy, befuddling interactions should clear up a lot today as Mercury pivots out of a mind-bending three-week retrograde that began in Sagittarius on November 9. With the silver-tongued messenger casting spells in Scorpio since November 18, nothing has been quite as it seems. Starting today, wires will slowly but surely uncross. Cutthroat dynamics could soften into healthy competition, but don't drop ALL self-protective shields. Mercury's backspin may have revealed some shady characters who don't deserve a second (third or fourth) chance. As Mercury continues its undercover crawl through Scorpio until December 11, continue to vet your engagements carefully and keep reading the fine print with a massive magnifying glass.

### VENUS-URANUS OPPOSITION

Assume nothing today...but expect anything! Controlling Venus in Scorpio is at loggerheads with bombastic Uranus in Taurus. Strong emotions might erupt like an active volcano under this explosive and unpredictable face-off. If people signal a need for "space," give it to them instead of frantically texting or pushing for a talk. Feeling the urge for more freedom? You don't have to throw out the baby with the bathwater. It's totally possible to create more space in a relationship without calling the whole thing off. Rule of thumb for the day? Assume nothing. And avoid making any unilateral decisions. Check in and get consensus (and consent) before taking action.

## NOV 30

### VENUS-NEPTUNE TRINE

Ooh la la! Venus in Scorpio gets in a flowing formation with enchanting Neptune in Pisces, spicing up the day. Their dynamic dance, which generally happens twice a year, sends seductive undercurrents rippling through the ether. Cast a spell with nonverbal cues, dab on a titillating fragrance; let a flash of colorful lingerie peek through your clothing. A little cat-and-mouse game can be arousing in affairs de coeur. Wait a little longer to reply to a new love interest's text—but not so long that they think you're uninterested. Uncertainty builds anticipation... and attraction. The only risk of a Venus-Neptune trine is that it can make boundaries a little hazy. Don't lose sight of all propriety in the heat of the moment. There's a time and a place for everything.

### VENUS IN SAGITTARIUS (NOV 30–DEC 24)

Ardent Venus swings into worldly Sagittarius, stirring up attractions across every aisle. After a bout of "Should I or shouldn't I?" you may feel ready to take a Vegas-sized gamble in the game of love. One way or another, candid confessions could come spilling out, blowing covers off of shady lovers everywhere. During this happy go lucky circuit it will be easier to brush off a "rejection" and keep on swiping... then probably laugh about it all and become BFFs with your now not-so-secret crush. Cross-cultural connections simmer with extra masala. If you can squeeze in a pre-Christmas baecation, even for a night or two, it promises to be epic. Close to home, you can find your romantic and artistic stimulation...anywhere BUT "the usual places."

# END OF YEAR INTENTIONS

# December

## MONTHLY HOROSCOPE

As December kicks off, you feel like winding down, reflecting and setting the stage for your next big chapter. With the Sun, high-octane Mars and glamorous Venus are swirling through your twelfth house of rest and release until the 21st, 15th and 24th, respectively, you're in a phase of deep contemplation and strategic plotting. Use this introspective energy to tie up loose ends, close any lingering chapters and prepare for a powerful new beginning when birthday season begins at the winter solstice this December 21st. Dreamy Neptune ends its five-month retrograde on December 10, shifting into forward motion in Pisces and your communicative third house. Suddenly, conversations flow more easily and any misunderstandings—especially with siblings or neighbors—begin to clear up, giving you the green light to express your thoughts with compassion and clarity. On the 15th, get ready for a surge of vitality as passionate Mars charges into Capricorn for the first time in two years, energizing you with motivation and drive. This momentum only intensifies as the Sun enters your sign on the solstice (December 21), and Venus follows on the 24th, adding a touch of glam to your assertive edge. You're stepping into your power, Capricorn, ready to wow the world as you close out 2025. With the planetary energy moving from your twelfth house into your first, it's time to put yourself front and center. Your ambitions are calling, and the universe is giving you a megaphone—don't be shy about letting your presence be known! When it comes to wrapping up the year, go for a celebration that truly honors you. Whether that's hosting an intimate but upscale birthday-slash-NYE gathering or heading out for an unforgettable night of club-hopping, ring in 2026 in a way that feels like a fresh start. Dance until dawn, fiercely declare your resolutions and step confidently into the new year knowing that it's yours to conquer!

*Read your extended monthly forecast for life, love, money and career! astrostyle.com*

# DECEMBER
## Moon Phase Calendar

| SUN | MON | TUE | WED | THU | FRI | SAT |
|---|---|---|---|---|---|---|
| | **1** ♉ 10:13PM | **2** ♉ | **3** ♊ 9:48PM | **4** ♊ Full Moon 6:14PM | **5** ♊ 8:54PM | **6** ♋ |
| **7** ♋ 9:48PM | **8** ♌ | **9** ♌ | **10** ♍ 2:20AM | **11** ♍ 4th Quarter | **12** ♍ ♎ 11:04AM | **13** ♎ |
| **14** ♎ ♏ 10:51PM | **15** ♏ | **16** ♏ | **17** ♏ ♐ 11:38AM | **18** ♐ | **19** ♐ New Moon 8:43PM ♐→♑ 11:53PM | **20** ♑ |
| **21** ♑ | **22** ♑ ♒ 10:52AM | **23** ♒ | **24** ♒ ♓ 8:09AM | **25** ♓ | **26** ♓ | **27** ♓→♈ 3:02AM ♈ 2nd Quarter |
| **28** ♈ | **29** ♈ ♉ 6:57AM | **30** ♉ | **31** ♉ ♊ 8:13AM | | | |

*Times listed are Eastern US Time Zone*

## KEY

| | | | | | |
|---|---|---|---|---|---|
| ♈ ARIES | ♌ LEO | ♐ SAGITTARIUS | **FM** FULL MOON | | |
| ♉ TAURUS | ♍ VIRGO | ♑ CAPRICORN | **NM** NEW MOON | | |
| ♊ GEMINI | ♎ LIBRA | ♒ AQUARIUS | **LE** LUNAR ECLIPSE | | |
| ♋ CANCER | ♏ SCORPIO | ♓ PISCES | **SE** SOLAR ECLIPSE | | |

12

*Supermoon*

DECEMBER 4, 6:14PM

## full moon in
# Gemini (13°04')

## GEMINI FULL MOON CRYSTAL

### DALMATIAN JASPER

This black-and-white-flecked stone helps balance the yin and yang of dualistic Gemini. Dalmatian Jasper can evoke a sense of childlike wonder along with bursts of hope and joy— all while supporting the release of anger and resentment.

---

*What's one thing you're celebrating under this full moon?*

---

## GEMINI FULL MOON = CELEBRATE!

*Friends who are always up for a hangout*

*The silly things that make you laugh*

*Your favorite local haunts*

*People who are easy to flirt with (no strings attached)*

*Inside jokes*

*Books, movies and experiences that stimulate your mind*

DECEMBER 19, 8:43PM

# new moon in
# Sagittarius (28°25′)

## SAGITTARIUS NEW MOON CRYSTAL

### LAPIS LAZULI

This bright blue, high-vibrational stone helps you tap into your inner wisdom and gain confidence with self-expression. Lapis Lazuli connects you to the Sagittarian values of integrity, clarity and intuition.

---

*What's one fresh intention you're ready to set under this new moon?*

---

## SAGITTARIUS NEW MOON = FOCUS

*Turn each day into an adventure*

*Travel to new places—locally and globally*

*Broaden your social horizons*

*Speak your truth while hearing new perspectives*

*Study and invest in self-development*

*Make media and share your message*

12

**December 2025** Longitude & Retrograde Ephemeris [00:00 UT]

| Day | Sid.time | ☉ | ☽ | +12h☽ | ☿ | ♀ | ♂ | ♃ | ♄ | ♅ | ♆ | ♇ | ☊ | ☊ | ⚸ | ⚷ | Day |
|---|---|---|---|---|---|---|---|---|---|---|---|---|---|---|---|---|---|
| 1 Mo | 04:40:26 | ♐09°02'23 | ♈13°27'36 | ♈20°40'59 | Ds 20°50 | ♐00°11 | ♐19°17 | ℞ 24°32 | ♓25°09 | ℞ 29°03 | ℞ 29°23 | ♒01°54 | ℞ 13°48 | ℞ 14°17 | ♏27°46 | ℞ 23°05 | 1 Mo |
| 2 Tu | 04:44:22 | ♐10°03'11 | ♈28°01'13 | ♉05°27'12 | ♏21°08 | ♐01°27 | ♐20°02 | ♋24°28 | ♓25°10 | ♉29°00 | ♓29°23 | ♒01°55 | ♓13°45 | ♓14°12 | ♏27°53 | ♈23°03 | 2 Tu |
| 3 We | 04:48:19 | ♐11°04'00 | ♉12°58'41 | ♉20°34'07 | ♏21°35 | ♐02°42 | ♐20°46 | ♋24°24 | ♓25°10 | ♉28°58 | ♓29°23 | ♒01°56 | ♓13°42 | ♓14°04 | ♏28°00 | ♈23°01 | 3 We |
| 4 Th | 04:52:15 | ♐12°04'49 | ♉28°12'47 | ♊05°52'48 | ♏22°09 | ♐03°58 | ♐21°31 | ♋24°19 | ♓25°11 | ♉28°55 | ♓29°23 | ♒01°58 | ♓13°39 | ♓13°54 | ♏28°07 | ♈23°00 | 4 Th |
| 5 Fr | 04:56:12 | ♐13°05'40 | ♊13°33'12 | ♊21°11'57 | ♏22°51 | ♐05°13 | ♐22°16 | ♋24°15 | ♓25°11 | ♉28°53 | ♓29°22 | ♒01°59 | ♓13°36 | ♓13°43 | ♏28°13 | ♈22°58 | 5 Fr |
| 6 Sa | 05:00:08 | ♐14°06'32 | ♊28°48'08 | ♋06°19'53 | ♏23°39 | ♐06°29 | ♐23°00 | ♋24°10 | ♓25°12 | ♉28°50 | ♓29°22 | ♒02°00 | ♓13°32 | ♓13°31 | ♏28°20 | ♈22°57 | 6 Sa |
| 7 Su | 05:04:05 | ♐15°07'25 | ♋13°46'32 | ♋21°06'39 | ♏24°33 | ♐07°44 | ♐23°45 | ♋24°06 | ♓25°13 | ♉28°48 | ♓29°22 | ♒02°02 | ♓13°29 | ♓13°21 | ♏28°27 | ♈22°55 | 7 Su |
| 8 Mo | 05:08:02 | ♐16°08'20 | ♋28°20'02 | ♌05°25'42 | ♏25°32 | ♐09°00 | ♐24°30 | ♋24°01 | ♓25°14 | ♉28°46 | ♓29°22 | ♒02°03 | ♓13°26 | ♓13°13 | ♏28°33 | ♈22°54 | 8 Mo |
| 9 Tu | 05:11:58 | ♐17°09'15 | ♌12°23'57 | ♌19°14'18 | ♏26°34 | ♐10°15 | ♐25°15 | ♋23°56 | ♓25°15 | ♉28°43 | ♓29°22 | ♒02°05 | ♓13°23 | ♓13°07 | ♏28°40 | ♈22°52 | 9 Tu |
| 10 We | 05:15:55 | ♐18°10'11 | ♌25°57'21 | ♍02°33'02 | ♏27°41 | ♐11°31 | ♐26°00 | ♋23°50 | ♓25°17 | ♉28°41 | ♓29°22 | ♒02°06 | ♓13°20 | ♓13°05 | ♏28°47 | ♈22°51 | 10 We |
| 11 Th | 05:19:51 | ♐19°11'09 | ♍09°02'13 | ♍15°25'00 | ♏28°51 | ♐12°46 | ♐26°45 | ♋23°45 | ♓25°18 | ♉28°39 | D 29°22 | ♒02°08 | ♓13°16 | ♓13°04 | ♏28°54 | ♈22°50 | 11 Th |
| 12 Fr | 05:23:48 | ♐20°12'07 | ♍21°42'27 | ♍27°54'45 | ♐00°04 | ♐14°02 | ♐27°30 | ♋23°39 | ♓25°19 | ♉28°36 | ♓29°22 | ♒02°09 | ♓13°13 | ♓13°04 | ♏29°00 | ♈22°49 | 12 Fr |
| 13 Sa | 05:27:44 | ♐21°13'07 | ♎04°03'00 | ♎10°07'25 | ♐01°19 | ♐15°17 | ♐28°15 | ♋23°34 | ♓25°21 | ♉28°34 | ♓29°22 | ♒02°11 | ♓13°10 | ♓13°03 | ♏29°07 | ♈22°47 | 13 Sa |
| 14 Su | 05:31:41 | ♐22°14'08 | ♎16°09'04 | ♎22°08'09 | ♐02°35 | ♐16°33 | ♐29°00 | ♋23°28 | ♓25°22 | ♉28°32 | ♓29°22 | ♒02°12 | ♓13°07 | ♓13°01 | ♏29°14 | ♈22°46 | 14 Su |
| 15 Mo | 05:35:37 | ♐23°15'10 | ♎28°05'38 | ♏04°01'39 | ♐03°55 | ♐17°48 | ♐29°45 | ♋23°22 | ♓25°24 | ♉28°30 | ♓29°22 | ♒02°14 | ♓13°04 | ♓12°57 | ♏29°21 | ♈22°45 | 15 Mo |
| 16 Tu | 05:39:34 | ♐24°16'13 | ♏09°57'05 | ♏15°51'58 | ♐05°15 | ♐19°04 | ♑00°31 | ♋23°15 | ♓25°26 | ♉28°27 | ♓29°22 | ♒02°15 | ♓13°01 | ♓12°49 | ♏29°27 | ♈22°44 | 16 Tu |
| 17 We | 05:43:31 | ♐25°17'17 | ♏21°47'05 | ♏27°42'22 | ♐06°33 | ♐20°19 | ♑01°16 | ♋23°09 | ♓25°28 | ♉28°25 | ♓29°23 | ♒02°17 | ♓12°57 | ♓12°38 | ♏29°34 | ♈22°43 | 17 We |
| 18 Th | 05:47:27 | ♐26°18'22 | ♐03°38'29 | ♐09°35'17 | D 08°01 | ♐21°35 | ♑02°01 | ♋23°03 | ♓25°30 | ♉28°23 | ♓29°23 | ♒02°19 | ♓12°54 | ♓12°26 | ♏29°41 | ♈22°42 | 18 Th |
| 19 Fr | 05:51:24 | ♐27°19'27 | ♐15°33'22 | ♐21°32'29 | ♐09°25 | ♐22°50 | ♑02°47 | ♋22°56 | ♓25°32 | ♉28°21 | ♓29°23 | ♒02°20 | ♓12°51 | ♓12°11 | ♏29°47 | ♈22°41 | 19 Fr |
| 20 Sa | 05:55:20 | ♐28°20'34 | ♐27°33'10 | ♑03°35'09 | ♐10°50 | ♐24°06 | ♑03°32 | ♋22°49 | ♓25°35 | ♉28°19 | ♓29°23 | ♒02°22 | ♓12°48 | ♓11°57 | ♏29°54 | ♈22°41 | 20 Sa |
| 21 Su | 05:59:17 | ♐29°21'40 | ♑09°38'56 | ♑15°44'14 | ♐12°15 | ♐25°21 | ♑04°18 | ♋22°43 | ♓25°37 | ♉28°17 | ♓29°24 | ♒02°23 | ♓12°45 | ♓11°43 | ♐00°01 | ♈22°40 | 21 Su |
| 22 Mo | 06:03:13 | ♑00°22'48 | ♑21°51'34 | ♑28°00'41 | ♐13°43 | ♐26°37 | ♑05°03 | ♋22°36 | ♓25°39 | ♉28°15 | ♓29°24 | ♒02°25 | ♓12°42 | ♓11°32 | ♐00°08 | ♈22°39 | 22 Mo |
| 23 Tu | 06:07:10 | ♑01°23'55 | ♒04°12'07 | ♒10°25'42 | ♐15°11 | ♐27°52 | ♑05°49 | ♋22°29 | ♓25°42 | ♉28°13 | ♓29°25 | ♒02°27 | ♓12°38 | ♓11°23 | ♐00°14 | ♈22°39 | 23 Tu |
| 24 We | 06:11:06 | ♑02°25'03 | ♒16°42'04 | ♒23°01'03 | ♐16°39 | ♐29°08 | ♑06°34 | ♋22°21 | ♓25°45 | ♉28°11 | ♓29°25 | ♒02°29 | ♓12°35 | ♓11°18 | ♐00°21 | ♈22°38 | 24 We |
| 25 Th | 06:15:03 | ♑03°26'11 | ♒29°23'24 | ♓05°49'01 | ♐18°07 | ♑00°23 | ♑07°20 | ♋22°14 | ♓25°47 | ♉28°09 | ♓29°26 | ♒02°30 | ♓12°32 | ♓11°15 | ♐00°28 | ♈22°38 | 25 Th |
| 26 Fr | 06:18:60 | ♑04°27'19 | ♓12°18'41 | ♓18°52'21 | ♐19°36 | ♑01°39 | ♑08°06 | ♋22°07 | ♓25°50 | ♉28°07 | ♓29°26 | ♒02°32 | ♓12°29 | D 11°14 | ♐00°34 | ♈22°37 | 26 Fr |
| 27 Sa | 06:22:56 | ♑05°28'27 | ♓25°30'50 | ♈02°14'01 | ♐21°05 | ♑02°54 | ♑08°51 | ♋21°59 | ♓25°53 | ♉28°05 | ♓29°27 | ♒02°34 | ♓12°26 | ♓11°15 | ♐00°41 | ♈22°37 | 27 Sa |
| 28 Su | 06:26:53 | ♑06°29'35 | ♈09°02'40 | ♈15°56'35 | ♐22°35 | ♑04°10 | ♑09°37 | ♋21°52 | ♓25°56 | ♉28°03 | ♓29°27 | ♒02°35 | ♓12°22 | ℞ 11°15 | ♐00°48 | ♈22°36 | 28 Su |
| 29 Mo | 06:30:49 | ♑07°30'43 | ♈22°56'23 | ♉00°01'36 | ♐24°06 | ♑05°25 | ♑10°23 | ♋21°44 | ♓25°59 | ♉28°02 | ♓29°28 | ♒02°37 | ♓12°19 | ♓11°14 | ♐00°55 | ♈22°36 | 29 Mo |
| 30 Tu | 06:34:46 | ♑08°31'51 | ♉07°12'37 | ♉14°28'38 | ♐25°36 | ♑06°41 | ♑11°09 | ♋21°37 | ♓26°03 | ♉28°00 | ♓29°28 | ♒02°39 | ♓12°16 | ♓11°11 | ♐01°01 | ♈22°36 | 30 Tu |
| 31 We | 06:38:42 | ♑09°32'59 | ♉21°49'42 | ♉29°14'38 | ♐27°07 | ♑07°56 | ♑11°55 | ♋21°29 | ♓26°06 | ♉27°58 | ♓29°29 | ♒02°41 | ♓12°13 | ♓11°05 | ♐01°08 | ♈22°36 | 31 We |
| Δ Delta | 01:58:15 | 30°30'36" | 398°22'06" | 398°33'38" | 36°17' | 37°45' | 22°37' | -3°02' | 0°56' | -1°04' | 0°05' | 0°47' | -1°35' | -3°11' | 3°21' | -0°28' | Delta |

Ephemeris tables and data provided by **Astro-Seek.com.** All times in UTC.

**DECEMBER 2025**

| S | M | T | W | T | F | S |
|---|---|---|---|---|---|---|
| | 1 | 2 | 3 | 4 | 5 | 6 |
| 7 | 8 | 9 | 10 | 11 | 12 | 13 |
| 14 | 15 | 16 | 17 | 18 | 19 | 20 |
| 21 | 22 | 23 | 24 | 25 | 26 | 27 |
| 28 | 29 | 30 | 31 | | | |

## WEEKLY INTENTION

## TOP 3 TO-DOS

○

○

○

1 MON

○♈
♉ 10:13PM

**2** TUE ○♉

---

**3** WED ○♉
♊ 9:48PM

---

**4** THU ○♊
**FULL SUPERMOON IN GEMINI**
(6:14PM; 13°04')

---

**5** FRI ○♊
♋ 8:54PM

---

**6** SAT ○♋
Mercury-Jupiter trine #3 of 3

**DECEMBER 2025**

| S | M | T | W | T | F | S |
|---|---|---|---|---|---|---|
| | 1 | 2 | 3 | 4 | 5 | 6 |
| 7 | 8 | 9 | 10 | 11 | 12 | 13 |
| 14 | 15 | 16 | 17 | 18 | 19 | 20 |
| 21 | 22 | 23 | 24 | 25 | 26 | 27 |
| 28 | 29 | 30 | 31 | | | |

## WEEKLY INTENTION

## TOP 3 TO-DOS

○

○

○

**7** SUN

☽ ♋
♌ 9:48PM
Mercury-Saturn trine #3 of 3

**8** MON

☽ ♌
Mars-Saturn square

**9** TUE ◐ ♌

---

**10** WED ◐ ♌
♍ 2:20AM
Neptune direct in Pisces (7:21AM)
Mercury-Uranus opposition

---

**11** THU ◑ ♍
Waning Quarter moon in Virgo (3:52PM)
Mercury-Neptune trine #3
Mercury in Sagittarius until Jan 1, 2026 (5:40PM)

---

**12** FRI ◑ ♍
♎ 11:04AM

---

**13** SAT ◑ ♎

| S | M | T | W | T | F | S |
|---|---|---|---|---|---|---|
|  | 1 | 2 | 3 | 4 | 5 | 6 |
| 7 | 8 | 9 | 10 | 11 | 12 | 13 |
| 14 | 15 | 16 | 17 | 18 | 19 | 20 |
| 21 | 22 | 23 | 24 | 25 | 26 | 27 |
| 28 | 29 | 30 | 31 |  |  |  |

## WEEKLY INTENTION

## TOP 3 TO-DOS

○

○

○

**14** SUN

♏ 10:51PM
Mars-Neptune square

**15** MON

Mars in Capricorn until Jan 23, 2026 (2:34AM)

**16** TUE  ◐ ♏︎
Sun-Saturn square

---

**17** WED  ◐ ♏︎
♐︎ 11:38AM

---

**18** THU  ● ♐︎

---

**19** FRI  ● ♐︎

**NEW MOON IN SAGITTARIUS**
(8:43PM; 28°25′)
♑︎11:53PM

---

**20** SAT  ● ♑︎
Sun-Neptune square

## DECEMBER 2025

| S | M | T | W | T | F | S |
|---|---|---|---|---|---|---|
|   | 1 | 2 | 3 | 4 | 5 | 6 |
| 7 | 8 | 9 | 10 | 11 | 12 | 13 |
| 14 | 15 | 16 | 17 | 18 | 19 | 20 |
| 21 | 22 | 23 | 24 | 25 | 26 | 27 |
| 28 | 29 | 30 | 31 |   |   |   |

## WEEKLY INTENTION

## TOP 3 TO-DOS

◯

◯

◯

**21** SUN

● ♑
Venus-Saturn Square
Sun in Capricorn (10:03AM)

## CAPRICORN SEASON UNTIL JAN 19, 2026

**22** MON

● ♑
♒ 10:52AM

12

**23** TUE ◑ ♒

---

**24** WED ◑ ♒
♓ **8:09PM**
Venus-Neptune square
Venus in Capricorn until Jan 17, 2026 (11:26AM)

---

**25** THU ◐ ♓

---

**26** FRI ◐ ♓

---

**27** SAT ◐ ♓
♈ **3:02AM**
Waxing Quarter moon in Aries (2:10PM)

**DECEMBER 2025**

| S | M | T | W | T | F | S |
|---|---|---|---|---|---|---|
|   | 1 | 2 | 3 | 4 | 5 | 6 |
| 7 | 8 | 9 | 10 | 11 | 12 | 13 |
| 14 | 15 | 16 | 17 | 18 | 19 | 20 |
| 21 | 22 | 23 | 24 | 25 | 26 | 27 |
| 28 | 29 | 30 | 31 |   |   |   |

## WEEKLY INTENTION

## TOP 3 TO-DOS

○

○

○

**28** SUN                    ☽♈

**29** MON                    ☽♈
                             ♉ 6:57AM

**12**

**30** TUE

○♉
Mercury-Saturn square

---

**31** WED

○♉
♊ 8:13AM

---

## NOTES & THOUGHTS

# DECEMBER
## MONTHLY HOTSPOTS

**12**

### DEC 4 FULL MOON IN GEMINI (6:14PM; 13°04'; SUPERMOON)

Wordplay, wit and wisdom! Everyone's got a story to tell under the loquacious full supermoon in Gemini. Articulate your dreams, desires and wishes aloud. Post about them on social media and see who wants to get help you manifest your vision. Gemini rules peers and platonic partnerships and under this lunation, a creative partnership could turn into an official dynamic duo. Plan a drop or debut or just get the buzz going! Need a new set of wheels? This full moon may light the way to the perfect car or mobile accessory for commutes. Surround yourself with uplifting people today because vibes are contagious. With nefarious Pluto and people-pleasing Venus influencing the supermoon, use your charm selectively. It's easy to tell people what they want to hear and even easier to lead them on. Stay on the side of good karma and be transparent.

### DEC 6 MERCURY-JUPITER TRINE #3 OF 3

Third time's the charm! With Mercury now direct in intense Scorpio, it's forming its third harmonious trine to expansive Jupiter in nurturing Cancer. You've had a chance to revisit and refine your ideas during Mercury's retrograde phase last month, and now everything's clicking into place. This celestial alignment opens the floodgates for big breakthroughs and aha moments. Dive deep into those meaningful conversations and brainstorming sessions—you've laid the groundwork, and now it's time to act. Opportunities that felt just out of reach might suddenly land in your lap. Just remember to pace yourself; while enthusiasm is high, steady steps will turn your grand visions into lasting realities. Embrace this momentum—you've earned it!

## DEC 7 MERCURY-SATURN TRINE #3 OF 3

Break out the fine-toothed comb. As analytical Mercury and mature Saturn form their third in a trio of alliances since late October, you may have a final draft that's ready to review. Whether you're making a big decision or finishing a project, make sure you've turned over every detail before you proceed. In emotional water signs—Mercury in Scorpio and Saturn back in Pisces—these planets prompt you to reach out to your inner circle for support. Has a close friend or wise relative been through something similar? Don't let pride stand in the way. Get their advice and opinion, even if it only winds up being food for thought.

## DEC 10

### NEPTUNE DIRECT IN PISCES

Wake up, Sleeping Beauty. Dreamy Neptune rises from its annual, five-month retrograde, which will change the current from downstream to upstream. Certain areas of life that have been mired in illusion or uncertainty begin slowly moving in a proactive direction. This year's U-turn is particularly poignant as it marks Neptune's final lap through its home sign of Pisces—the seas it's been paddling through since 2011! The world has become a lot more spiritual and psychedelic since this transit began raising the collective vibration fourteen years ago. What mystical adventures await you now? Is there a spiritual experience you want to have? An artistic milestone you'd like to achieve? Neptune in Pisces is your muse until January 26, 2026, when the compassionate planet heads back into Aries for thirteen years. Add some soul to your goals. Tap into your creative right brain (and the divine flow) with journaling, meditation or visualization exercises.

### MERCURY-URANUS OPPOSITION

Get ready for a mental shake-up! When Mercury in deep-diving Scorpio faces off with wildcard Uranus in stubborn Taurus, surprises are bound to pop up. Expect intense, no-BS conversations that could turn into power struggles—especially if you're clinging to the old while craving change. Shocking news or revelations might rock your world, but they can also free you from stuck situations. Stay grounded before making any impulsive moves, especially with money. While this transit might feel like a cosmic curveball, it's clearing space for breakthroughs and fresh perspectives. Embrace the disruption—it's leading you to transformation!

## DEC 11

### MERCURY-NEPTUNE TRINE #3

Ask, believe, receive! As Mercury forms its third trine to mystical Neptune since late October, it's time to harness that dreamy, intuitive energy and turn it into something tangible. You don't need to grind away to get what you want—instead, go with the flow and use the Law of Attraction to manifest your desires. Visualize your goals clearly and let the universe handle the details. With Mercury and Neptune in water signs, your intuition is next-level psychic, so trust your gut. Sure, check the facts, but don't overthink it. Your inner guidance knows the way better than any data report!

### WANING QUARTER MOON IN VIRGO (3:51PM)

Don't sweat the small stuff, but don't ignore it either. Fine lines and wrinkles can interfere with plans as the quarter moon in Virgo plays inspector for the day. Proof your work before sending it off, making sure everything's spellchecked, accurate and up to date. Ask an eagle-eyed friend to read your text before you impulsively fire it off. Falling prey to perfectionism? Adjust your expectations instead of comparing and despairing. Are you asking more of people than they can humanly provide? Today's moonbeams may guide you to more qualified service providers who can help you get the job done to code. But even then, get real. Timelines and budgets may also need adjusting unless you're willing to simplify your strategy.

### MERCURY IN SAGITTARIUS (DEC 11–JAN 1, 2026)

Dream it, do it! The messenger planet jets back into Sagittarius, picking up plans that got sidelined when Mercury turned retrograde in this sign back on November 9. Go big and bold with your 2026 resolutions! Between now and New Year's Day, you'll be able to articulate some of your grandest dreams in colorful detail. But don't waste your best material on people who don't get it. Wait until you find the perfect audience to share your genius. With worldly Sagittarius energy flowing, they might be located 50, 500 or 5,000 miles from your front door!

## DEC 14 MARS-NEPTUNE SQUARE

It may seem thrilling to take a gamble today, but that's a slippery slope. Unless you have all the facts in front of you, hedge your bets! With the most active planet (Mars) at loggerheads with the most passive one (Neptune), you could take yourself on a wild ride of impulsivity and skewed intuition. Go back to the drawing board and do some quality research. With Mars in impulsive Sagittarius and Neptune in slippery Pisces, don't assume that a "maybe" is a "yes" until you've 100 percent confirmed it. Moreover, don't let anyone sweet talk you into making decisions, especially if they involve a financial transaction.

## DEC 15–JAN 23, 2026 MARS IN CAPRICORN

How obsessed are you with success? You're about to find out as goal-getter Mars leaps into ambitious Capricorn and brings out your desire to do, be, and have, the best. Mars is exalted in Capricorn, meaning it's one of its most powerful positions on the zodiac wheel. Harness the red planet's power to finish the year strong—and start 2026 even stronger. The cream always rises to the top! Remember: Grabbing the brass ring isn't just about laser focus and tireless hustle. The endorsement of prestigious people may be your golden ticket into the big leagues. Use the holiday season to mingle with the influencers or begin next year joining an industry group where you can casually rub shoulders with the VIPs. Already in the VIP lounge?

## DEC 16 SUN-SATURN SQUARE

Too much too soon? This twice-a-year battle between the optimistic Sun and speed-checking Saturn can make you feel a little stressed about the future. It's also an important reality check—and a necessary one with the Sun in optimistic Sagittarius and Neptune in unrealistic Pisces. You might not be able to realistically deliver what you're promising within the budget and timeline, so better to speak up now. Instead of getting discouraged, tighten up your blueprint. Consider this brief pause a blessing in disguise. You could spot an error just in the nick of time.

## DEC 19
## NEW MOON IN SAGITTARIUS (8:43PM; 28°25')

Borders become bridges as today's new moon in Sagittarius sets the stage for multicultural mingling and cross-cultural collabs. Better yet? Harmonious, loving Venus is co-piloting the mission, helping patch over any conflicts that may have flared during last month's Mercury retrograde. With healing Neptune and serious Saturn squaring the new moon, don't gloss over any structures that need to be put in place moving forward. Sagittarius rules travel. Switch to a wide-angle lens and zoom in on other parts of the world, from Perth to Portugal. Searches could turn up virtual connections or the perfect Airbnb to book for your winter vacation. Even though it's almost time for a holiday break, this new moon brings a burst of "cosmic capital" for start-up initiatives. Entrepreneurs, give your vision some thought today. What benchmarks would you love to achieve over the coming six months? Even taking one small action to move the needle today can send a strong signal to the universe that says, "I'm ready for this journey!"

## DEC 20

### SUN-NEPTUNE SQUARE

Hit pause and take stock of how realistic your ambitious ideas are. As the holiday timeline kicks in, people are just not eager to take on a big project. While you don't want to limit yourself, hazy Neptune in Pisces clashing with the confident Sun in Sagittarius can obscure facts or draw in people who over-promise under the twinkling lights. Err on the side of caution and scale down anything that's become overly complex. Stressing people out with elaborate party instructions or over-the-top dress codes, for example, can cause a ripple of tension that kills the fun of getting together. This cosmic clash can create a foggy atmosphere, making it hard to see the full picture. Get clear about other people's boundaries and time limits—and be up front about your own.

## BLACK MOON LILITH IN SAGITTARIUS (DEC 20, 2025–SEP 14, 2026)

Break free from limiting "norms" and restrictive expectations. Black Moon Lilith goes on a freedom-fighting spree through Sagittarius, the sign of fierce independence. This nine-month truth-seeking cycle invites you to design a life on your own terms and discover what truly sets you free. Globally traditional roles and beliefs could come under fire. (Sorry, #tradwives, you're, uh, just not fondue-ing it for us anymore.) Since Sagittarius rules religion, Lilith here could fire back at fundamentalist regimes that restrict women's rights, sexuality and freedom. Same for governmental laws that oppress and limit women's independence. Whatever fires you up, this take-no-prisoners Lilith transit makes everyone a whole lot more outspoken and ready to challenge the status quo. Time to boldly take up space, expand your horizons, and live on your own terms.

## DEC 21

### VENUS-SATURN SQUARE

Speed check! If you've been cruising along with your holiday season indulging, today's Grinchlike aspect between hedonistic Venus in Sagittarius and dour Saturn in Pisces could slam on the brakes. Even at this "most wonderful time of the year," it's possible to have too much of a good thing. Go easy on the sugary treats, boozy libations and sloppy mistletoe moments. Self-control is sexy today. Smart too, since this transit may reveal how close you've gone to being over budget. Think twice before going overboard with the hand-blown ornaments and stocking stuffers that will only wind up in people's junk drawers. Find your "enough" button and hit it fast!

## DEC 21–JAN 19, 2026 SUN IN CAPRICORN (10:03AM)

It's beginning to look a lot like solstice! The Sun enters Capricorn today, marking the shortest day of the year for those living in the northern hemisphere. Carve out space to meditate, reflect and find gratitude for the high points of your 2024. Then, clarify what you'd like to leave behind as you enter 2025. What golden lessons are you excited to bring with you into the New Year? The winter solstice always coincides with the Sun's move into grounding, elegant Capricorn. And since the celestial Sea Goat is the governor of goalsetting, how perfect is it that we get to make our resolutions under these rays every year? Get a running list going in your Notes app for now, so you can enjoy the holidays pressure-free. Capricorn season rallies on until January 19, 2026, so fear not! You're not going to lose your momentum (or your "high pro glow") if you start building your supersized visions after NYD.

## DEC 24

### VENUS-NEPTUNE SQUARE

Christmas Eve is meant for relaxing in the spirit of joy and togetherness. Try not to blow the assignment as people-pleasing Venus squares boundary-challenged Neptune. In your desire to play Santa for everyone you love, you could exhaust yourself wrapping presents instead of putting them in bags or sacrificing your family time to pick a friend up from the airport who is perfectly capable of taking a Lyft. With Venus in maximizer Sagittarius and Neptune in sacrificial Pisces, it will be hard to know where your limits lie. No one will be mad if you pick up a pie from the bakery instead of trying to play pastry chef in the eleventh hour! Create space to be with your favorite people.

### VENUS IN CAPRICORN (DEC 24–JAN 17, 2026)

Nothing wrong with a little strategic placement of the mistletoe this Christmas Eve. With amorous Venus settling into Capricorn's VIP lounge until January 17, your tastes could elevate as sky-high as the Star of Bethlehem. Defining nebulous situationships could be a fun game of "You show me your bucket list, I'll show you mine!" Or, if you're the type who doesn't even think about bucket lists, well, maybe it's time to write one up along with your New Years resolutions. With driven Capricorn ruling romance for the next few weeks, couples could achieve something memorable—and profitable—as a pair. No apologies for being attracted to status now. Couples can align around your shared future, discussing your 2025 dreams by the fireplace. If you're single and looking, search for someone who is ready for meaningful co-creation, like now.

## DEC 27 WAXING QUARTER MOON IN ARIES (2:10PM)

Chasing after shiny objects is not recommended under today's moderating quarter moon in Aries. It's fine to be attracted to the sparkliest person in the room or the most expensive item on the shelf. But weigh that impulse against your long-range plans. Rushing can backfire, so ease slowly into any new arrangements. Test the waters with a trial run. It's a lot less expensive than buying a season pass, especially if you've never tried an activity before. If you've been scattering your energy this month, take a pause to assess what's really in alignment with YOU. Devote more time to a few key interests instead of attempting to learn everything all at once!

## DEC 30 MERCURY-SATURN SQUARE

Reality check! With Mercury in adventurous Sagittarius squaring off against Saturn in dreamy Pisces, those grand New Year's Eve plans might need a little fine-tuning. Sure, the idea of a big celebration sounds great, but have you thought about the practical details? Last-minute complications could pop up, so double-check your reservations, confirm the guest list, and set realistic expectations. This transit urges you to end the year with a mix of optimism and realism. It's not about canceling the fun—just making sure it's grounded in what's actually doable. Start 2026 on solid ground, not lost in a cloud of wishful thinking.

Made in USA - Kendallville, IN
20504_9781966096085
11.18.2024 2136